ISBN 978-1-5277-6154-4
PIBN 10888400

English
Français
Deutsche
Italiano
Español
Português

www.forgottenbooks.com

Mythology Photography **Fiction**
Fishing Christianity **Art** Cooking
Essays Buddhism Freemasonry
Medicine **Biology** Music **Ancient
Egypt** Evolution Carpentry Physics
Dance Geology **Mathematics** Fitness
Shakespeare **Folklore** Yoga Marketing
Confidence Immortality Biographies
Poetry **Psychology** Witchcraft
Electronics Chemistry History **Law**
Accounting **Philosophy** Anthropology
Alchemy Drama Quantum Mechanics
Atheism Sexual Health **Ancient History**
Entrepreneurship Languages Sport
Paleontology Needlework Islam
Metaphysics Investment Archaeology
Parenting Statistics Criminology
Motivational

ANGLING;

OR,

HOW TO ANGLE, AND WHERE TO GO.

BY

ROBERT BLAKEY,

AUTHOR OF

THE "HISTORY OF THE PHILOSOPHY OF THE MIND," "SHOOTING," ETC. ETC.

A New Edition, with Illustrations.

LONDON:

ROUTLEDGE, WARNE, & ROUTLEDGE,

FARRINGDON STREET;

NEW YORK: 56, WALKER STREET.

1862.

CONTENTS.

PART I.—HOW TO ANGLE.

PART II.—WHERE TO GO.

ANGLING.

PART I.—HOW TO ANGLE.

CHAPTER I.

INTRODUCTORY OBSERVATIONS.

THE art of angling is one of the most ancient amusements and practices of which we have any record in the history of the human family. We read of it in the Old Testament; and in the records of ancient Egypt, Assyria, and the whole of the eastern section of the globe, once the seat of powerful empires, and of a civilized people, we have innumerable testimonies in their several sepulchral and architectural remains, that angling—as we angle at this day— was an art well known, and generally practised, both as an amusement, and as a means of support. In the polished and literary states of Greece and Rome we have still more pointed and irrefragable testimony of the high antiquity of the art. The bucolic writers of Greek poetry descant upon the subject in a variety of forms; while graver historians among that singular and enlightened people dwell upon the art as one firmly embedded in the permanent customs and habits of the nation. The literature of Rome likewise portrays the existence of the gentle art among the warlike conquerors of the world. Not only formal works were composed on the subject, but we find that the classic poets, both serious and comic, make many direct allusions to the amusement of the rod-fisher, and to the fish he was in the habit of catching.

From the Christian era, and during the first centuries of the decline of Roman power and conquest, we find that angling continued to be one of the common pursuits of many nations, then in a state of transition from barbarism to refinement and knowledge. Pliny wrote on fish; and Ausonius, between the third and fourth century, expatiates with rapture on the abundance of fine salmon that were caught in the "blue Moselle;" a river in France, that

                                                                B

flows into the Rhine on the northern frontier of the country. The old chroniclers and scholastic writers often mention the piscatory art; and the Church, then in full power, took the subject of fish generally under its own guidance, and regulated both the sport in taking them, and the using of them for food. In every country in Europe, where any degree of progress had been made in learning and civilization during the middle ages, we find numerous traces of fishermen and their labours, even long before the art of printing became known and practised.

It is now an established fact, admitted by all writers, that the English nation has been, from the earliest days of its history, the most distinguished and zealous propagators of the art of rod-fishing. And it is interesting to remark, in passing, that the historical memorials we possess, of the state of the angling art among the Anglo-Saxon tribes who first settled in this country, throw a great light on the origin of this striking predilection for the sport. The Anglo-Saxons, we are told, ate various kinds of fish, but the eel was a decided favourite. They used these fish as abundantly as swine. Grants and charters are sometimes regulated by payments made in these fish. Four thousand eels were a yearly present from the monks of Ramsay to those of Peterborough. We read of two places purchased for twenty-one pounds, wherein sixteen thousand of these fish were caught every year; and, in one charter, twenty fishermen are stated, who furnished, during the same period, sixty thousand eels to the monastery. Eel dykes are often mentioned in the boundaries of their lands.*

In the dialogues of Elfric, composed for the use of the Anglo-Saxon youth in the learning of the Latin tongue, we find frequent mention made of fishermen, and matters relating to their craft. In one dialogue the fisherman is asked, "What gettest thou by thine art?" "Big loaves, clothing, and money." "How do you take them?" "I ascend a ship, and cast my net into the river; I also throw in a hook, a bait, and a rod." "Suppose the fishes are unclean?" "I throw the unclean out, and take the clean for food." "Where do you sell your fish?" "In the city." "Who buys them?" "The citizens; I cannot take so many as I can sell." "What fishes do you take?" "Eels, haddocks, minnows, and eel-pouts, skate, and lampreys, and whatever swims in the rivers." "Why do you not fish in the sea?" "Sometimes I do; but rarely, because a great ship is necessary here."†

The historian Bede tells us, that Wilfrid rescued the people of Sussex from famine in the eighth century, by teaching them to catch fish : "for though the sea and their rivers abounded with fish, they had no more skill in the art than to take eels. The servants of Wilfrid threw into the sea nets made out of those by which they had obtained eels, and thus directed them to a new source of plenty."‡

* Dugdale's Monas., p. 244.
† Turner's Anglo-Saxons, vol. iii. p. 23.　　　‡ Bede, lib. 4.

It is an article in the *Penitentiale* of Egbert, that fish might be bought, though dead. In the same work, herrings are allowed to be eaten; and it states that, when boiled, they are salutary in fever and diarrhœa, and that their gall, mixed with pepper, is good for a sore mouth.*

Such are the historical relations between our Saxon forefathers and the art of angling; and we can trace no abatement in the original impulse to cultivate and extend its practice in the subsequent epochs of our nation. We carry, at this moment, a love of the sport to every quarter of the globe, wherever our conquests and commercial connections extend. In fact, we are the great *piscatory* schoolmasters that "are abroad," teaching all mankind how to multiply their rational out-door pleasures, in the pursuit of an amusement that is at once contemplative, intellectual, and healthful.

Nor are there any good grounds for complaining that other nations have been slow or dull scholars in taking advantage of our zealous labours and instructions. Within the last forty years, since the intercourse with our continental neighbours has been upon the most intimate and visiting footing, there has been a very marked improvement, not only as it relates to the practising of rod-fishing itself, in all its various forms, but likewise in the spirit in which the amusement is followed, and the literary taste evinced in describing and treating it. In Belgium and the Rhenish provinces generally, we have at this hour angling clubs in almost every locality contiguous to where there are eligible fishing-streams, all conducted upon the same principles, and influenced by the generally prevailing sporting sentiments which regulate similar institutions in our own country. Here a free and gentlemanly intercourse takes place among the brethren of the angle; fishing exploits and adventures are rehearsed over for the common amusement of the members; and we have had, of late years, some specimens of the poetic efforts made to grace the meetings of this order with something of the sentimental and humorous vein. In every department of France there has likewise been, since the close of the last general war, a great increase in the number of rod-fishers. The English modes of angling, especially for trout, have obtained considerable attention, and in some of the finest river-fishing districts are now commonly in vogue among all amateur or professed piscatorians. Many books on the art have also issued from the Paris and provincial presses, containing much useful information, and written in a truly genial and literary spirit; and, on the whole, there has been a very great change in reference to the extension of this out-door species of amusement among all classes of the people.

In Italy, Switzerland, and even in Spain, there has been a considerable augmentation of piscatorians within the last century. Some of the rivers in these countries are most munificently supplied with fine, rich trout; and, in their higher localities, the scenery upon

* Wilkins, Conc. p. 123.

some of their banks presents some of the most bewitching
views to the eye of one who has any artistic idea of landscape
sketches.

In the northern countries of Europe, angling, chiefly by English
sportsmen, has been successfully practised to a great extent. In
Sweden, Denmark, Norway, and even in Russia, the British mode
of angling is now well known, and even followed with enthusiasm,
by many of the nobles of those respective countries.

But the most cheering view for the angling enthusiast in England,
who revels in the delightful anticipation of seeing his favourite
sport becoming universal, is the rapid progress which the amusement has made in the United States of America. Here we see the
accounts daily, from the provincial prints in every section of the
Union, that angling clubs, and gatherings, and parties, are now
becoming quite fashionable in every direction where there are fishable streams and rivulets. Almost the entire district, from the
New England States to the foot of the Rocky Mountains west, and
even to the very shores of the Pacific Ocean in the Columbian district, has been visited, within the space of a few years, by professed
anglers. And it is no uncommon thing to undertake a fishing tour
of a month or two, and devoting the chief portion of the time to
the search of new and unfrequented localities for the prosecution
of future piscatory pastimes. We read in a recent number of a
Cincinnati newspaper, that Mr. Such-and-such-a-one had just arrived
at his own place of abode, all well, after a two months' fishing excursion; and that there would be a meeting of the friends of the
art, who lived in the town, to congratulate him on his return. The
angling literature of the States is increasing daily, and assuming
that scientific form and polished taste which show that the mass of
the people look upon the art as a truly improvable and intellectual
one. We find, in the American fishing-books, a number of spirited
angling songs, worthy of taking their place among the very best
specimens of lyrical composition either in the English or any other
language; and, with respect to prose compositions on angling
topics, few English writers have come up to the spirit and life
which the Americans embody. Witness the following description
of an angling tour, written by the late Hon. Daniel Webster, one
of the most able legislators and men of genius of whom the United
States can boast:—

"We were lost standing," says he, "at the upper part of Sage's
ravine, with some forty trout in our basket, when the time was up,
the mail must go, the article must be cut short, and all the best
parts of it, that for which all the rest was but a preparation, must
be left unwritten. The same visitor never comes twice to the eye
of the pen. If you scare it away, you might as well fish for a
trout after he has seen you, and darted under a stone, or beneath
his overhanging bank or root. But trouting in a mountain brook
is an experience of life so distinct from every other, that every
man should enjoy at least one in his day. That being denied to

most, the next best I can do for you, reader, is to describe it. So then come on.

"We have a rod made for the purpose, six feet long, only two joints, and a reel. We will walk up the mountain road, listening as we go to the roar of the brook on the left. In about a mile the road crosses it, and begins to lift itself up along the mountain side, leaving the stream at every step lower down on our right. You no more see its flashing through the leaves; but its softened rush is audible at any moment you may choose to pause and listen.

"We will put into it just below a smart foamy fall. We have on cow-hide shoes, and other rig suitable. Selecting an entrance, we step in, and the swift stream attacks our legs with immense earnestness, threatening at first to take us off from them. A few minutes will settle all that, and make us quite at home. The bottom of the brook is not gravel or sand, but rocks of every shape, every position, of all sizes, bare or covered; the stream goes over them at the rate of ten miles an hour. The descent is great. At a few rods cascades break over ledges, and boil up in miniature pools below. The trees on either side shut out all direct rays of the sun, and for the most part, the bushes line the banks so closely, and cast their arms over so widely, as to create a twilight—not a gray twilight, as of light losing its lustre, but a transparent black twilight, which softens nothing, but gives more ruggedness to the rocks, and a sombre aspect even to the shrubs and fairest flowers. It is a great matter to take a trout early in your trial. It gives one more heart. It serves to keep one about his business. Otherwise you are apt to fall off into unprofitable reverie; you wake up and find yourself standing in a dream—half seeing, half imagining—under some covert of overarching branches, where the stream flows black and broad among rocks, whose moss is green above the water, and dark below it. * * * * But we must hasten on. A few more spotted spoils are awaiting us below. We make the brook again. We pierce the hollow of overhanging bushes—we strike across the patches of sunlight, which grew more frequent as we got lower down towards the plain; we take our share of tumbles and slips; we patiently extricate our entangled line again and again, as it is sucked down under some log, or whirled round some network of broken beechen roots protruding from the shore. Here and there we half forget our errand as we break in upon some cove of moss, when our dainty feet halt upon green velvet, more beautiful a thousand times than ever sprung from looms at Brussels or Kidderminster. At length we hear the distant clamour of mills. We have finished the brook. Farewell, wild, wayward simple stream! In a few moments you will be grown to a huge mill-pond; then at work upon its wheel; then prim, and proper, with ruffles on each side, you will walk through the meadows, clatter across the road, and mingle with the More-brook—flow on toward the Housatonic—

lost in its depths and breadths. For who will know thy drops in the promiscuous flood? Or who, standing on its banks, will dream from what scenes thou hast flowed—through what beauty— thyself the most beautiful."

Such writing as this shows the refined and healthy tone of the angling literature and taste among our American cousins. With respect to the angling prospects of our own country at the present day, they are the most encouraging and hopeful. At no previous time of our history has the amusement been pursued with a keener relish than in the present age; and works on this subject are constantly appearing, which demonstrate the firm hold that it has on the public sentiment and feeling.

CHAPTER II.

ON TACKLE AND BAIT FOR ANGLING.

HOW TO ANGLE?

THIS question or proposition embraces two or three very obvious divisions. First, our rod and tackle, then our baits, and then our fish. We shall in this chapter keep to the consideration of the two first items. These constitute the materials of angling—the instruments or contrivances by which fish are commonly captured.

A considerable variety of articles are required for an angler's complete outfit: that is, to place him in a position to be ready at an hour's notice for angling any river or piece of water in any section of the kingdom. But there are more limited establishments which can answer all the rational ends or purposes of an angler, whose real sport does not depend upon, nor is regulated by the extent, variety, and cost of his stock of implements. Where economy or necessity demands a more curtailed stock of materials, the energetic and zealous rod-fisher will prosecute his favourite amusement with ardour; and invention and contrivance will, for the most part, supply the place of a more formal and ostentatious assortment of fishing-tackle. We shall give a list of a few articles which most anglers consider requisites.

Rods for salmon and trout fishing, trolling, worm, and fly-fishing, spinning the minnow and the bleak.

Hair lines, Indian weed, plaited silk and hair, and patent and other lines for trolling.

Reels for running tackle.

Hooks for trolling on wire or gimp, for the gorge or the snap.

Plummets.

Floats.

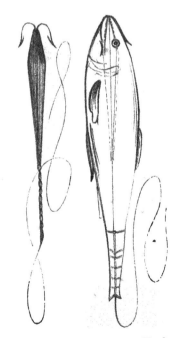

Eel Spear.

Fixing the Bait on the Hook.

Minnow, gudgeon, and bleak tackle, and baiting needles of different sizes.

Loose hooks of all kinds.

Paternosters for perch-fishing.

Cobbler's wax, sewing silk, and a few balls of small twine.

Floats of various sizes, and plenty of spare caps for floats.

Split shot and bored bullets of various sizes.

Disgorger, and clearing ring and drag.

Landing net, a gaff, and kettle for live bait.

Gentle-box and bags for worms.

A fishing-basket, creel, or game pouch.

A pair of pliers, a pair of scissors, and a good pocket-knife, both with large and small blades.

A parchment book of artificial flies.

A parchment book for general tackle.

A book for containing the various articles requisite for making artificial flies; the following list of materials is necessary for this purpose.

Cock and hen feathers or hackles of all colours; as red, ginger, black, dun, olive-grizzle, and stone-colour. Peacock's herl, copper-coloured, green, and brown. Black ostrich's herl. Fowls' spotted feathers.

The feathers of the turkey, the partridge, the grouse, ptarmigan, pheasant, woodcock, snipe, dotterel, landrail, starling, golden plover, common pee-wit, wild mallard, bustard, sea-swallow, wren, jay, blackbird, thrush, blue pigeon, silver-pheasant, parrot, and the tame and wild duck.

The fur of the water-rat, and hare's ears.

Mohair dyed all colours.

Fine French sewing silk of all colours.

Flos silk of all colours.

German wools of all colours.

Silk twist and bee's-wax.

A pair of pliers, a pair of fine-pointed scissors, a small slide vice, and a few fine-pointed, strong dubbing needles.

Silkworm gut, from the finest to the strongest; and salmon gut single and twisted.

Length of the white and sorrel hairs of stallions' tails.

And lastly, a variety of fly-hooks.

Of course fancy has a great deal to do with all arrangements of this kind. We find no two fishers alike in this instance. Some anglers prefer one kind of hooks, some another; we have the London hooks, the Kirby sneck, and the Limerick bend. A fair assortment of essentials should be the guide.

FISHING RODS.

A good fishing-rod is one of the essential instruments for the angler, and one to which he commonly pays the greatest attention; and this is more particularly the case in London, and in other large towns, where articles of this kind can be procured of the best quality and most polished workmanship. But in remote country districts, where there is often the best angling, we may daily meet with the frequenter of the streams, furnished only with a straight hazel rod, or perhaps two rudely spliced together, following his vocation with ardour and success. It is often surprising, and not a little instructive withal, how necessity sharpens the intellect of the angler; and how he shifts on, from the simplest and rudest implements, and really procures a fair day's sport under the most apparently discouraging circumstances. Every person who has visited the rural districts of England and Wales, with the rod in his hand, must have seen many instances of this kind, and felt a sort of inward self-reproach, that with all his superior outfit, he could not hope to surpass the success of the simple, but indefatigable rustic craftsman.

The qualities which a good and handy rod must possess, will, of course, vary with the nature of the angling. There need be no very great difference between a salmon and a trout rod, for fly fishing, except you fish in very wide streams, or on lakes in open boats. In such cases, we would recommend a good double-handed rod, from sixteen to eighteen feet in length, as the best that could be made for salmon fishing, in such kinds of water as we have just noticed. A rod of this size, and for this specific purpose, ought to have a free and equal spring in it, from the butt end to the top. This is of vital importance in dealing with large fish, whether hooked and run in rivers or in lakes.

A single-handed fly rod ought to be from twelve to fifteen feet in length. It should be as elastic as possible, and constructed of such materials as will unite lightness and elasticity with durability and strength. An experienced fly fisher can never get hold of a rod that is too light and springy, although a rather stiffish weapon is better for a beginner. The most beautifully elastic rods we have ever seen, were those made of ash and lance-wood. All rods with metallic root-pieces must necessarily be of uneven suppleness, although of late years, the manufacture of this description of rod has very materially improved, with reference to this radical defect.

There are many expert anglers, particularly those who have been constantly resident in the vicinity of narrow and thickly wooded streams, who can use no other but a single-handed fly-rod. The mode of fishing in such limited, and often very clear waters, is quite different from that which a man has to practise in more spacious and stronger rivers. But a good lengthy rod, where it is

Fishing Rod.   Hoop and Net.

Winch.

not too heavy for the single hand, gives the angler a greater command over the water, and enables him, not only to throw his flies
more lightly, but often to reach distant spots, where fine fish are
lying, without either overreaching himself, or having recourse
to wading.

Accidents to rods should be always calculated upon, whenever
we go to the waters. They often arise from the simplest circumstances or casualties. The salmon and trout fisher especially,
ought always to be provided with two or three spare top-pieces, in
case of any mishap from loss or breakage.

A trout rod for trolling for with minnow, should be from twelve
to fourteen, or even sixteen feet in length, of a good firm build, not
by any means so elastic as a fly rod. A rod for worm-fishing
ought to be stoutly and firmly constructed, of the same length as
a fly-one, and to feel, when placed in the hand, pretty stiff and tidy.
For what is called "bush-fishing," with the worm, a much shorter
rod will answer the purpose; and the stiffer and stronger it is the
better.

A pike rod ought to be very strong and stiff, and as straight as
an arrow. The length should not be more than about fourteen feet;
though, for our own part, we have often used rods of only ten feet.
The rings through which the line travels should be strong and
large; and, in our opinion, the fewer the better.

The rod for spinning the minnow is recommended by some
experienced anglers to be made of bamboo cane, and to be from
eighteen to twenty feet long, with a stiff top. A similar kind of
rod, but only about twelve feet in length, is used in angling with
the ledger bait for the barbel.

The rod adapted for roach and dace varies according to the
nature of the fishing ground. If the angler has to pass over high
banks, or lofty reeds, the rod should not be less than twenty feet,
and very light; but if the sport be pursued from a boat, or even on
water of easy access, a rod of twelve or fourteen feet will be
long enough.

For the convenience of travelling, either in England or on the
continent, what is termed "a general rod," is the most eligible.
It is so contrived, by means of top joints of various degrees of
length and elasticity, to answer the several purposes of fly-fishing,
trolling, or bottom-fishing. The whole affair may be packed up as
to be no more trouble than a single rod, and is often put into the
same dimensions of an ordinary walking stick.

FISHING LINES.

Fishing lines are made of various materials, and of various degrees of strength and length, depending entirely upon the kind of
angling for which they are required.

For salmon and trout-fishing, whatever length or strength we may fix upon, nothing is so good, in our humble opinion, *as a pure horse-hair line.* If you have a line for fly-fishing with any portion of silk in it, you can never throw a line of any considerable length with the requisite steadiness and precision. The reason is obvious. When the line has been a short time in the water, the silk gets *soaked*, becomes soft and flabby, and consequently falls heavily on the water. On the other hand, a good hair line invariably preserves its firmness and elasticity under all states and circumstances.

If the angler be fishing on lakes, or in large rivers, for salmon, he will require from eighty to one hundred yards of line; but if on a moderate-sized stream, from forty to fifty will be quite sufficient. We have seen, however, two hundred yards used in boat-fishing on a lake, and this quantity was not too much.

Some fly-fishers have their lines tapered at the bottom, in order to connect the gut and flies more immediately with it, and, indeed, this plan is now quite the fashion. But with all due deference to the prevailing mode, we ourselves prefer the old " cast line " of about four or five feet in length, and from four to six or eight hairs in thickness, on which to place the gut and flies. A line thus prepared can be thrown much truer to any given point, and possesses also other advantages over a tapered running line.

Lines for trolling are made of silk, silk and hair, and various other materials. In the process of trolling, the lightness and elasticity of the line are not of so much consequence as in fly-fishing; but, for our own part, we prefer hair lines before any other, even for this sport of trolling.

The line called a paternoster for perch fishing, is made of strong gut or gimp, on which are suspended, at certain distances, three or more hooks; the whole is connected with the wheel-line by a small swivel.

FISH-HOOKS.

There are two celebrated localities where the best hooks are manufactured—London and Limerick; and the majority of hooks assume the name of these respective places.

Good hooks are of essential importance to the angler, and we would most earnestly recommend all our countrymen who visit the Continent for the purpose of fishing, to provide themselves amply in England with these necessary articles, of all sorts and sizes.

There is some difference of opinion among experienced anglers as to hooks—some liking the bended ones, some the straight. Fancy, or custom, has had a good deal to do with the judgments in such conflicting determinations. We wish not to speak dogmatically on the subject, but only to crave the liberty of stating that we prefer the straight hook, both for flies and for bait, to the bent ones. In fly-fishing we have always found, or at least fancied we found, that we lost more fish by the crooked than the straight hooks; and in reference to bait, the bent part of a hook generally, if the bait be worm, breaks through and seriously damages it. This is the result of our own experience, and we state it for the guidance and consideration of others.

FISHING FLOATS.

Floats are necessary things in certain kinds of angling, and in some particular kinds of water; but they are, nevertheless, as all our best brethren of the craft will admit, necessary evils. We feel the operation of a prejudice when we see them in use. They bring to our minds, by the power of association, the infantile or youthful periods of our angling history, and when lofty and dignified sport has been long enjoyed, it is scarcely possible to bring us back to the idea that such appendages are useful.

LANDING-NET AND GAFF.

These things are absolutely requisite in some particular rivers and waters, where, owing to the nature of the banks and sides, it is difficult to land large fish. When made in a portable manner, so as to be carried in a fishing-basket, or creel, they prove occasional useful adjuncts to an angler's equipment. We think them, however, unnecessary articles in streams which have a broad and channelly bed; and we would never recommend them in such situations, for this plain reason, that the fish are easily enough brought to shore from waters of this description, by any angler of average skill and experience. Besides, there is more art required in capturing a fish with the slight tackle of a fly-line, and landing him, without any extraneous assistance. It should always be borne in mind, that the uncertainty and suspense connected with an angler's amusement, constitute some of the prime elements of his pleasure, and ought never to be materially diminished by mechanical contrivances.

ON THE METHOD OF MAKING FLIES.

The intelligent reader will bear in mind that all verbal or written instructions on this mechanical process must necessarily be very imperfect. Fly-making is just one of those delicate and minute matters which can be learned effectually only by imitation; just, in fact, as a man can be taught to make a shoe, a basket, a chair, or a table. You will learn more in an hour by the eye, than in a twelvemonth by the understanding. The best thing, therefore, a young angler can do, who is anxious and ambitious to excel in this department of the craft, is to get some friend who understands making artificial flies to instruct him in the business. Any one may soon acquire the requisite degree of knowledge; and a little patient practice will speedily render him an adept. To those who have witnessed professional fly-makers, nothing so strikingly shows the power gained by having the mind and fingers confined to one set of thoughts and actions. The rapidity of movement, the facility of handling the small and delicate materials, and the general winding up, and polishing off the entire fly, however small and complicated its shades and colours, seem to uninitiated persons as the effect of magic.

But in conformity with the general practice observed in constructing treatises on fishing, we shall here subjoin a few directions in detail for making artificial flies. We take the account from Captain Richardson and others, because anything like originality is quite out of the question in an operation so purely imitative and mechanical.

The surest way to complete a number of flies is to have every necessary material arranged immediately under your eye; every article separate and distinct so as to be grasped in a moment; and all the hooks, and gut, or hair, wings, hackles, dubbing, silk, and wax, neatly assorted, and prepared for instant use. The hooks require to be sized for different flies; the gut demands the most careful examination and adjustment; the hackles must be stripped, and the dubbing well waxed; the silk must be carefully assorted, and of the very finest texture; and the wings must be tied the length of the hook they are to be fastened to, in order that the fibres of the feathers may be brought into the small compass of the hook. This previous care and trouble not only save time in the process, but ensure a degree of neatness in the execution that is otherwise almost unattainable.

The tying of the wings is thus performed. A piece of well waxed silk is laid in a noose on the forefinger of the left hand; the wings, or feathers, are put in the under part of the noose, and at the distance of the length of the wing required; the thumb is then applied closely to the feather, and with one end of the noose in the mouth, and the other in the right hand, the noose is drawn quite tight, and the silk is then cut within an inch of the knot, thus leaving a handle by which to hold the wing. If the thumb be not firmly pressed, the feathers will be pulled away, and the article will be useless.

First Method.—How to make a fly with the wings in the natural position in the first instance.

Hold the hook by the bend, with the point downwards, between the forefinger and the thumb of the left hand. With your waxed silk in your right hand, give one or two turns round the bare hook, about midway, lay the end of the gut along the upper side of the hook (if tied on the under side the fly will not swim, but continually revolve), and wrap the silk firmly until you get within a few turns of the top. Then you must take the wings, lay them along the shank with your right hand, and hold them stiffly in their place to the hook with the left hand. This done, tie the feathers tightly at the point of contact with two or three turns, cut off the superfluous ends of the feathers; and, tying the head of the fly tight, you must carry the silk round the hook, until you come to the knot which fastens the wings. Divide the wings equally, and pass the silk through the division, alternately, two or three times, in order to keep the wings separate and distinctly from each other.

Now prepare the hackle, by drawing down the fibres, taking care to have two or three less on the but, on that side of the feather which comes next to the hook, in order that it may revolve without twisting away.

Tie the but-end of the hackle close to the wings, having its upper or dark side to the head of the fly. The Scotch dressers of flies reverse this, and tie the hackle with its under side to the head, and also strip the fibres entirely from that side which touches the hook. Take the dubbing between the forefinger and the thumb of the right hand, twist it very thinly about your silk, and carry it round the hook as far as you intend the hackle or legs to extend, and hold it firm between the forefinger and thumb of the left hand, or fasten it at once. Then, with your pliers, carry the hackle round the hook, close under the wings, down to where you have already brought your silk and dubbing; continue to finish your body, by carrying over the end of the hackle, and when you have made the body of sufficient length, fasten off, by bringing the silk twice or thrice loosely round the hook, passing the end through the coils to make all snug and right.

Some finish the body of the fly thus:—When the hackle is fastened, after it has made the legs of the fly, the bare silk is carried up to the legs, and there fastened.

Second Method.—This manner of proceeding differs from the first in the fixing on of the wings. When you have fastened the gut and hook together to the point where the wings are to be tied, apply the wings to the hook with the but of the feather laying uppermost; then, when the wings are well fastened, pull them back into the natural position alternately; and, having your silk firmly tied to the roots of the wings (and not over the roots), the fly is to be completed as in the first method, having cut off the roots of the feather.

Third Method.—This includes the Irish mode of tying flies, and is the plan generally adopted in those places where flies are manufactured extensively for sale.

There are two ways of finishing a fly under this head.

If the wings are to be reversed or turned back, they are to be tied to the hook first, but not immediately turned back; the silk is carried to the tail of the fly, when the dubbing is carried round the hook until the putting on of the hackle; the hackle is tied by the point, and not by the but. Having finished the body, twist on the hackle close up to the wings, and fasten by one or two loops; then divide the wings, and pass the silk between them, pulling them back to their proper position, and finishing the head; fasten off by one or two loops.

The Irish tie over the roots of the wings, which interferes with their action in the water and renders them lifeless.

If the wings are placed at once in their natural position, and the fly is to be finished at the head, the gut must be tied on the hook, beginning near the head, and finishing at the tail; twist on the body up to the legs, fasten on the hackle by the point, finish the body and the legs, and then apply and fasten the wings; and, when properly divided, cut off the but-ends, finish the head, and fasten off your silk by one or two loops. This concludes the method of making the winged fly.

TO MAKE THE PALMER OR HACKLE FLY.

The making of the *Palmer* or *Hackle-fly*, with the cock's or hen's feathers, is simply as described in the foregoing methods, namely, by twisting on the legs and body, taking care that the hackle has fibres as long as, or rather longer than the hook it is to be twisted upon.

But in making hackle-flies with the feathers of other birds, such as the snipe, dotterel, &c., the feather is prepared by stripping off the superfluous fibres at the but-end, and then drawing back a sufficient quantity of fibre to make the fly. Take the feather by the root, and put the whole of the fibres into your mouth and wet them, so that they may adhere together, back to back. When the gut is fastened to the hook, then twist it twice or thrice round the hook, and fasten it by one or more loops; the fibres of the feather will then lie the reverse way. Cut off the superfluous parts of the feather that remain after tying, and twist on the body of the required length; fasten by two loops; draw down the fibres of the feather to the bend, and the fly is finished.

If the tinsel, or gold, or silver twist be required for the body of the fly, it must be tied on after the hackle, but carried round the body before the hackle makes the legs. If the tinsel be required only at the tail of the fly, it must be tied on immediately after the gut and hook are put together, the hackle next, then the body, &c. &c.

And here we think is the proper place to make an observation or two about the fitness or expediency of making tackle at home. Many things have altered their aspects within the last half-century, and fishing-tackle making and selling is one of these. In former times—and the thing is now the case in remote districts of the country—a fisher was almost laid under a fixed necessity to manufacture his own rods, and lines, and flies; but now the

London trade, in all the materials connected with the piscatory art, is so wonderfully extended, and has now such a general and easy mode of transacting business in country districts, that it has become a matter of pure prudence and economy whether it is not better to buy than to make one's fishing outfit. It is now argued —and argued fairly and rationally—that the perfection to which the London tackle-making trade has brought everything they manufacture, and the low prices at which they are disposed of, forbid every man whose time is worth anything, from wasting it on making his own implements of fishing. If all the materials he requires were purchased with a view of making, instead of buying, fishing tackle, the maker would find the cost much heavier than it would be worth after it was used up, and made; without taking into consideration that there could not be that skill, neatness, delicacy, and soundness, which the tackle-makers of the present day guarantee in every article they send out of their premises. The waste of time is saved by judicious purchases, and one can scarcely hesitate to pronounce that the best home-made rod that was ever made was vastly inferior to those manufactured by first-rate workmen in the craft, wno have made the profession their study, and worked at it all their lives. Such persons become possessed of such a keen professional eye, that no improvement can escape them. There are many establishments in London, and even in provincial towns of any considerable magnitude, where every description of fly, every kind of line, and all the various patterns and sizes of hooks, floats, rods, &c., can be found, and at a price, too, which none but those who manufacture extensively for wholesale purposes can produce them at; and where every contrivance for taking fish and securing them may be purchased as good as the best materials and workmanship can procure. "Where, then," it is asked, "are the inducements for making our own?" None but the distance a man may be from a tackle-warehouse when he wants it; and considering that most things may be transmitted in a single post, there can be very little inducement under any circumstances. Our advice is, that persons at a distance from London or country tackle-shops, should lay in a plentiful stock of those articles which take but little room, and cost but little money. Gut and hair hooks, flies of all kinds, floats, two, three, or four yards lengths of gut, which are always kept in readiness regularly tapered, the heaviest being at the upper end, and each link gradually diminishing, some very strong and others light, a clearing ring, and other smaller matters of this kind. The lovers of angling may take our word that, however wise it may be to repair accidents, and re-whip a hook occasionally, it is better to be provided with every thing ready for use. Every leisure day at home these things should be examined, and whatever runs short should be ordered at once. It is bad policy, or no policy, to be short of any thing, and particularly of what cannot be procured without delay."

So much for the cause of the fishing-tackle shops. We are anxious that the fullest knowledge on the subject should be generally known among anglers; and this is our chief reason for submitting these statements without note or comment.

BAITS.

Baits are the next important things to speak about, next to tackle. They are of different kinds, and are, on the whole, very numerous. They demand the particular attention of the angler. We shall, at present, and under this head, merely give an enumeration of baits, leaving the specific application of them individually to that part of our work which treats of the different kinds of fish, and how to take them.

ARTIFICIAL FLIES.

These are very numerous; and the varied materials of which they are composed may be best obtained from a plain and simple catalogue of them. We therefore submit the following to the reader's attention.

1. THE CHANTREY.—This fly was a great favourite with the late Sir Francis Chantrey, and is an excellent killer. *Imitation.*—Body, copper-coloured peacock's herl, ribbed with gold twist; legs, a black hackle; wings, partridge's or brown hen's feather, or pheasant's tail. Hook, No. 9, or No. 10.

2. HOFLAND'S FANCY may be used after sunset with success in any part of the kingdom, and in any season. *Imitation.*—Body, reddish brown silk; legs, red hackle; wings, woodcock's tail; tail, two or three strands of a red hackle. Hook, No. 10.

3. MARCH BROWN, also called the Dun Drake, appears about the latter end of March, and continues in season till the beginning of May; it will be found a very killing fly, in many lakes in Wales, from March to September. *Imitation.*—Body, fur of the hare's ear, ribbed with olive silk; legs, partridge hackle; wings, tail feather of the partridge; tail, two or three strands of the partridge feather. Hook, No. 8, or No. 9.

4. BLUE DUN.—Appears in March, and generally upon the water in dark, windy days, may be used with success till October. *Imitation.*—Body, dubbed with water-rat's fur, and ribbed with yellow silk; legs, dun hen's hackle; wings, from the feather of the starling's wing; tail, two strands of a grizzle cock's hackle. Hook, No. 10.

5. FOR CARSHALTON AND THE TEST.—I am not acquainted with a proper name for this fly, but it is much used at Carshalton, and on the Test in Hampshire, and is a well-dressed fly, likely to kill in other streams. *Imitation.*—Body, black silk, ribbed with silver twist; legs, a dark grizzle hackle; wings, the dark

feather of the starling's wing, made spare and short. Hook, No. 10.

6. CARSHALTON COCK-TAIL.—A dun fly, and will be found a good killer in other streams as well as the Wandle. *Imitation.* —Body, light blue fir; legs, dark dun hackle; wings, the inside feather of a teal's wings; tail, two fibres of a white cock's hackle. Hook, No. 9, or No. 10.

7. THE PALE YELLOW DUN.—Excellent from April to the end of the season. *Imitation.*—Body, yellow mohair, or marten's pale yellow fur, tied with yellow silk; wings, the lightest part of a feather from a young starling's wing. Hook, No. 12.

8. THE ORANGE DUN.—Another fly in request on the Test and other southern streams. *Imitation.*—Body, red squirrel's fur, ribbed with gold thread; legs, red hackle; wings, from the starling's wing; tail, two fibres of red cock's hackle. Hook, No. 9.

9. THE COACHMAN.—*Imitation.*—Body, copper-coloured peacock's herl; legs, red hackle; wings, from the landrail. Hook, No. 8.

10. COW-DUNG FLY is in season throughout the year, and is used chiefly in dark, windy weather. *Imitation.*—Body, dull lemon-coloured mohair; legs, red hackle; wings, from feathers of the landrail, or starling's wing. Hook, No. 8, or No. 9.

11. THE HARE'S-EAR DUN.—A killing fly, and in great favour in Hampshire. *Imitation.*—Body, the fur of the hare's ear; wings, the feather from a starling's wing; tail, two fibres of the brown feather from a starling's wing. Hook, No. 10.

12. EDMONDSON'S WELSH FLY.—Constantly used in Wales by the skilful fly-fisher and tackle-maker whose name it bears, Mr. Edmondson of Liverpool. A killing fly in most of the large lakes and rivers of Wales, and would answer for many of the lakes of England, Scotland, and Ireland. *Imitation.*—Body, dull orange mohair; legs, the black feather of a partridge; wings, the feather from a woodcock's wing, or the tail of a hen grouse. Hook, No. 8.

13. THE KINGDOM OR KINDON.—Much in use in the Hampshire streams, and is a good general fly also. *Imitation.*—Body, pale yellow silk, ribbed with crimson silk; legs, black hackle; wings, the feather of a woodcock's wing. Hook, No. 9.

14. BROWN SHINAR is a favourite with the Welsh anglers, also excellent for the rivers and lakes of Cumberland. *Imitation.*— Body, peacock's herl, twisted spare, with a grouse-hackle over it.

15. GRAVEL, OR SPIDER-FLY, appears towards the latter end of April; where it is met with, it may be fished with all day, and the trout take it freely. *Imitation.*—Water-rat's fur; legs, black hackle; wings, the feather from a partridge. Hook, No. 10, or No. 11. It may also be made with a dark dun hackle, which I prefer instead of the partridge feather.

16. THE IRON BLUE is in season from April till July, and

c

may be again used in September and October. *Imitation.*—
Body, the fur of the water-rat; legs, a light dun hackle; wings,
the tail feather of a tom-tit, or of an American robin. Hook, No.
12, or No. 13.

17. THE GREAT RED SPINNER may be used as an evening fly
during the whole summer season. *Imitation.*—Body, hog's wool,
red and brown, mixed, ribbed with gold twist; legs, bright red
cock's hackle; wings, the light feather of the starling's wing;
tail, three strands of a red cock's hackle. Hook, No. 7.

18. BLACK GNAT.—A capital fly for dace as well as trout, and
may be used from April to the end of the season. *Imitation.*—
Body, black hackle, or ostrich herl, tied with black silk; wings,
the feather from a starling's wing. Hook, No. 13.

19. WREN-TAIL is an excellent killer in small, bright streams,
and is in great favour in the northern counties. *Imitation.*—
Body, dark orange silk, with wings and legs of a wren's tail.
Hook, No. 12.

20. THE BRACKEN-CLOTH is a kind of beetle. If made upon a
large hook it will be found an excellent fly for the lakes in
Scotland. *Imitation.*—Body, peacock's herl, dressed full, and
tied with proper silk; wings, feather of a pheasant's breast.
Hook, No. 9, or No. 10; for lake fishing, No. 6, or No. 7.

21. RED ANT.—This is the small red ant, and there is another
of the same size, called the black ant, and two others, named
the large black and red ants. *Imitations.*—Body, peacock's herl,
made full at the tail, and spare towards the head; legs, red, or
ginger-cock's hackle; wings, from the light feather of the starling's wing. Hook, No. 9, or No. 10.

22. THE SAND-FLY.—Equally good for trout or greyling, from
April to the end of September. *Imitation.*—The fur from a hare's
neck, twisted round silk of the same colour; legs, a ginger-
hen's hackle; wings, the feather from the landrail's wing. Hook,
No. 9.

23. THE STONE-FLY is one of the larger kind of flies, and
appears in April; it is used in windy weather, and is a good fly
in May or June, early in the morning or late in the evening.
Imitation.—Body, fur of hare's ear, mixed with brown and yellow
mohair, and ribbed with yellow silk; the yellow colour towards
the tail; legs, brownish-red hackle; wings, the dark feather of the
mallard's wing; tail, two or three fibres of the mottled feather of
a partridge. Hook, No. 6.

24. ALDER-FLY.—Makes its appearance early in May, and may
be used through June; it is an excellent fly during the drake
season, and will tempt the trout, even where the may-fly is strong
on the water. *Imitation.*—Body, peacock's herl, tied with dark-
brown silk; legs, coch-a-bonddu hackle; wings, the brown-
speckled feather of a mallard's back. Hook, No. 8.

If this fly be dressed on a No. 6 or 7 hook, and winged with the
red rump-feather of a pheasant, it will be found an excellent lake fly.

25. GREEN DRAKE.—Appears late in May or early in June. This short-lived insect is not to be found on every stream : I have never seen it on the Wandle. *Imitation.*—Body, yellow flos silk, ribbed with brown silk; the extreme head and tail, coppery peacock's herl; legs, a red or ginger hackle; wings, the mottled wing of a mallard, stained olive; tail or whisk, three hairs from a rabbit's whiskers. Hook, No. 6.

26. GREY DRAKE.—*Imitation.*—Body, white flos silk, ribbed with dark brown or mulberry-coloured silk; head and top of the tail, a peacock's herl; legs, a grizzle cock's hackle; wings, from a mallard's mottled feather, made to stand upright; tail, three whiskers of a rabbit.

27. THE BLACK PALMER is a standard fly, and its merits are too well known to need description. It is a valuable drop-fly in dark, rainy, or windy weather, and in full water. *Imitation.*—Ostrich's herl, ribbed with silver twist, and a black cock's hackle over all.

28. THE SOLDIER PALMER.—This fly (and its varieties) may be considered the most general fly on the list, and many anglers never fit up a fly-link without having a red hackle, of some kind, for a drop-fly. *Imitation.*—Body, red mohair, or squirrel's fur, ribbed with gold twist, and red cock's hackle over all.

29. THE GOVERNOR is used on the Hampshire rivers. *Imitation.*—Body, coppery-coloured peacock's herl, ribbed with gold twist, tipped with scarlet twist; legs, red or ginger hackle; wings, the light part of a pheasant's wing. Hook, No. 9.

30. FOR LOCH AWE.—*Imitation.*—Body, orange mohair; legs, ginger hackle; wings, from the feather of the pheasant's tail. Hook, No. 8.

31. SECOND FLY FOR LOCH AWE.—*Imitation.*—Body, copper-coloured peacock's herl; legs, black hackle; wings, the feather from a water-hen's wing. Hook, No. 7.

32. FOR THE RIVER DEE.—This, and the following will be found to be killing flies in the River Dee. *Imitation.*—Body, dull yellow mohair; wings, hackle from the neck of a pale dun hen. Hook, No. 9.

33. ANOTHER FLY FOR THE RIVER DEE.—*Imitation.*—Body, peacock's herl; legs and wings, a dark dun hen's hackle, dressed rather full. Hook, No. 9.

34. A FLY FOR LLYN OGWYN.—This fly, and those recommended for Loch Awe, will ensure sport on this most sporting lake. *Imitation.*—Body, peacock's herl; legs, black hackle; wings, the dark copper-coloured feather of the mallard. Hook, No. 8.

35. COCH-A-BONDDU is a well-known favourite throughout the United Kingdom, though not always under the same name. *Imitation.*—Body, peacock's herl; legs and wings, red and black, or coch-a-bonddu hackle. Hook, No. 8 or 9; and in the north of England, for clear streams, it is sometimes dressed on a No. 12 hook.

36. THE YELLOW SALLY continues in season from May to July, in warm weather. *Imitation.*—Body, pale yellow fur, or mohair, ribbed with fawn-coloured silk; legs, a ginger hackle; wings, a white hackle, dyed yellow. Hook, No. 9.

COMMON BAITS AND GROUND BAITS.

It is well known that fish take such baits as the season affords, as worms, insects, &c.; and worms may be used all day in spring and autumn, but in summer only early in the morning and late in the evening.

Lob-worms.—These are the largest worms that are found in digging up a garden. They are often full six inches long, and are good bait for large greyling, trout, perch, bream, and eels.

The *brandling-worm* is a striped one, which smells strongly, and is found in rotten dung, and is a very seductive and killing bait for most fish.

Red-worms are found in rotten dung also, but are smooth, of a bright pink colour, and are a first-rate bait for roach, dace, perch, carp, tench, bream, trout of moderate size, barbel and most other fish, which will frequently take it when they cannot be tempted with any other.

The *marsh*, or *meadow-worm*, is also occasionally a good bait for trout, greyling, perch, bream, and gudgeons.

When you have procured fresh worms, put them in a box or jar of damp moss; they will clean themselves in a few hours and improve for several days, becoming brighter and tougher.

To keep worms for any length of time, they should be placed in a box with a few inches thickness of rich soil, such as dung rotted to mould, and then scour them, a few at a time, as wanted. Mr. Blaine, however, gives the following, though not in so few words:—

"*To preserve worms for use*, shred some mutton suet and chop it into small pieces; let it boil slowly in water until the suet is dissolved, and then, having ready some clean well-beaten hempen sacking or wrapper, dip it into the liquor. When well soaked in it, and having become cold, mix some fresh mould with the worms and put the whole into a tub, and over the top tie a linen cloth that will admit air, and yet prevent them escaping. Place them in a cool situation, and the worms will feed and cleanse themselves, and keep lively and fit for use for many months."

Gentles are a favourite bait, especially for roach, dace, and barbel. In fact, at times any fish will take it. Gentles may be bred by hanging up a piece of liver till it putrifies. They should be kept in sand. The largest should be chosen.

The *beetles* found in a cow-dung, and *wasp-grubs*, also constitute good bait.

The *caddis*, which is found at the shallow sides of rivers, stony brooks, and ditches, is a good bait for every fish in the water the caddis is found in.

Flag-worms, which are found amongst flags, in pits, or ponds, are good for the fish.

Caterpillars, cabbage-worms, &c., are good for trout, chub, roach, and dace, dropped on the surface of the water.

Salmon-spawn is a superior bait for trout, chub, roach, &c., and may be bought ready preserved.

Carpenter says, "Having obtained a pound of it, about September or October, put it into hot water, and having boiled it for about ten minutes, wash and clean it; rinse it well with cold water, and dry it. When dried, take two ounces of salt and a quarter of an ounce of pounded saltpetre, and mix it up with the spawn, after which it should be spread out on a dish or board before the fire, until it becomes quite stiff. Then put it into jars or gallipots, pouring over the top of each melted mutton suet, and covering with a bladder."

Paste is a good bait in still, quiet waters, with a small hook and a light float. See that it is clean, or the fish will not take it.

A good paste for carp, roach, tench, and chub, is made of crumb of white bread.

A good paste, especially for chub, is made of rotten Cheshire cheese and crumb of bread.

Greaves paste—that is, a paste made of white bread dipped into the liquor in which greaves have been boiled—is a killing bait for barbel, but wheat paste is a favourite bait in some parts of the country, as is also pearl-barley. The wheat should be freed from the husks by keeping ten or twelve hours in water, and then par-boiled, which will swell it to twice its natural size. Malt and pearl-barley may be prepared in the same way. They may be crushed and used like a paste, or a single grain be taken and put on the hook, after the manner of baiting with a gentle.

Ground-baiting should be done the night before, when it is practicable.

Greaves boiled, and worked up into balls with clay and bran, is a good ground-bait for barbel.

White bread soaked in water, and mixed up with bran and pollard, is a ground-bait for carp, roach, dace, and chub.

Clay and bran mixed together, and made into small balls, may be used for roach, dace, and bleak.

Carrion gentles, or *worms cut into pieces,* are sometimes used with great success in still waters.

For roach, dace, bream, and every other fish in still water, bread chewed till it sinks is the very best ground-bait; or, if it be too much trouble, knead some very moist, that it may partly separate as it sinks. Use this in small quantities upon the very spot you fish.

For roach-fishing in rivers, bread and bran kneaded together till they are sticky or clammy, and put a coating of a quarter of an inch thick round good-sized pebbles.

BAITING THE GROUND.

Those who live near a river, and especially those whose premises adjoin it, should select an even bottom and a place moderately deep, and regularly feed the fish. Make everything convenient for the sport; put up a hurdle, if there be no bushes, and tuck evergreen branches between the bars: make it fast in the ground, rather leaning over the water. If there be an eddy, or scarcely any stream, you may hang up a liver or a dead cat on a sloping stick for want of a tree, so that the maggots may drop from it in such a spot that they will get to the bottom about where you fish; or it is better to provide carrion gentles, and worms, and bait the place exactly day after day. If there be a stream, make balls of clay, maggots, and worms, bread, greaves, snails, and any living things you can get, only use enough clay to sink them—in other words, make the ground-bait rich: when you are going to fish, put the same quantity of bait, but make it poor, and you are as sure of sport as you wet your line. Whoever fishes a pond or river often should prepare a place; and the object of the hurdle is to place a complete screen between you and the fish, and it will be the fault of the angler if he is seen at all. Land your fish beyond the hurdle, on the side which is most handy. When you are on your own ground, if there be no holes or deep places, make one at any cost; and this is especially necessary in some ponds which are shallow at the edge. When there are many weeds, have them cleared, if possible, altogether. If no other way presents itself, use your drag, but it should be done days before you fish. Make but a hole, or small deep, form a good screen, regularly feed the fish, and with good clean baits and appropriate tackle you will take some of the best in the water.

Before closing this account of tackle and baits, we beg to remark that attention to these respective objects is of great importance to the angler, and a very necessary ingredient of his success in the pursuit of all kinds of fish. We like to see care bestowed on this part of piscatory duty. We never see a tidy and neat rod fisher, but the simple and expressive lines of old Doctor Cotton rush into our mind; written more than two hundred years ago, yet full of freshness and meaning at the present hour. We shall transcribe them for the reader's pleasure and instruction.

> " Away to the brook,
>   All your tackle out-look,
> Here's a day that is worth a day's wishing.
>   See that all things be right,
>   For 'twould be a spite
> To want tools when a man goes a fishing.

" Your rod with tops two,
　　For the same will not do,
If your manner of angling you vary;
　　And full well may you think,
　　If you troll with a pink,
One too weak will be apt to miscarry.

" Then, basket, neat made
　　By a master in's trade,
In a belt at your shoulders must dangle;
　　For none e're was so vain
　　To wear this in disdain,
Who a true brother was of the angle.

" Next, pouch must not fail,
　　Stuffed as full as a mail,
With wax, crewels, silks, hairs, furs, and feathers,
　　To make several flies
　　For the severe skies,
That shall kill in despite of all weathers.

" The boxes and books
　　For your lines and your hooks,
And, though not for strict need notwithstanding,
　　Your scissars and hone
　　To adjust your points on,
With a net to be sure of your landing.

" All these being on,
　　'Tis high time we were gone,
Down and upwards, that all may have pleasure,
　　Till, here meeting at night,
　　We shall have the delight
To discourse of our fortunes at leisure."

Having now mentioned the principal matters connected with
rods, and tackle generally, it is proper we should say a word or
two on the modes of using them, or, perhaps, more fitly, the
mechanical art of angling itself.

It must always be borne in mind that the gentle art is an *imitative* one. It is best learned by looking at others fishing, and
making accurate observations from what experience teaches.
This must ever be the grand school for the angler. All that books
on the subject can do, is to lay down such general rules as may
guide the understanding in the use of instruments, and keep
young beginners from falling into egregious errors at the commencement of their career. Most anglers have begun to frequent
the rivers when young; and youth in general is the aptest time for
learning many things; but persons considerably advanced in years

may soon render themselves respectable fly-fishers by paying a little
attention to it, by going a few times with a person who is himself
acquainted with the art. We have taught three or four gentlemen
the amusement who had never before thrown a single fly into the
water, and they were, in point of age, full fifty, or even more. The
chief matter is the *desire* to learn. Where this exists in any great
vigour, and proper means be adopted, success becomes almost
certain.

The two leading points connected with fly-fishing for salmon and
trout are the casting of the flies, and the acquirement of that peculiar
knowledge or tact which enables the skilful angler to recognise,
at a glance, those parts of a river or stream where such kinds of fish
are likely to lie during particular parts of the day or season.

One of the first maxims a learner should fix in his mind is, not to
have *too long* a line. He should not attempt too much at once.
To acquire the steady and efficient command of the rod is a vital
matter. To throw long lines steadily and lightly is an art which
can only be acquired by considerable practice and observation;
therefore, a learner should never feel discouraged should his progress in this angling accomplishment not keep pace with his san-
guine expectations. A cast line, with gut and flies, should be just
the length of the rod, and no longer; and all first efforts in the
art should be confined to the employment of a very few yards
more in making casts upon the water; and as the pupil progresses
in adroitness and skill, he can, of course, lengthen his line
accordingly.

There is a great comfort and convenience connected with the
use of a single-handed fly-rod. In small rivers, particularly if the
banks are lined with brushwood, and the water is reedy, and the
bottom full of roots of trees, &c., the angler should learn the habit
of what may be called "chucking" his fly into those parts of the
stream which run under bushes, and form strong ripples and currents beneath overhanging boughs. In such situations, the trout
are generally numerous, and of the first size and quality. We
have seen many good two-handed fly-fishers who lost ranges of the
finest water on account of not being able to fish narrow and
woody streams. In rivers which run through a bed scooped out
by mountain torrents, two or three times as broad as the quantity
of water which they commonly supply, the fly-fisher has plenty of
elbow-room, and can use a long rod and line, which require both
hands, with good effect; but in smaller waters, such as those just
described, there is nothing like a single-handed rod; it gives you
greater power over the stream, and enables you, as it were, to pick
fish out of places that the double-handed artist must invariably
pass by.

To measure distances by the eye with accuracy, is an essential
part of the fly-fisher's profession. This can only be acquired by
close attention to the subject, and constant practice. No written
or verbal rules of direction can possibly reach it; and yet any

one may attain a high degree of excellence in this respect, if he devote himself patiently to the subject; and one or two seasons' free range with the fly will enable a man to hit his point to a hair's breadth in every cast of the line.

In the progress of the art of angling, many crotchety and fanciful rules are laid down with sufficient dogmatism. Amongst these, that which recommends fishing *up* a stream instead of down it, still retains its advocates and defenders. We do not hesitate to say, nothing can be more preposterous than this notion. If the angler will observe attentively the manner in which flies lie on the water, when the line is thrown up against the current, he will see in an instant the *almost impossibility* of the trout seizing the fly in such a position. But even if the fish should take it, the power is greatly weakened, if not entirely lost, to retain him; for the tightness and tenacity of the line are destroyed by the captive rushing down the stream, right into your face as it were.

The best, pleasantest, and indeed the only efficient mode, is to fish *down* the river; and where it is possible, fish each stream in it right across. To do this, begin at that part of the stream which is nearest to you, and trail or draw your line at a considerable angle to the other, or *vice versa*, as the case may be. If the fish rise when your tackle is in this position, there is a far greater probability of his hooking himself, than if any other direction were taken; and, when hooked, his rushes and plunges down the stream, bring him in direct opposition to the strain of the line and the spring of the rod, and so expedite his capture. If it should happen, as it often does, that you have a strong head-wind against you in descending a river, then you must make the best of your situation, and contrive to throw your line at as slight an angle in an upward direction as the breeze will permit you. Steady practice and perseverance, however, will enable you to overcome all difficulty arising from this source, unless you encounter a downright hurricane.

To have, what may be called, an *angler's eye*, is of great importance in fly-fishing, and indeed in fishing of all kinds. This consists in perceiving at a glance where the fish may be presumed to be, in any stream or water. This apparently intuitive knowledge, is solely the result of observation and experience, and no written or verbal directions can convey it to the young beginner. Still without it no man can hope to make any satisfactory progress in the art. An expert angler, if he sees a brother of the craft flogging away in certain parts of the water, detects in a moment that he can have no correct notions on the subject, and is, in this matter, a veritable ignoramus. "For, to an angler's eye, it is requisite that a stream ever should have a certain shape—a contour, a physiogonomy, a character—to solicit his attention and favour. Every disciple of the rod carries about with him an *ideal* figure of a perfect stream, where, in all rivers—under every parallel of latitude and longitude—he is morally certain to find the object

of which he is in quest. This beau ideal of watery conformations
is not a variable or uncertain thing; it has in every one's eye the
same general outline and expression. We know that what is at
this moment prefigured to our imaginations as the height of perfection, is the same as that which occupies the mind of every other
angler in the kingdom, who is entitled to the appellation. A fine
fishing stream has all the standard elements of permanent beauty
that appertain to the beautiful in every branch of art or science
whatever."*

The trout observes the same rule as the salmon, with respect
to his haunts and places of abode. The latter never ventures
into very shallow water, at a great distance from a deep place
of shelter; and thus long, shallow streams, situated at a considerable distance from a range of deep water, are seldom frequented by large trout, except at night in the summer season,
when they often run a considerable distance up such places in
pursuit of minnows. Those streams, therefore, are the best which
lead immediately into tolerably deep water.

It is a good general rule in fly-fishing, *never to remain very long at
one particular spot*. When you have the water before you, take
the best streams, and fish them carefully, but as quickly as you
can. Remember *a trout never can be enticed*. All his movements
are impulsive and prompt; and if you cast your fly where he lies,
he will generally dash at it at once; but should he miss it in his
first eagerness, do not tempt him again for a few minutes; rather
recede from the spot a little to allow him time to regain his former
position, and then you will stand a fair chance of getting hold
of him at the next attack. Many an excellent trout has been
caught in this manner, which would have been lost altogether, if
the angler had persisted in thrashing away at him after his first
unsuccessful rise.

We shall proceed no further with our general remarks on the
purely mechanical and prudential rules relative to the art of
angling at the present time. We shall have to state several
matters of importance to the practical fisherman when we come to
treat of the various kinds of fish contained in our list.

* Guide to the Rivers and Lochs of Scotland. London, 1854.

Salmon, p. 27

Trout, p. 37.

Pike, p. 53.

CHAPTER III.

OF THE DIFFERENT KINDS OF FISH.

THE SALMON.

THE Salmon is the noblest of fresh-water fish, and stands highest in the angler's estimation. He is the prince of the streams; and his title to precedence has never yet been questioned. His magnitude, his keen and lively eye, his muscular powers, his rapid and graceful motions, his beautiful proportions, his shining silvery scales, his intellectual instinct, and his superior, rich, delicate flavour, all unite in establishing superiority over all other fish. Neither should it be forgotten that salmon-fishing is considered the angler's highest sport, whilst it affords the best criterion of his professional skill. Indeed, angling for this noble fish, may be deemed the measure or standard of the angler's dexterity, the test of his art, the legitimate object of his loftiest aspirations; affording an undeniable proof of his fitness to take his stand amongst the most accomplished adepts of this interesting craft.

The Salmon was not known to the ancient Greeks. The first notice we have of it is in Pliny's "Natural History" (9, 12), and the first regular account we have of it in any Latin classic author, is contained in the "Mosella" of Ausonius. Here we have the progressive stages in the growth of the fish. The *salar* is the sea-trout, the *fario* is what in Scotland is called the grilse, and the *salmo* is the full-grown fish. A recent writer on the subject says,—

"It is pretty certain that the ancients knew some members of the salmon family; as to that prince of river fish, however, salmon—the glory and representative of this large family—the Greeks have left us no extant proof that they were at all acquainted with it; and though we know that many of their treatises on fish, wherein mention of the salmon might have occurred, have not come down to us, we can hardly imagine such a noble species, if at all known in Greece, should by any possibility have escaped alike the notice of Aristotle, and of the host of *diepnosophist* fish fanciers, quoted in Athenæus. Among the Latins, Pliny is the only author who makes a cursory mention of the *salar*, and he does not speak of it as an Italian fish, but as frequenting the rivers Dordogne and Garonne, in Aquitaine. It was thus, before the days of 'Kippes,' plainly out of the reach of the luxurious Romans, whatever favourable reports they may have received of its merits from passing tourists."[*]

The natural history of the salmon is still wrapped in considerable mystery, though successful attempts have, within the last ten years, been made in clearing up some important facts connected with their migratory habits, modes of propagation, and ratio of growth. They resemble in their movements some of the feathered creation, such as the swallow for example. Salmon have a strong inclination to return to their last year's quarters, but are often diverted from their course by any slight alterations in the course of the river, or any new obstacle, as buildings, dams, &c., placed across their path. In the history of the salmon-fisheries in Great Britain, many curious facts are recorded about them as to these particulars. Although a northern fish, and abounding in high latitudes in great profusion, yet naturalists tell us that they are not partial to a very cold stream, but prefer that one whose waters are warmer, and where the rays of the sun have free access to it. "There are two rivers in Southerlandshire," says Sir William Jardine, "one, the Oikel, rising in a small Alpine lake; the other, the Shin, a tributary about five miles from its mouth, coming out of Loch Shin, a large and deep lake connected with other deep locks; in early spring most of the salmon turn up the Shin, which is the warmer of the two, while very few prosecute the main current until a later period of the year."

The salmon spawns generally in the months of September and October, but there is a difference in this respect in different rivers. This fact has been fully established in Parliamentary records, framed with a direct reference to projected laws for the preservation of this kind of fish. It is during this particular season of the year that the salmon are seen passing up the rivers in enormous shoals, and leaping over every obstacle which lies across their path. The extraordinary power and agility the fish display in these remarkable leaps, have long been the wonder of the naturalist, and the theme of admiration and surprise to the angler. They will spring over rapid falls from seven to ten feet in height, and force their way against a powerful volume of descending water. It is when the salmon are running up streams of this description, broken by rapids, and crossed by cataracts, and when they thus meet with apparently insuperable obstacles to their progress, that enormous quantities are killed by poachers and fish-hunters, with spears, leisters, and nets. We have frequently seen a band of men come down to celebrated salmon-rivers, in the North of England and in Scotland, with a cart and horse, and in a very short space of time catch as many as the animal could draw. In fact the destruction of salmon at this season of the year is quite appalling; and were it not for the vigilance of the guardians of the rivers, and the strictness of the laws, the species would scarcely be able to exist, under the constant repetition of practices so manifestly destructive and unfair.

The mode in which the salmon disposes of its spawn has been often dwelt upon and discussed by scientific anglers. But, as the subject does not immediately and necessarily come across the path of the sportsman, we shall not enter upon any elaborate description of this peculiar process, but rather content ourselves with a few general observations on the matter.

For the secure and effectual depositions of its spawn, the salmon invariably selects pure running streams, with gravelly bottoms. All slow, stagnant, sluggish, and clayey bedded rivers, are carefully avoided, or at most very, very seldom entered. In their choice of the stream, the fish never make any very serious mistake, but are conducted by an almost infallible instinct to a safe and suitable deposit, with all the certainty and regularity that experience and reason could themselves confer. Salmon generally swim pretty close to the bottom of the river, and pursue their onward course with rapidity and decision; and, indeed, some naturalists have affirmed that they frequently run at the rate of five-and-twenty miles an hour, in waters where they encounter no obstacles.

When the gill, or male fish, finds a proper place, he works in the ground with his nose, until he has made a hole or bed sufficiently large for the reception of the spawn; and when this subaqueous nuptial couch is all prepared, he looks out for his mate, and they jointly take possession of their temporary residence. When the process is finished they both return to their haunts in the river, or dash back to the sea on the first favourable opportunity. This is substantially the state of the case, as far as the mere act of depositing the spawn is concerned. It has been more minutely described by some naturalists and angling writers than by others, but the general result is comprised in the statement now made.

But here a controversy starts, which has of very recent years been carried on, but without the main questions having been as yet brought to a satisfactory and general decision. What becomes of the salmon-fry when hatched into life? What shape, colour, size do they assume? How do they regulate their movements? These are still, in some measure, debateable and unsettled questions. The old opinions used to be these:—After the roe had been deposited by the parent fish a sufficient length of time in the bottom they had channelled out, it became quickened into life by some hidden and inscrutable process, and became *salmon fry*, which attained a length of from four to seven inches by the months of March or April. They then, in a flooded state of the waters, made their way down to the sea, and in the months of June, July, and August, returned again to their native streams, increased by a very rapid growth, and the fattening powers of the salt water, to a weight varying from two to six or seven pounds.

Every one who has angled in a river where salmon frequent in any considerable numbers, knows, that in the spring months, that is in March, April, and part of May, he meets with immense swarms of *smelts*, or *smoults*, or *parr*, that these take the artificial fly most greedily, and that they afterwards seem to disappear, or, at least, are but comparatively seldom met with in fishing the

streams. The law forbids the taking of these small fry, but as far
as our experience has gone, we have seldom seen this enactment
obeyed to any extent, even by the most scrupulous and high-minded
anglers. With the mass of fishermen, the maxim, unhappily, holds
good almost everywhere, that " all are fish that come into the net."
To justify the infraction of this law, it has been often contended
that the *par,* or smoult, was a minute but distinct species of the
salmonidœ, and that its capture was both fair and reasonable.

This matter was examined into. It was affirmed that these
swarms of small fish were nothing more nor less than the salmon
itself in the infant stage of its being. Mr. Shaw, manager of the
Duke of Buccleugh's salmon fisheries in Scotland, instituted, a
short time back, experiments on the subject upon an extensive
scale. This gentleman asserts, that what is commonly called the
parr, is the salmon fry in the first stage of their development.
That in this state, as parr, they remain in the river in which they
were brought forth for one whole year; that in the second year
their outer covering of scales is moulted off as it were, and they
then assume the character of graveling or smoults, which was formerly supposed to be the first stage of the salmon's existence;
that when they are two years old, being still in the dress or outward covering of a smoult, and averaging from five to seven inches
in length, they descend to the ocean, and in the course of a few
months or weeks, re-enter the river as grisle, or salmon-peal, and
weighing from two to five or six pounds, according to the time
they have remained in the salt water.

These experiments, though apparently very carefully and honestly
conducted, did not give general satisfaction. Mr. Andrew Young
entered into the controversy, and he maintained that there was no
doubt but that the *parr* were the young salmon, but disputed the
other fact attempted to be established by Mr. Shaw, that they
remained two years in the river. Mr. Young says they only remain one year, and has cited various facts in confirmation of this
position.

Another question has arisen, and is at this moment zealously discussed, connected with the salmon and other kinds of fish, of which
it is proper we should here give some brief account. The question relates to the production of salmon artificially. On the banks
of the rivers Tyrie and Faig, experiments have been recently instituted by Mr. Young, of Inverness-shire, of transferring the salmon
spawn into localities where the fish is not found. These experiments have been partially successful. This of stocking rivers
was practised two thousand years ago by the Romans, and is
largely treated of Columella and other ancient writers. After a
lapse of many centuries, it has been revived again, and with great
success in France. Two fishermen of the Vosges, named Gehin
and Remy, have succeeded in propagating salmon, carp, pike,
tench, and perch, and they maintain that the plan is applicable to
those fish which live partly in fresh water and partly in the sea,

as well as to those that live entirely in fresh water rivers and lakes. The streams and rivers over a large extent of France have now been abundantly stocked with a variety of fish from this ancient process, more particularly in the vicinity of Allevard, Vazille, Pontcharra, Sessenage, Veary, Bouig d'Oisons Rivis, Pont-en-Royans, Paladru, Lemps, St. George, Avandon, La Buisse, Grenoble, and in many other departments of the Allier, the Lozere, the Mense, the Mensthe, and Hant Saone.

At the moment we are penning these lines, we copy from the pages of a public journal, that this mode of propagating salmon is being adopted on the river Tay, in Scotland, on a pretty extensive scale. As the account must be interesting to all the disciples of the rod and line, we make no apology for transferring it here as it is given :—

"THE SALMON MANUFACTORY ON THE TAY.

" The ponds for this purpose are situated on the river bank, near Storemountfield, the spawning-boxes being 16 feet above the summer level of the river. The water which supplies the ponds is taken from Storemountfield lake (but owing to the impurity of the Tay during spates, a supply is also to be taken from a neighbouring spring), by a pipe with a valve, into a filtering pond ; thence it is carried by a canal along the upper end of the spawning-boxes, through which it runs. These boxes are 84 feet long by one foot six inches broad, and three deep. They are placed with a fall of six inches, so as to allow the water to flow freely through them, and are partly filled, first with a laying of fine gravel, next coarser, and lastly with stones somewhat coarser than road metal. In distributing the ova, it is gradually poured out of the vessel at the upper end of the box. The water flowing downwards carries it among the stones, under which it settles down, and by gently applying a few buckets of water at the upper end of the boxes, the ova are taken down and distributed equally among the gravel. When the young fry are in a proper state, they are allowed to escape into a pond situate at a foot lower level than the boxes, where they will be fed, and allowed to remain, until such time as they are in a fit state to be turned into the river. This pond is not yet made, but will be finished by the time the fry are hatched. Great care has been taken to prevent any animal entering with the water that would prey upon the fish. Mr. Ramsbottom, from Clitheroe (who has experimented successfully for the Messrs. Ashworth, on the Lough Corrib waters, in Ireland), has the sole management of the Tay ponds. Saturday was a remarkably fine day for the season, and we were privileged in being present at the operation of stripping the fish. When we arrived, Mr. Ramsbottom had already got about 15,000 ova in round tin cans, and he showed us an oval-shaped tin box with a lid, which contained a small male fish swimming in water, which, he said, was waiting for his mate. Presently the net was shot in the Tay at the mouth of the Almond, when two fine female fish ripe for spawning, from 18 to 20 pounds' weight, along with a small male fish, were caught. Mr. Ramsbottom having taken the largest female in his left hand, drew his fingers down both sides of the belly of the fish, when the ova flowed in a stream into the tin box formerly mentioned, in which there were a few inches of water. The fish was instantly returned to the river, and, after a short time, sailed off as if nothing had happened to it. After the ova had been washed, by water being poured on and off—care being taken never to allow it to be exposed to the air—the male fish was brought (which all this time had been in the river under a fold of the net), and manipulated in the same manner as the female, only a small portion of the milt being required. On the milt being shed, a slight change was seen to take place in the colour of the ova, which became paler. Water was again poured on and off, when the operation was complete. The ova were then poured into round tin cases and carried to the ponds. When we left the river-side, upwards of 400,000 ova in fine condition had been obtained. We observed that a few of the ova, after impregnation, turned white, instead of being a fine salmon colour. Mr. Ramsbottom said they were barren ova. In the month of March, the fry will have burst their shells, when we hope to report further.*

But leaving these controversial points on the habits, and natural history of the salmon, which, however, must be allowed to have a direct bearing on the angler's amusement, as a practical art, seeing that legislative enactments are essentially guided by them;—let us direct the reader's attention to the mode of catching this monarch of the streams. First, as to bait. We shall confine ourselves principally to the artificial fly. This is the only kind of bait, in our apprehension, worthy of the regard of the genuine angler, or which will secure his unvarying success, and confer real pleasure in his exploits. We have always considered the employ-ment of any other bait or artifice for luring this noble inhabitant of the deep, as directly implying something frivolous and debasing; alike unworthy of the angler's reputation, and the nature and character of the fish. It must always be borne in mind, that the real angler has a certain kind of fame or reputation to support. And it is on this ground, that an angler, having what the old Scottish divines called "the root of the matter" in him, will, on all occasions, be remarkably particular and sensitive to all the movements and appliances connected with his cherished amuse-ment. There must be nothing low and grovelling, nothing which may seem to involve an idea that he is pursuing his fascinating calling under the influence of any motive, *but the pure love of the sport*. Better lose a thousand fish a day, than adopt or sanction any practices which may have the most distant appear-ance of running counter to the high principles of his profession.

* See Note A at the end of the volume.

The size and colour of the flies to be employed in salmon-fishing, must always vary according to the nature of the waters, the state of the wind, the season, and the depth and brilliancy of the stream. There are scarcely any rules of an absolute or universal character to be laid down. They are all subjected to modifications and exceptions. It is the knowledge when general rules are to be followed, and when they are to be departed from, that constitutes such an essential part of an angler's skill, and stamps him as a master of his art. Experience must be our sole guide in this important matter.

Some gentlemen of an extensive and admitted piscatory knowledge, uniformly fish with dull-coloured flies; others again, whose claims to respect are equally high, employ extremely gaudy ones. As far as our observation and practice go, we submit the following list as the most likely to prove successful, when the waters are in good order; for this is an essential matter.

No. 1. Limerick.—A red cock hackle, ribbed with gold twist, with drake wings of a tolerable length, and standing well out from each other.

No. 2.—Body—orange mohair ribbed with gold twist; legs—a black hackle, and mottled grey feathers of the mallard's wing.

No. 3.—A red cock hackle, ribbed with gold twist, and wings of the woodcock, set considerably apart.

We have never known, of our own personal experience, very large flies do much execution. The conformation of most of the rivers in Great Britain and Ireland, which contain salmon, is, in our humble opinion, decidedly unfavourable to the employment of such kinds of flies. Indeed, in many streams, unless they are very much ruffled by heavy winds, the expediency of using them becomes very questionable; and for this single reason—if any angler look steadily and attentively at a large fly when in the water, he will discover that it does not lie evenly upon it, so as to preserve the shape of a natural fly; the hook is too heavy for the superstructure of feathers, and hence the fly rolls about in a very awkward and unnatural manner. This, it will be readily admitted, defeats the great end and object of fly-fishing—*deception.*

The practice, however, in Ireland is, to use very large and gaudy flies; and it is but natural to infer that the general practice arises from a conviction of their utility. O'Shaughnessy, of Limerick, has the reputation of making those most used and esteemed in this country.

Mr. Hansard, in his work "On Trout and Salmon Fishing in Wales," recommends the following flies for that particular country.

For the Spring.—Wings, dark brown, mottled feathers of the bittern; body, orange silk or worsted, with gold broad twist; and a smoky, dim hackle for legs.

For Summer.—Wings, the brown, mottled feather of a turkey cock's wing, with a few of the green fibres selected from the eye of

D

a peacock's tail-feather; body, yellow silk and gold twist, with a deep blood-red hackle for legs.

Every fly-fisher who is experimentally acquainted with salmon-fishing in Scotland, must have often observed what an immense variety of flies are commonly used, and with almost equal success by the numerous anglers who throng the streams in that country on the height of the fishing seasons. We have seen salmon caught in the Tweed, the Esk, the Dee, and the Clyde with the rudest possible imitation of flies, shining in all the colours of the rainbow. Indeed we have witnessed this fact so repeatedly, as to found upon it an opinion that this species of fish are caught here with much ruder implements, and with far less skill and dexterity than in any other country with which we are acquainted. This may seem fanciful; but, nevertheless, circumstances have fixed upon us the belief. We once saw a shepherd boy, in Peebleshire, kill a prime salmon, of twelve pounds weight, with a common hazel rod, and an extraordinary hair line, without a reel or winch of any kind upon it, and with a fly exactly like a large humble bee. He hooked the fish in the deep part of a strong stream, and had the sagacity and promptitude of action to throw his rod imme-diately into the water after the rushing and powerful fish. The force of the current took it down to the calmer end of the stream, where the stripling caught hold of it again, and instantly suc-ceeded in running the salmon into the next stream, and so on, till he had artfully exhausted his captive, and forced him into a shallow part of the water. Here he got him stranded with great adroitness, and eventually conquered him in capital style.

Instances of this kind are common all over the mountainous parts of Scotland, where the greater portion of the rural popu-lation, who are fond of fishing, use very homely and rude materials.

The flies to be used in Scotland in ordinary salmon-fishing, may be enumerated as follows; the angler filling up the catalogue according to his own fancy or experience.

No. 7. Limerick.—The body, claret and orange mohair, or red cock's hackle, with green tip, ribbed with gold twist; legs, black hackle; wings, turkey feather with white tip.

No. 5.—Body, greenish yellow mohair, ribbed with gold twist and red tip; legs, black hackle; wings, mottled grey.

No. 4.—Body, one half pale red, the other half orange mohair with gold twist; tip, turkey's wing; legs, red hackle; wings, the black and white tail feather of the turkey.

In English rivers where salmon-fishing prevails, the general run of flies employed is seldom so large as those employed in Scotland, but are used of a great variety of colours. The best method, perhaps, is to get flies dressed on such sized hooks, and in such colours, and of such makes, as will answer generally for salmon, sea-trout, common trout, &c., at all seasons of the year.

As a general principle, it may safely be stated, that a certain degree of gaudiness is indispensable in all salmon-flies; and the angler will find from experience that the light-coloured and showy bodies, and gray-coloured wings, are never-failing instruments of success, where fish abound and are on the feed. This principle, it is true, may be modified in various ways and degrees; but it can never be entirely departed from without mortification or disappointment.

Thus much for the fly-baits. Though we have spoken disparagingly of bait-fishing for the salmon, we still think the matter is worthy of a passing notice. The following has been of late years recommended by fishers of experience in this line. A raw cockle, or mussel, taken out of the shell; prawns, minnows, and worms have likewise been used with occasional success. The mode of angling with these is to cast the line, which must be without shot, into some shallow at the edge of a hole, permitting the bait to be carried in by the current. When the fish has taken the bait, give it full time to swallow it properly and securely; after this, fix the hook firmly by a gentle twitch. On the first sensation of pain, the captive will probably plunge or spring in the air; but by keeping the rod firmly, he will be captured without the same degree of trouble or risk that there is in pure fly-fishing. Salmon prefer little fish and worms best on their first arrival in the fresh water.

When the salmon takes a fly, the angler must immediately give him line, and particularly bear in mind that the slightest degree of rashness at this crisis will set him at liberty again. No matter how seasoned or strong your tackle may be, no one can ever succeed in turning a salmon when he is first hooked. It is only by giving comparatively gentle tugs, or letting him feel the weight and pressure of the rod and line at short intervals, that you can make him rush about backwards and forwards, so as to exhaust his strength. Many fishers turn excessively nervous after hooking a good-sized fish. We once knew one of the boldest officers of the Indian army, one who had braved the rampart in its most fearful thunder and carnage, with the most undaunted courage, who never got hold of a salmon (for he was an enthusiastic brother of the craft) without showing the symptoms of almost excessive trepidation; and this is by no means a very uncommon occurrence. All experienced anglers know, from their own history, and from what they daily see around them, how very exciting the sport really is when you get fairly engaged in it.

The most unreserved patience and coolness are, therefore, indispensable. Many fish will require unremitting care and skill for two or three hours before they will yield; and few of any size can be landed as they ought to be in less than an hour. When the river the angler is fishing has a broad shelving bed on each side the stream between the water and the banks, and there are no trees nor bushes to hamper and perplex his operations, then his work is comparatively easy and expeditious; but, on the contrary, when the river is narrow in its channel, and fills it completely up, and when timber and brushwood abound, is always a work of some difficulty and uncertainty to kill a large salmon with the fly; and if the bottom of the stream be full of roots of trees, large stones and reeds, the case becomes still more desperate and hopeless.

When the fish bounds repeatedly out of the water, the chances are that he will succeed in breaking his hold, either by the main force of his fall into the stream, or by tumbling across the line; the latter accident scarcely ever fails to set him free. There is a remarkable difference in salmon in reference to their particular movements after being hooked; some never leap at all, while others are continually at it. When the fish takes what is called the *sulks*, the chances of killing him, when the bottom of the water is not favourable, are very problematical.

A salmon will rise again and again at the fly after he has once missed it. In this respect he differs widely from the trout. We have seen the salmon miss the fly a dozen times in succession, and at last take it greedily. Should he, however, be slightly hooked in any instance, and break off, he will come no more—at any rate, not for a considerable time.

It is an essential part of an angler's knowledge to be able to detect, with a glance of an eye, the most probable places where salmon may be expected to lie. When fishing in lakes, he must necessarily take the water at hazard; but in rivers and smaller streams, a considerable latitude is afforded him for a display of judgment and skill. It is not often that the fish are to be found in long straggling streams, comparatively shallow, and not leading directly into a longer or shorter reach of deep and still water. They are always very shy in trusting themselves in such places; on the contrary, a rapid stream running directly into a sheet of deep and still way, is the most probable haunt for fish. Many large fish, however, never go into the streams at all; they keep in deep water amongst large stones, brushroots, and old sunken roots of trees. When, therefore, there is a fine and brisk curl on the surface of the water, and it is otherwise in good condition, the deeps are the places for finding fish. The shallow end or tail of a good long stretch of water where there is a broad bed of gravel or slopes, is, in all salmon rivers, a favourite locality for the fly-fisher.

CHAPTER IV.

THE TROUT.

NEXT in importance to the salmon, in the estimation of the genuine angler, stands the trout. He is the standard commodity of the enthusiastic rod-fisher. There are many expert and experienced fly-fishers who never enjoyed the unique and exciting luxury of hooking and killing a salmon; but no man can fairly lay claim to the appellation of an "angler," if he cannot kill trout with the rod and line, in some way or another. There is something about trout-fishing which has exalted it in all eyes above every other branch of the art, except, of course, that of salmon-fishing. If we attempt to analyse this preference, we shall find it resolve itself into something appertaining to the attributes, qualities, or habits of this beautiful and interesting fish. He is an intellectual kind of creature, and has evidently a will of his own—he looks sagacious and intelligent : he sedulously avoids thick, troubled, and muddy waters, loves the clear mountain stream, displays an ardent ambition to explore the rivers to their very source; is quick, vigourous, and elegant in his movements — likes to have the exclusive command of the stream — keeps up a rigid system of order and discipline in the little community of which he is a member—exhibits a remarkable degree of nicety and fastidiousness about his food—is comparatively free from vulgar, low, and grovelling habits—entices his pursuer into the loveliest scenes of nature's domain—calls forth from man, his great enemy, the utmost efforts of his ingenuity and skill; and, in a word, in every stage of his existence, preserves a superior and dignified demeanour unattainable by any other living occupant of the streams.

These may be styled the social and intellectual qualities of this glorious fish. His physical constitution is equally entitled to our respectful consideration. He boasts a prepossessing and fascinating figure, moulded in strict conformity with the most refined principles of symmetrical proportion, sparkles in all the gorgeous colours of the rainbow, and occupies a distinguished position in the important science of gastronomy.

These seem to be the most prominent reasons why the trout holds so high a rank in the angler's estimation. There must be *mind*, real or imaginary, in everything which enjoys human attention, in order to fix our serious consideration and secure our lasting esteem.

The trout, in disposing of its spawn, follows the identical rules which govern the salmon in this important process. He runs up rivers, and torrents, and brooks in the months of September and October, and seeks out the most retired water, flowing over gravelly bottoms, for this annual operation. Like the salmon, he leaps over formidable obstacles in his progress, although he cannot cope, in point of muscular agility, with the prince of the waters; still, in proportion to his size, the trout possesses quite as much physical vigour and daring as the lordly salmon. The leaps the trout will take when ascending the rivers in autumn are really quite astonishing. If we examine even the smallest rivulet, or burn, which runs into any good trout stream, we shall find it full of small trout-fry, the produce of the spawn which the parent fish had, under the pressure of apparently insuperable difficulties, contrived to deposit. A trout of a pound weight will often clear a leap of four feet high.

The period of the year in which trout are in the finest condition varies in different countries, and even in different rivers of the same country. The seasons also exercise a considerable influence. If the winter has been open and mild, the trout will be in fine order much earlier than if there had been long sharp frosts and heavy falls of snow. We have in some rivers, such as the Tweed and Coquet, caught trout in tolerable condition in the months of February and March. In 1851, we caught burn-trout in the Esk, Haddingtonshire, as red as crimson, in the last day of January. In the months of June and July, trout are generally, in all the rivers of Europe, supposed to arrive at their highest degree of perfection in strength, richness, and flavour.

This fish varies in size in different rivers and different countries, from the small Welsh trout of a few ounces to the giants of some foreign rivers, which occasionally reach a weight of twenty or thirty pounds; but the general run of fish in trout-streams averages from half a pound to a pound and a half. In waters where they are very numerous, the number caught below half a pound will, in ordinary cases, far exceed those caught above that weight. It is almost a universal rule or condition of existence, that where trout are large they are scarce.

The age which trout generally attain has been a long disputed, and is as yet an undecided, question among naturalists and anglers. Experiments have been made in ponds to settle this point; but such tests are not quite satisfactory, inasmuch as they are, in some degree, artificial contrivances, and place the fish out of their usual haunts, habits, and modes of life. There can be little doubt, we apprehend, that the longevity of the trout varies with the country, and the nature of the stream it inhabits.

We shall here recite two instances relative to the age of this fish, which have been noticed in other works on fishing. The first is the statement that a trout died in August, 1809, which had been in Dumbarton Castle for eight-and-twenty years; the other account is taken from the *Westmoreland Advertiser* of some years ago. "Fifty years since, the proprietor of Bond Hall, near Broughton, in Furness, when a boy, placed a male Fellbeck trout in a well in the orchard belonging to the family, where it remained till last week, when it departed this life, not through any sickness or in-

firmity attendant on old age, but from want of its natural element
—water, the severe drought having dried up the spring—a circumstance which has not happened for the last sixty years. His lips
and gills were perfectly white, although his head was formerly
black, and of a large size. He regularly came, when summoned by
his master by the name of 'Ned,' to feed from his hand, on snails,
worms, and bread. This remarkable fish has been visited, and
considered a curiosity by the neighbouring country for several
years."

The progress of trout towards maturity has also been a fruitful
topic of discussion, and, indeed, remains undecided at the present
hour. Some contend that they grow comparatively quickly; others,
on the contrary, maintain the opposite notion, and affirm that their
growth is singularly slow. For our own part, we conceive them to
be fish of slow growth, and we also imagine that many of them
never attain any great size. We advance this opinion on the
strength of two or three general facts, which have been repeatedly
verified during an experience of forty years' standing; and which
also may be tested by the experience and observation of every
inquisitive angler who will direct his attention to the subject.

In the first place, in really good streams, you will always find,
year after year, the great mass of the fish nearly about the same
size, no matter in what particular year you angle, or what kind of
bait you employ. We could name twenty trout-streams in England
and Scotland, where ten out of every twelve fish caught in all seasons will be within an ounce or two of each other. Now, this conformity among such numerous tribes can only be rationally accounted
for on the supposition that they are of slow growth, and remain
long stationary at the same size. If there were always a progressive increase going on, even according to the most moderate scale
of advance, we should not find this uniformity or fixity of bulk;
but we should see trout of all sizes, and this, too, in regular and
equal proportions.

In the second place, we find that large trout are seldom caught
in rivers which abound with this fish. A fish of unusual size is
one in perhaps twenty thousand; and the number of intermediate
grades of dimensions is very small indeed.

And, in the last place, from a careful personal observation of
bright, clear rivers, in dry hot seasons, you will perceive that the
trout are all about the same size; and should you detect any rare
instances of difference among them in point of bulk, you will,
perhaps, be inclined to agree with us, that the very diversity is
strikingly confirmatory of the slow and almost imperceptible
growth of these interesting fish.

Trout congregate together, and keep up a regular system of
discipline and order among their tribes. This is easily discernible
in clear bright streams during fine sunny weather. You will
sometimes see a dozen or dozen and a half of trout arranged,
according to their sizes, in exact order. The largest of the troop

take the lead, and the others fall behind, two and two, or three
and three; the smaller fellows being always stationed at the
bottom of the line. We have seen fish remain in this position for
many hours without moving a single inch. If a little food be
dropped in among the number, the largest always claims; and is
invariably allowed the privilege of first taking possession.

All trout have their holds, or haunts, or places of retreat.
These are commonly some large stone, or trunk of a tree, or old
timbers about mills, or overhanging rocks. Each fish has his
regular track or portion of water to range about in, and seldom
trespasses on the liberties of his neighbours. If one of these
sections or divisions of water become vacant, it is soon filled up
by a new occupant. These habits and facts respecting the trout
were noticed two hundred years ago by Giovanni Villifranci, in a
work published at Venice, in 1614, called "L'Armaranto Favola
Piscatoria."

Trout will remain for some weeks in precisely the same spot.
In the hot and dry summer of 1826, we observed a large fish about
four pounds weight, which, for ten weeks, never moved, that we
could ascertain, out of a small but rather deep stream. We tried
him at intervals, both early and late, with fly, worm, and minnow,
but all to no purpose. Soon after a flood came down the stream,
and we saw him no more. Nearly about the same time, a large
trout, under precisely the same circumstances, was observed for a
long time near to one of the arches of Felton Bridge, on the river
Coquet. He took up a sort of permanent abode there; had often
anglers paying him a visit, but all their subtle arts proved unavail-
ing, and he was captured at last by a simple country lad, with a
miserable rod and line, with a plain red worm. His weight was
five pounds.

It is by taking cognizance of these holds or haunts that an
angler, who knows a river well possesses such a decided advantage
over a stranger, however skilful and expert. The former knows
to a certainty where the fish are lying; and if he be unsuccessful
on one occasion, he is almost sure to succeed on another.

Trout pair at the latter end of June, and the whole of the month
of July, and are invariably nearly of the same size. They roam
together, feed together, exist together, and seem to delight in
each other's society. We have sometimes fancied that they express feelings of commiseration and affection for each other in
times of peril and danger. The Italian author just named noticed
this fact in the trout of Italian streams, and treats of it under the
name of the "Loves of the Fishes."

There can be no doubt, we apprehend, that trout are remarkably
susceptible of atmospheric influences. It is, perhaps, impossible
to explain this; but our opinion is founded on circumstances like
the following, which have fallen under observation over and over
again in many parts of Great Britain. We have started some
beautiful morning, with rod and fly, anticipating noble sport

from the favourable aspect of the weather; the sky, perhaps,
clear and settled, with a gentle breeze from the west or south-
west—a more promising day could not well be imagined. The
river was fished with uncommon care and assiduity; all kinds of
flies were tried in their turn, and every dodge which experience
teaches was successively resorted to, but never a fish could be
hooked; miles of ground were walked over, but not even a solitary
rise could be obtained, and the fellow-craftsmen whom we met in
our rambles were in precisely the same predicament. The waters,
in fact, appeared as still, and quiet as if there was not a single
trout in them to disturb the calm surface. Well! in a short time,
out comes the explanation. The next day is ushered in by a
violent storm of snow and rain; the waters rise, the floods come
down, and the fish get gorged with food to their heart's content.
Now, in our humble opinion, for we speak with diffidence on the
subject, this is a striking exemplification of the existence of a
powerful instinct for a given end or purpose. The secret influences of the atmosphere, imperceptible to man, intimate to the
wakeful and conscious fish that an abundant supply of food is at
hand; and, on this account, they have no inclination to forestall
the copious repast which awaits them. We may add to these
statements, that we never saw trout take freely immediately before
or during powerful thunderstorms.

And we may observe in passing, that these statements we have
here made, grounded on our experience, as well as on that of other
anglers, have lately received great weight in our minds from a fact
connected with the history of angling literature in Italy, during the
middle ages. It was then the custom to have *Piscatory Dramas*
acted, and in one of these pieces we have a song comparing the
ordinary journey of human life to the art of angling. It is clear,
from the general scope and bearing of the sentiment of this poetical
effusion, that the fact of fishermen experiencing what appeared to
them unaccountable disappointments in their amusements, must
have been known and observed as a regular condition of the art as
then practised. We shall cite these few lines, and the reader will
be the better able to judge whether our conjectures are borne out
by the historical testimony of bygone ages :—

" How oft times with my rod in hand,
    In wandering by the stream,
I've liken'd the angler's magic wand
    To life's deceptive dream !

" The sky, perchance, looks fair and bright,
    The breeze curls on the brook,
The waters ting'd to please the sight,
    Trout waiting for the hook !

"We plunge and strive from spot to spot,
  But not a fish will rise—
In wonderment at our ill-luck,
  Turn up our wistful eyes.

"In daily life the same we see,
  When hope mounts on the wing;
Our means to ends may not agree,
  And griefs from labour spring.

"Again, sometimes, the day is sour,
  And darkened is the sky;
Fair sport seems not within our power,
  Though artful be our flies.

"But here, again, at fault we are,
  Success attends our skill,
And fish in scores come wide and far,
  Our fishing creel to fill.

"In life's career the same we see,
  When hope flags in the near,
And dark's the shade of destiny
  When our success is near.

"A moral, too, your line may point,
  When tangl'd is the hair;
Let patience with her oil annoint,
  'Twill save you from despair.

"The same in life when ills assail,
  Perplex'd with mischiefs rank,
Patience and skill will seldom fail
  To unloose the knotted hank."*

Trout-fishing is the very principle of life to the practised and enthusiastic angler. It is that which gives vitality and animation to all his movements, and constitutes him what he really is. Without the trout and salmon he would be, in many respects, a truly pitiable object—nearly reduced to that degraded state which would justify Dr. Johnson's snarling definition of the angler's profession.

Fishing for trout may be comprehended under three heads:—Fly-fishing, trolling, and worm-fishing. Other modes are known and sometimes practised, and we shall mention them incidentally, but we shall confine the general burden of our suggestions and remarks to these three leading divisions of our angling art. In doing so we shall be chiefly guided by our own experience in a variety of waters, both at home and abroad.

* Eclectic Review for July 1853.

FLY FISHING

Is the most successful, and, by immeasurable degrees, the most delightful mode of angling for trout. It is graceful and gentlemanly, and can be enjoyed by all who exhibit any anxiety to acquire the art. It is also the most independent mode. You take your rod, fishing-creel, and fly-book, and roam away over half a kingdom, without any further trouble about baits, or incumbrance from nets, or fish-kettles, or other trumpery. In point of exciting the mind and sustaining a joyous hilarity, it is infinitely preferable to all other modes of exercising the gentle art. The constant attention which the angler must pay to his flies as they glide on the water, the repeated changes of locality, the calm and placid pleasure infused into the soul by sparkling and gushing streams, the constant exercise of his skill in casting and drawing his line, the gentle tantalisings of his hopes by frequent unsuccessful risings at the fly, the dexterity and management requsite in killing a fish with such delicate materials, and the uncertainty which always hangs over his successful capture, all tend to awaken and keep alive that feeling of the mind on which rests the whole charm of the art. In short, in fly-fishing all the elements are judiciously combined, which contribute to render angling an agreeable and healthy amusement.

Before we enter into any detail with reference to the application of artificial flies, we beg to make a few preliminary observations, which may possibly be of use to the unexperienced angler.

This mode of fishing has given birth to an enormous mass of discussion and conjecture, as to the best kinds of flies for particular countries and waters, so cumbrous and voluminous as to be quite forbidding and confounding to the younger professors of the art. Imagination has been allowed to usurp the place of judgment; and trifling theories, that of comprehensive and well-digested experience. A fly-fisher goes to the waters agitated by a thousand fancies, as to what kind and colour of fly the fish are likely to take; and if he be not successful in hooking fish after three or four casts, down he squats and puts on another set of flies. This sort of thing occupies nearly the whole day; he is constantly shifting his tackle, so that in the evening, his creel is as empty as it was in the morning.

Now, we have long arrived at the conclusion, *that anglers are vastly more fastidious about the shape and colour of their flies than trout are.* The fact seems to be, that when trout are inclined to feed on this kind of bait, it does not much signify what shape or colour your fly is, provided the *size* be strictly attended to. Any great disproportion in this particular, will decidedly mar all chances of success. When a stream has been completely covered with what is called the "May-fly," and the fish rising at them in all directions, we have often and often filled our creel in quick time with other kinds of flies as opposite as possible, both in shape and colour, from this particular insect.

Now, it is a commonly received notion among many expert anglers, that when trout are rising at these flies, they will scarcely look at anything else. Nothing can be more erroneous, as experience will amply testify if proper means be employed. True it is, we have occasionally met with a few instances, where trout, dashing rapidly at the natural fly, have obstinately refused the artificial fly; but in all such cases as have come under our own observation, we have, upon inspection, invariably found the rejected fly *too large in size*. On the substitution of a *small one*, somewhat in conformity perhaps, as to shape, though it may be decidedly opposite in colour to the insect on which the fish were feeding; *the evil has been immediately rectified*, and trout taken with great rapidity.

But we consider almost decisive in this question, is this: when we traverse a fine trout stream, we often meet in the course of our rambles, ten or a dozen brother anglers, all well skilled in the craft, and employing an endless variety of flies. If the fish be in good humour, the whole fraternity bear testimony to the fact; the difference in the number of the fish each one has got, will be but very trifling, and may well enough be considered referable to the difference of time they may respectively have been on the rivers, or to the casual advantages which some might enjoy over others, by falling in with better streams. Mutual congratulations and compliments are here the order of the day, and the superior excellence of particular flies eagerly commented on. But, on the other hand, when the fish have no inclination for the fly, we find the reverse of all this. Every one shakes his head in despair, and swears he has tempted them in vain with every conceivable object in his fly-book. Now all this, which is an everyday occurrence, is inexplicable, except upon our theory, that when the fish are inclined to feed, they are not nice to a shade of colour; and when they are not, the highest ingenuity of man may be displayed to no purpose.

We fished for five or six successive seasons, some of the finest and most prolific rivers in England and Scotland, in company with one of the very best fly-fishers in Great Britain, and the author of many papers in popular periodicals on the art; and we invariably used different coloured flies. It was quite astonishing to see how nearly, on finishing in the evening, we were to each other in point both of number and quality of fish. If one had a bad day, so had the other; and if good, both participated in the success.

In the north of England, and in Scotland, there are angling matches very frequently, between two first-rate fly-fishers, to decide who shall kill the greater number of fish on a given day, both traversing the same tract of water, taking the streams alternately as they come to hand, and beginning and finishing at certain points of the range of waters, and at a certain hour. These exploits generally attract a good deal of attention for a considerable distance round the country. We have, ourselves, witnessed four of such contests; and on these occasions, the difference between the rivals never exceeded eight or ten fish, out of a day's sport, yielding from eight to ten dozen each; and, in only *two* cases, had the contending parties *a single fly alike*.

In addition to these cases, we may be allowed to add, that we fished one entire season for trout, with only two kinds of flies— the red and black palmer; and we were as successful on the whole period as any of our angling competitors.

Now, these statements and facts are introduced, not with a view of enforcing, in a dogmatical spirit, any general rules for the government of fly-fishers, but solely to guard young beginners from falling into a fidgetty and fastidious habit of perpetually changing flies, whenever their success is not commensurate with their hopes. We never knew a fancy angler with an old bit of gut. The fact is, there are general rules in this art as well as in every other; but they must be deduced from carefully collated facts. One grain of reasoning founded on experience is worth a ton of theory and speculation in such cases.

There is a fertile source of deception as to the trout's fondness for particular flies, which deserves our notice; it is this: having cast our line over a stream, when we draw it across, the bob-fly is the first which by the mechanical process can solicit the attention of the fish. When, therefore, trout are in the humour, this will, in the majority of cases, *appear* to be the favourite fly, and the angler notes down on the "tablet of his memory," that such is really the case. We have often changed the flies on this account, with a view of testing the fact. That which seemed to be the favourite fly, was put on the stretcher, and an entirely different fly mounted as the bob one; and yet the result was just the same; the latter became, apparently, the favourite fly, and the stretcher was apparently neglected.

This we feel confident arises solely from the mechanical arrangement of the flies, and the manner in which the line is thrown. The bob comes over the nose of the fish first, and he takes it immediately, never calculating on what may be behind him. We would, therefore, advise all young anglers to pay strict attention to this matter before they adopt any hasty conclusion as to the preference which the fish may seem to give to any particular fly.

In conformity with an inference deducible from these general observations, we shall not furnish the reader with a very long list of flies, but confine ourselves to such standard and every-day articles of sport as will not, we hope, disappoint the angler, provided he is content to put up with the solid, though, apparently, homely bill of fare.

The RED HACKLE, and RED PALMER flies, on No. 6, Limerick, will prove killing baits in all parts of the kingdom, particularly in the early part of the season. As summer advances, the same flies, on hooks two sizes less, will answer the purpose well; if

ribbed with gold and tinsel, they will be still better in the months
of May and June.

THE DOTTEREL HACKLE is a sure fly : the body made of yellow
silk, and the legs and wings of the feather of the dotterel. The
sizes of the hooks may vary from 6 to 10, according to the condition and clearness of the water.

A black cock's hackle body, with wings from the woodcock's
wing, on Nos. 6 or 8, will be very suitable for April and May in
most of the rivers in England and Wales.

A red cock's hackle body, with wings of the gray drake, on No.
4 to 10, is a standard fly, both for salmon and trout, nearly all the
year round, in all the waters of Great Britain.

A body made of copper-coloured peacock's herl; legs a black
cock's hackle ; and wings either of the water-hen's wing, or from
the woodcock's breast. This fly, if slightly ribbed with gold
tinsel, will answer admirably in June and July, after a flood. It
may be wrapped on hooks, from No. 6 to 10.

The flies now mentioned are favourable for all waters, both in
Great Britain and Ireland ; but in addition to them, we shall add
the following more copious catalogue of what we consider the best
flies for all rivers and all seasons ; and we doubt not, the angler,
who is not over fastidious, will find it sufficiently ample for all
effective purposes.

THE CHANTRY FLY.—Body, copper-coloured peacock's herl,
ribbed with gold twist ; legs, black hackle ; wings, partridge's
brown herl feathers or pheasant's tail. Hooks, No. 9 or 10.

MARCH BROWN.—Body, fur of the hare's ear, ribbed with olive
silk ; legs, partridge hackle ; wings, tail-feather of the partridge ;
tail, two or three fibres of the partridge feathers Hooks, No.
8 or 9.

THE BLUE DUN FLY. — Body, dubbed with water-hen's hackle ;
wings, the feather of the starling's wing ; tail, two fibres of a
grizzled cock's hackle. Hooks, Nos. 9 and 10.

THE CARSHALTON COCK-TAIL FLY.—Body, light blue fur ; legs,
dark dun hackle ; wings, the inside feather of a teal's wing ; tail,
two fibres of a white cock's hackle. Hook, No. 9 or 10.

THE PALE YELLOW DUN FLY. — Body, yellow mohair, or mar-
tin's pale yellow fur, tied with yellow silk ; wings, the lightest part
of a feather from a young starling's wing. Hook, No. 12.

THE ORANGE DUN FLY.—Body, red squirrel's fur, ribbed with
gold thread ; legs, red hackle ; wings, from the starling's wing ;
tail, two fibres of red cock's hackle. Hook, No. 9.

THE GREAT RED SPINNER.—Body, hog's wool, red and brown
mixed, ribbed with gold twist ; legs, bright red cock's hackle ;
wings, the light feather of the starling's wing ; tail, three fibres of
a red cock's hackle. Hook, No. 7.

THE BLACK GNAT FLY. — Body, black hackle or ostrich's herl,
tied with black wings ; wings, the feather from the starling's wing.
Hook, No. 9 or 10.

THE RED ANT FLY.—Body, peacock's herl, made full at th tail, and spare towards the head, red or ginger cock's hackle wings, the light feather of the starling's wing. Hook, Nos. 9 and 10.

THE LAND FLY. — Body, the fur from the hare's neck, twisted round with silk of the same colour; legs, a ginger hen's hackle; wings, the feather from a landrail's wing. Hook, No. 9.

THE ALDER FLY.—Body, Peacock's herl, tied with dark brown silk; legs, cock's hackle; wings, the brown speckled feather of a mallard's back. Hook, No. 8.

THE GREENDRAKE FLY. — Body, yellow gloss silk, ribbed with brown silk; the extreme head and tail coppery peacock's herl; legs, a red and ginger hackle; wings, the mottled wing of a mallard stained olive; tail, three hairs of a rabbit's whiskers. Hook, No. 6.

THE GREY DRAKE.—Body, white flos silk, ribbed with dark brown or mulberry-coloured silk; head and tip of the tail pea-cock's herl; legs, a grizzled cock's hackle; wings, a mallard's mottled feather made to stand upright; tail, three whiskers of a rabbit. Hook, Nos. 6 and 7.

THE GOVERNOR FLY. — Body, coppery-coloured peacock's herl, ribbed with gold twist; legs, red or ginger hackle; legs, the light part of a pheasant's wing. Hook, No. 9.

THE COACHMAN FLY. — Body, copper-coloured cock's herl; legs, red hackle; wings, the light feathers of the landrail. Hook, No. 8.

COW-DUNG FLY.—Body, dun lemon-coloured mohair; legs, red hackle; wings, a feather of the landrail or starling's wing. Hook, Nos. 8 and 9.

TROLLING FOR TROUT.

This mode of trout-fishing has become very common in Great Britain within these thirty years, and is a very successful one, particularly in the spring of the year, and in most rivers after a summer flood. Trolling, however, has long lain under a species of reproach, as being of a poking, poaching, interloping character; and on this account it is, in some districts of England, strictly pro-hibited. This stigma is not a modern thing—it is mentioned in angling satirical songs 250 years ago; and in one poetical piece, which we shall here insert, by Llewellyn, in his "Men Miracles" (1646), we find trolling is severely handled, along with other unfair modes of fishing:—

"You that fish for dace and roches,
Carpes and tenches, bonus noches,
Thou wast borne betweene two dishes,
When the Fryday signe was fishes.

Anglers' yeares are made and spent,
All in Ember weekes and Lent.
   Breake thy rod about thy noddle,
   Throw thy worms and flies by the pottle,
   Keepe thy corke to stop thy bottle,
   Make straight thy hooke, be not afeared
           To shave his beard;
   That in case of started stitches,
   Hooke and line may mend thy breaches.

"He that searches pools and dikes,
Halters jackes, and strangles pikes,
Let him know, though he think he wise is,
'Tis not a sport, but an assizes.
Fish to hooke, were the case disputed,
Are not tooke, but executed.
   Breake thy rod, &c., &c.

"You whose pastes fox rivers throat,
And make Isis pay her groat,
That from May to parch October
Scarce a minnow can keep sober,
Be your fish in open thrust,
And your own red-paste the crust.
   Breake thy rod, &c., &c.

"Hookes and lines of larger sizes,
Souch as the tyrant that troules devises,
Fishers nere believe his fable,
What he calls a line is a cable;
That's a knave of endless rancour,
Who for a hooke doth cast an anchor.
   Breake thy rod, &c., &c.

"But of all men he is the cheater,
Who with small fish takes up the greater;
He makes carps without all dudgeon,
Makes a Jonas of a gudgeon;
Cruell man that stayes on gravell,
Fish that great with fish doth travel.
   Breake thy rod, &c., &c."

A trolling-rod, as we have already mentioned, should be pretty long and stiff, with a line a shade stronger than that used for the artificial fly. The best minnows for the purpose are those of a moderate size, their bellies and sides being of a pearly whiteness. If the angler has conveniences, they are all the better for being kept a few days in clear, sweet, soft water: this process renders them firmer and brighter.

There are numerous modes of baiting with the minnow; but they all resemble each other so nearly, that a minute description of each is quite unnecessary. Some trollers employ six or seven hooks, and others only two or three. This is, in a great measure, a matter of taste and fancy. As a general rule, however, it may safely be determined, that in those rivers of Great Britain and Ireland which run deep with a swift current, have a muddy, weedy bottom, and whose sides are covered with brushwood, that kind of trolling-tackle is the best which is the strongest, and mounts the greatest number of hooks. It is only by jerking and holding the fish tight by the head that it is possible to catch it; for if you allow him to run in such situations, he will soon smash your tackle to atoms. But in fine clear streams, with gravelly and pebbly bottoms, fewer hooks will answer better, inasmuch as *deception* is more effectively preserved.

Here we find a radical difficulty in explaining, in writing, the acquisition of a purely mechanical art. By once or twice *looking* at a good troller, the youthful angler will obtain more real insight into this mode of trout-fishing than by perusing an entire volume on the subject. All that a writer can do is to deal in general description, and this always falls far short of elucidating a matter depending more upon artistic adroitness than upon abstract principles. Old Izaak Walton's mode of trolling is thus stated:—
"And then you are to know that your minnow must be put on your hook, that it must turn round when it is drawn against the stream; and, that it may turn nimbly, you must put it on a big-sized hook, as I shall now direct you, which is thus: put your hook in at the mouth, and out at the gill; then, having drawn your hook two or three inches beyond a-through his gill, put it again into his mouth, and the point and beard out at the tail; and then tie the hook and his tail about very neatly with a white thread, which will make it the apter to turn quick in the water; that done, pull back that part of your line which was slack when you did put your hook into the minnow the second time. I say pull that part of your line back, so that it shall fasten the head, so that the body of the minnow shall be almost straight on your hook; this done, try how it will turn by drawing it across the water, or against the stream; and if it do not turn nimbly, then turn the tail a little to the right or left hand, and try again till it turn quick, for, if not, you are in danger to catch nothing; for know, that it is impossible that it should turn too quick." This was Walton's method, two centuries and a half ago.

The mode of baiting with minnow, and managing the rod and line in trolling, followed in the North of England, and in most parts of Scotland is substantially the following:—A gilse hook (No. 3 or 4), is placed at the end of the line, but wrapped firmly and carefully on the end of the shank to make it secure, and to leave as much room as possible to bait. At the distance of an inch, or little more, from the shank end of the gilse hook, a strong

E

hook must be tied on, about half the size of the other. This being done, the point of the large hook must be placed in at the mouth of the minnow, and out at the tail, on the right side of the minnow, bending it half round as it is put in ; then the other hook must be put in below the under chop, which has the effect of keeping the minnow's mouth quite close.

When the angler is not pressed for time, the hook and tail should be tied together with a little white thread. Before the little hook is entered, the minnow must be drawn up to its full length, and made to fit the bending of the hook, so that it may properly twirl round in the water when drawn through it. When all this is finished, the angler takes the line in his left hand, a little above the bait, and throws it underhand, lifting up the right and the rod, in order that the bait may fall as gently on the water as possible. He stands at the top of the stream, as far off as his tackle will permit, and lets the bait drop in a yard or so from the middle of it. The minnow must then be drawn by gentle pulls, of about a yard at a time, across the stream, turning the rod up the water within half a yard of its surface, keeping an eye steadily fixed on the minnow.

When a trout seizes the bait, he is commonly firmly hooked by the very act, but most fishers give a smart strike, and if he feels firm after that, it may be confidently assumed that he is securely hooked. The troller throws three or four times at the upper part of the stream, but never twice in the same place, but a yard lower every cast. He should throw quite over the stream, but let the bait cross it in a round, like a semicircle, about a foot below the surface, with two shot, No. 3 and 4, placed nine or ten inches from the hooks, which will sink the apparatus to a proper depth in the water. In the act of drawing the bait across the stream, the top of the rod must be kept within less than a yard from the water, and drawn downwards, that the bait may be the greater distance from the angler, and be placed as the first thing that the fish will see. It often happens in this kind of fishing that the troller sees the fish before he takes the bait; when this is the case the rod must be given in a little, that the minnow may appear, as it were, to meet the trout half way; but should the trout appear shy, it is best to pull the line away, and do not throw it in again for a short time. Many fine trout are taken by this manœuvre. The twisting of the bait is the chief beauty in this mode of angling; the fish sees it at a great distance, and fancying it is making all possible haste to escape, the trout makes the same haste to overtake it.

WORM FISHING FOR TROUT.

Worm fishing for trout may be divided into two kinds : one, the angling in streams, both when they are full and flooded, and in clear weather when they are purer, and much reduced in bulk;

the other, shade-fishing, which is practised in the hottest and brightest days, when the rivers are nearly dried up, and sport can be obtained by scarcely any other means.

Some anglers are very expert at both these methods, and often kill considerable quantities of fish when the fly-fisher can do nothing. The great secret is to know where the fish lie, to keep the line as perpendicular as possible, and when the water is clear and bright, to have the lightest and finest tackle consistent with the requisite strength.

The red-worm, which has been sufficiently scoured in moss, is the very best that can be used. Some, indeed, prefer the brandling, but it never stands the water so well as the red worm. There is a good worm to be found under old cow-dung in the fields, but these are not always to be got when wanted. The worm ought not to be large, for in bright days, when the streams are clear and sparkling, the trout will scarcely even look at a big worm.

The hooks for worm fishing should always be straight. Those with a bend generally break the worm speedily, and in clear weather this is fatal to success. The hooks ought always to be as small as is compatible with the easy threading on of the worm.

In a suitable stream, shade or bush-fishing is one of the most agreeable and amusing modes of angling for trout. It is the only method which gives you an insight into the instincts and habits of the fish. In the months of July and August, when the weather is dry and hot, and the sun shines finely over head, and the streams are nearly dried up, and ordinary anglers smile in derision, that any one should be fool enough to take a rod in hand, go out with some small red worms, to a shady part of the stream where there is a fine stony or gravelly bottom, and as great a depth of water as you can find. Here worm your way into the very thickest part of the bushes, taking care to have the sun in your face; for, if you get with your back to the luminary of day, the shadow of yourself and rod falling on the water will entirely defeat your object. Your rod must be short and stiff, and the rings rather large, in order that, when you hook a fish, there should be no obstacle in the way to your giving him whatever length of line his size may require.

When you have taken up the desired position, peep cautiously into the deep water, and you will soon perceive fish. Bait your hook, and let it drop into the water, without any shot, as snugly and lightly as possible; you will soon see how greedily the bait will be seized.

Though deep water is of course preferable, still, if the water be only six inches in depth, it will answer your purpose. In such situations, if you perceive trout, you will observe that almost every fish has a certain space of water to himself, about which he takes his regular rounds, always returning to the exact spot from whence he set out. Watch when he starts from this position, and then throw your bait behind him, in the spot he has just left, so that when he returns, it may be lying still at the bottom. He will gaze at it for a moment, hold it in doubt as if startled; and, when he fancies all is safe, he will gobble down the worm, shake his head when he finds something appending to it, and then plunge off with all speed.

The bush-angler should carefully contrive to keep the end of his rod exactly parallel with the edge of the water, for if he allow it to hang over the bank or bushes, the fish will see it, take fright, and fly off without ceremony. In drawing the line out of the water, care should be taken to avoid lifting it up perpendicularly, it should rather be drawn out in a slanting direction, and then the water will not be so much disturbed.

When the weather and water are best adapted for shade or bush-fishing, the trout are often very hungry; and if you can only contrive to keep yourself and tackle well out of sight, you may safely calculate on good success. In order to show to what extremities this fish is sometimes reduced, we shall relate an incident which fell under our own observation in 1826. This was a remarkably hot and dry summer; many rivers in England were nearly dried up; and the fish in some of the shallower streams were entirely destroyed for want of water. We had gone out one fiercely hot day, to the distance of ten miles, in the North of England, to a favourite spot for bush-fishing. When we arrived at the water, we found, to our dismay, that we had left our worm-bag behind us. Our mortification was extreme. To get a worm of any kind was next to impossible, for there had not been a drop of rain for three entire months, and the fields were burnt up like the deserts of Africa. We happened, by mere chance, to have an old bait-bag in our pocket, in which there were about twenty old dried up, shrivelled worms, so dry, indeed, that they almost crumbled into powder between the finger and the thumb. We steeped them in water as a desperate resource, and contrived to thread them on a very small hook. The expedient proved successful; and we returned home with a very fine basket of trout.

The French anglers catch hundreds of trout in the months of May and June with the natural May-fly. They put it alive on a small hook, and let it float down the stream, and are generally very successful. They throw or spin their fly into particular spots of the river, especially where they see that a fish is rising, with considerable dexterity; but this mode of angling terminates when the May-fly is gone. Many of the English residents in France follow this practice. There is a plan analogous to this adopted by persons in this country. They make a pair of wings of the feather of a landrail, and on the bend of the hook put one or two caddis; the head of the caddis should be kept as close to the wings as possible. The bait is then allowed to float down the stream just below the surface, then gently drawn up again with a gentle degree of irregularity effected by the shaking of the rod; and some fishermen maintain that if there be a trout in the place it will be sure to take it. Some place two caddis with the wings.

the hook being put in at the head and out at the neck of the first, and quite through the other from head to tail. Two brandlings, or small red worms may be fished with in the same manner.

There are other modes of fishing for trout besides these first mentioned, varied by the kinds of bait employed. The salmon-roe is one of these. It is a singular article for the seductive and. deadly influence it exercises over the fish. We have witnessed some striking examples of its killing properties. We once saw two countrymen on the river Tweed, kill as many trout with this preparation in a few hours, as filled a good-sized sack. We have occasionally used it ourselves, both in spring and autumn, but we must confess we do not approve of its use. There is something low, revolting, and unsportsmanlike, about it. It is really not *angling*, in any honest or proper sense of the word.

The roe is used in two different states; the one preserved as a paste; and the other, the plain roe taken out of the fish, with a little salt sprinkled over it, and kept for a few days. We prefer the latter preparation; but this is only to be obtained in the latter portion of the fishing season; that is in August, September, and October. In fishing with roe, some tact is requisite, The bait should be about twice the size of an ordinary horse-bean; and when put upon the hook, should be fastened with a single fibre or two of common sheep's wool. When the fish bites, he must be struck sharply immediately. The best localities are the foot-waters of good streams; and when the colour of the water is whitish, after rain, and subsiding a little, the trout can be most readily caught.

CHAPTER V.

THE PIKE.

PIKE fishing has become of late years, a very fashionable and general branch of angling; not so much for the edible qualities of the fish, as for the sport which attends his capture, particularly in some of our larger rivers and lakes, where the fish attains to a considerable size.

All the writers on the natural history of the pike, tell many wonderful stories about him. It does not appear that he was known to the Greeks and Romans—at least Aristotle and Pliny do not speak of him. The first author who formally treats of the pike, is Ausonius, who flourished about the middle of the fourth century, and who does not appear to have entertained very favourable opinions of either the kindly dispositions, or gastronomic excellencies of the fish. He holds him forth in a poetic strain under the name of *Lucius*.

> " Lucius obscurus ulva lacunas
> Obsidet. His nullos mensarum lectus ad usus,
> Fumat fumosis olido nidore popinis."

> " The wary *luce* 'midst wreck and rushes hid,
> The scourge and terror of the scaly brood ;
> Unknown at friendship's hospitable board,
> Smokes 'midst the smoky tavern's coarsest food."

The pike has uniformly acquired the reputation for extraordinary and shark-like voracity. Anecdotes illustrative of this peculiarity, are detailed by numerous authors; and indeed everybody at all familiar with the habits and practices of this fine fish, must have witnessed some remarkable proof of the accuracy of the general opinion. The author of *British Fish and Fisheries*, says, " Shrouded from observation in his solitary retreat, he follows with his eye the motions of the shades of fish that wander heedlessly along; he marks the water-rat swimming to his burrow—the ducklings paddling among the water-weeds—the dab chick, and the moorhen leisurely swimming on the surface ; he selects his victim, and, like the tiger springing from the jungle, he rushes forth, seldom indeed missing his aim ; there is a sudden rush, circle after circle forms on the surface of the water, and all is still again in an instant."

A few years ago, in a preserve in Lincolnshire, a large pike was seen to snap at a swallow, as it poised lightly over the water in search of flies ; and a friend of ours, once took seven or eight right good fish out of a pool at the tail of a lock, not far from the Earl of Winchelsea's seat in that county, with a few pieces of uncooked bacon. He went to the spot—a well-known resort for pike in those days—unprovided with bait ; and, on his arrival, owing to the extreme clearness of the water, and the coldness of the day, he was unable to procure any with his cast-net. The lock-keeper urged him to try a lump of his bacon. In despair of getting any better bait, and unwilling to leave a favourite spot without a trial, he adopted the suggestion, and in a very short time, despoiled the pool of its occupants, consisting of seven or eight respectable fish.

Hundreds of stories of a similar kind are commonly related, and may be found in ordinary fishing-books ; but notwithstanding the numerous undoubted instances of his remarkable and fearless voracity, we have always found the pike a very dainty fish, and very difficult to catch in those preserves and pet-waters where small silvery roach are very numerous. He can, in such situations, procure a delicate and plentiful repast whenever he wants one ; for, greedy as he is, he does not, like the human glutton, eat for mere eating's sake. The one eats to live, the other lives but to eat ; and, therefore, the fish may be considered the more respectable gourmand of the two. When the appetite of the pike is on, he is furious ; when it is appeased, he is scarcely to be tempted. Practised trollers are well aware of this, and thoroughly understand the difference between the *"runs,"* when he is hungry and in earnest, and when he is neither one or the other. When not stimulated by hunger, he is anything but voracious, and will mouth a bait and play with it for a quarter of an hour, in sheer sport, without the slightest intention of swallowing it. In this condition, he will often allow himself to be hauled about, and quietly pulled up to the surface of the water, and then, with a careless flap of his tail, he coolly drops the bait from his jaws, and lazily rolls down again into deep water.

This daintiness of food has been often noticed by very ancient writers. Several of the scholastic divines, in their general summaries of matters of natural history mention the fact. They sometimes go very minutely into his peculiarities of taste. They maintain there are some particular articles they are passionately fond of; among these are the following :—A swan's head and shoulders, a mule's lip, a Polish damsel's foot, a gentleman's hand, tender kittens before their eyes are opened, and the fleshy parts of a calf's head. There are likewise things to which he evinces a great dislike. "In the midst of a banquet of frogs, throw him a toad, and he turns from it loathing; put a slimy tench near his muzzle, and he will recoil from the nauseous creature; and if compelled by strong necessity, as the scarcity of all other more acceptable food, to dine on a perch, he holds it shudderingly under water, at the greatest possible distance transversely in his jaws, whilst any life remains, and having next carefully put down the offensive spines on the back, proceeds to pouch it with address, but leisurely, and not without manifest reluctance. The sticklebacks are held in yet greater abomination than perch by old pikes, and not without good reason, seeing the havoc they commit amongst the young and unwary pickerels. It is only by personal suffering, that fish, any more than men, buy wisdom ; our young pikes no sooner begin to feel hunger, and to find they have large mouths, well furnished with teeth, provided on purpose to cater for it, than they proceed at once to make essay upon the bodies of the smallest fish within reach. These are commonly the *gasterostei* or sticklebacks, who, on observing the gaping foe advancing against them, prepare for the encounter by bristling up their spines in instinctive readiness to stick in his throat, instead of going smoothly down into his stomach."

We shall make no apology for inserting a few additional observations from Mr. Goose's "Natural History of Fish," relative to the voracity and modes of feeding of the pike.

"The voracity of the pike is shown by a circumstance of no infrequent occurrence in Sweden. Large perch often swallow the baited hooks of stationary night-lines, and then enormous pike gorge the hooked perch in their turn. In this case, though the pike himself is seldom or never actually hooked, yet on the fisherman's drawing in his line, the perch sets so fast in the greedy throat of the finny tyrant that he has been unable to get rid of it, and both are taken.

"O'Gorman gives some examples of the same ravenous appetite. One which he killed with a roach for a bait, had in his maw a trout of four pounds weight, evidently just taken; and another seized a trout of more than six pounds. But these examples yield to what he said he witnessed on Dromore. A large pike having been hooked and nearly exhausted, was suddenly seized in the water and carried to the bottom. Every effort was made for nearly half an hour to bring this enormous fish to shore, but to no purpose; at length, however, by making a noise with the oars and pulling at the line, the anglers succeeded. On getting up the pike which they had been playing, it was all torn as if by a large dog, but really, doubtless, by another fish of the same species; and as the pike so ill-treated weighed seventeen pounds, the rapacious fish that had held it so long must have been indeed a monster!"

Mr. Lloyd informs us that it is not an uncommon thing in the north of Europe for even the voracious pike to become the prey of a feathered enemy. Eagles frequently pounce on these fish when basking near the surface; but when the pike has been very large, he has been known to carry the eagle under water; in which case the bird, being unable to disengage his talons, has been drowned. This traveller was informed by Dr. Mellerborg, that he had himself seen an enormous pike, with an eagle fastened to his back, lying dead on a piece of ground which had been overflowed, but from which the water had then retreated. Captain Eurenius informed the same author that he was once an eye-witness of a similar circumstance. In this instance, when the eagle first seized the pike, he succeeded in lifting him for a short distance into the air; the weight of the fish, however, combined with its struggles, soon carried both down again into the water, under which they disappeared. Presently the eagle was seen at the surface, uttering piercing cries, and apparently making great efforts to extricate its talons; all, however, were in vain, for after a long continued struggling, he finally disappeared in the depths of the river.

The pike is generally believed to be a long-lived fish. Numerous stories are recorded more or less authentic confirmatory of the prevailing opinion; and there can be little doubt, perhaps, that he will live to a very great age, if well fed and undisturbed. This fish, however, has too many enemies to allow him to survive many seasons, except in stews and private waters, where he can remain secure and unmolested.

Many anecdotes are preserved respecting the size which the pike is supposed to be capable of attaining. Wales is said to contain numerous enormous fish in its deep mountain tairns; and Ireland —that land of exaggeration—boasts o fish of the extraordinary weight of seventy or eighty pounds. In the spring of 1843, a pike was exhibited in London, at a fishmonger's in Piccadilly, which was caught in some private preserve. He was immensely long, and was *ticketed* to weigh sixty-nine and a half pounds. How far such statements are to be believed one can scarcely determine; because no one seems to have taken the trouble properly to authenticate any remarkable instance. Some time in, or about the year 1820, a pike, said to be thirty-six pounds, was taken out of Whittlesea Mere, in Huntingdonshire, and exhibited alive in a small brewing tub at Trinity College, Cambridge, on the morning of the audit day. Whether or not he was served up at the capital dinner which occurs on this occasion, we do not remember; but perhaps the ravages of thirty years may have spared some old "blue-gown" who may have a more perfect recollection of the circumstances.

But what are these pigmies, compared with the monster whose carcase was preserved at Mannheim, and may be there yet for anything we know to the contrary? Part of the story has been a pet affair with most of the book-makers on fishing, from Walton downward; but all of them have shrunk from the *entire* narration in sheer despair, it is presumed, of being able to stuff it down the throats of their readers. Monsieur Passon Maisonneuve, in a third edition of his "Manuel du Pêcheur," has no such foolish scrupulosity; so he ventures on the following story, citing Eleazar Bloch, who published a magnificent work on ichthyology, under the auspices of the then King of Prussia, as his authority for the singular story. "In 1497, a person caught, at Kaiserslautern, near Mannheim, a pike which was nineteen feet long, and which weighed three hundred and fifty pounds! His skeleton was preserved for a long time at Mannheim. He carried round his neck a ring of gilded brass, which could enlarge itself by springs, and which had been attached to him by order of the Emperor, Frederick Barbarossa, *two hundred and sixty-seven years before.*" Monsieur Pesson Maissonneuve concludes the anecdote with this apposite and truly pathetic explanation: "What a tremendous quantity of animals, more weak and feeble than himself, he must have devoured, in order to nourish his enormous bulk during so long a series of years."

In March, if very warm, and in April, these fish leave their accustomed deep and quiet haunts and seek for gullies, creeks, broad ditches, and shallow reedy or pebbly places, in order to deposit their spawn, which they leave near the surface to be acted upon by the rays of the sun. It is said, but, perhaps, without much truth, that when thus obeying the impulses of nature, such is their lazy and absorbed condition, that they may be taken by the hand, much in the same way that trout are occasionally tickled.

The spawning season occupies from two to three months; the younger female fish, of about three or four years old, taking the lead; and when they have all been all safely delivered, the dowagers, or frog pikes, (so called from their period of spawning), succeed them. During this period, pike should never be molested or disturbed; and, indeed, until this peculiar season is entirely over, the fish is not worth catching.

The pike, like some other fish, is supposed to be affected in his hues by the complexion of the water in which he lives. However this may be, it is unquestionably true that pike taken out of canals, rivers, and rapid streams are generally of a brighter colour, and more brilliant in their tints than those which frequent deep pools, and large weedy lakes. The latter are commonly much darker, and their sides tinged with a deep yellow; and some of these taken out of the *marais* of France, are frequently quite tawny, and striped across the back and sides like a Bengal tiger. The river and running water fish have, too, a finer flavour, and are in every respect, both for the sportsman and the cook, far superior to their brethren of the pond and the pool.

Formerly, the pike was a scarce and expensive fish in England. During the reign of Edward I., about the close of the thirteenth century, jack was so dear that few could afford to eat it; the price, says Mr. Yarred, was double that of salmon, and ten times higher than that of either turbot or cod. In 1466, pike was one of the chief dishes in the high church festivals given by George Neville, Archbishop of York. In Henry the Eighth's time, these watery tyrants fetched as much again as house lamb in February; and a very small pickerel would sell higher than a fat capon. Now, however, the pike is to be found in most of the British waters adapted to his nature and habits; and there is scarcely a private pond in the kingdom, of any respectable dimensions, which is not well stocked with these noble fish.

When the pike is in season, he is a good, firm, and, if cooked *brown*, after the French fashion, a very fine, and, indeed, most excellent fish. When out of season, he is about as filthy a compound as can well be tasted. But, perhaps, there is no fish whose culinary qualities have met, at different times and in different places, with a greater diversity of opinion. The sentiment of Ausonius is, we have just seen, strongly against it; and in the part of France to which he belonged, there is, to this day, a great repugnance to the pike as an article of food; whilst at Chalons-sur-Saone, on the other hand, the fish is in high repute. In Italy, pike are but rarely eaten; and the Spaniards reject them entirely. In the northern countries of Europe, their reputation rises. Those taken from some of the large lakes of Germany are highly esteemed; and even in our own country, where once this fish was a first-rate favourite when taken out of clear waters, he is still held as a gastronomic luxury. Those caught in the Norfolk Broads are considered very rich and delicate eating; and the smelt-fatted pike of the Medway stand high in popular estimation.

Superstition, which has touched everything connected with this world, more or less, has not spared the pike. A little bone, in the form of a cross, which is said to be discoverable in the head of the fish, has been worn by the credulous as a sort of talisman against witchcraft and enchantment. In some of the districts of Hungary and Bohemia, it is considered an unlucky omen to witness before mid-day the plunge of the pike in still waters or ditches.

Medicine, too, has had its weaknesses and delusions on subjects of this kind. The heart of the pike is recommended to be eaten against the paroxysms of fevers; his gall to be used as a liniment in affections of the eyes; his mandibulæ, dried into dust, against pleurisy; and little fishes found in his belly were prescribed, when dried, as a draught for poor persons in consumption. These follies, have now, however, nearly passed away; but still the age which patronises the absurdities and extravagances of mesmerism, spirit rapping, &c., is scarcely in a condition to brag very loudly of its superiority in matters of this kind.

We shall now describe the various methods of capturing this ravenous and singular fish.

There are various methods of catching pike. He may be snared, trimmered, angled for with the float, huxed, trolled, snapped, shot, and, unfortunately, in the open rivers of England, he is remorselessly and illegally netted.

The trick of *snaring* used to be—and we suppose is now—done to perfection in the small streams which drop into the Ouse in Huntingdonshire, and in the large ditches and drains in the fens about Ely, Soham, Whittlesea, &c., &c. A strong, short, stiff aspen bough, or rough rod, about ten or twelve feet in length, is generally used for this purpose. From the thinner end of it is suspended a thread of copper wire, about three feet in length, with a running noose kept wide open. This wire must be previously burned in hay, which renders it ductile and pliable as a thin piece of lead, and takes off all the glare and shine. When the pike is discovered basking in the water, the noose is cautiously slipped over the head of the fish—an operation requiring considerable dexterity, owing to the refraction of the rays of light in the water; and as soon as it clears the gills, a sharp jerk fixes the snickle, and the fish is dragged out of the water by main force, the wire often cutting deep into his flesh when he is of some magnitude. Hundreds of fish are taken in this manner, in the calm, sunny days, when they are basking in still water, and can be easily seen.

The *trimmer* is a fatal weapon, more destructive than any other, but considered by many as utterly unworthy of a real sportsman. It requires no skill, no patience, and very little attention; well adapted for poaching, and very convenient to gamekeepers. A double hook, with a twisted wire shank about five inches long, having a loop at the end, must be baited with a bright, shining roach or gudgeon, alive or dead, it does not much signify which. The wire must be put down its throat and drawn through at the vent, the hooks being neatly placed on either side the mouth, with the point downwards. This wire must be attached to a strongish line of common twine about sixteen or twenty yards in length. About three or four feet above the bait, the line should pass through the centre of an ordinary-sized bung, a small moveable peg being thrust in with it to keep it fast: this peg should be fastened to the bung with a thin thread of twine, which should pass round the rim of the bung to keep it from splitting. Eight or ten inches further from the bait, a very small cork tied to the line will prevent it from twisting. These floats are often painted of different colours, which give them a showy appearance in the water. The line thus prepared, must be fastened at the other end to a strong peg, six or eight inches long, which must be driven into the ground, on which, when the trimmer is taken up, the line can be wrapped. When the bait is thrown into the water, a few yards of the line should be coiled neatly against the peg, in order to allow the fish to run off with a little more line if necessary. The trimmer is better without shot or weight of any kind.

Another kind of trimmer, called the "floating trimmer," is also a very killing affair, and is thus constructed. A small roll of wood, seven or eight inches long, has a small groove cut round the middle, and a small slit, about half an inch deep, sawn across one of the ends. To the groove in the centre, a line of about fifteen or sixteen yards in length is firmly tied; and when baited as before described, is wound round the roll of wood, with the exception of three or four feet or more above the bait; it is then drawn through the slit, but not too tightly, so that when a fish seizes the bait he may instantly release it, and run off the roll without the slightest resistance. Some make these trimmers in a fanciful style, using large round bungs, painted different colours on the different sides, with the line so fixed that when the pike takes the bait the trimmer may roll over, and betray the run by the altered colour. This is said to be occasionally amusing; for our own part, we consider it but a very childish affair.

The pike is angled for with a large float and a live bait, the hook being thrust under the back fin, or through the nose of a strong gudgeon or roach. A strong gimp hook must be used; a small bullet to keep down the bait; a stiff rod, and a pretty strong line. The bait should swim about mid-water if shallow, and not more than three or four feet under any circumstances. In weedy waters, this mode of fishing is worse than useless. The float will not allow the line to run freely through the weeds when the fish bolts off to gorge, and the chances are, that in nine cases out of ten you will not only lose your fish, but injure him also, and damage your tackle as well. Even at the best, and under the most favourable circumstances, it is but a bungling piece of business, fit only for schoolboys and small amateur anglers.

Huxing is done by fastening a live bait to a large distended ox bladder, and throwing them into the water as a sort of floating trimmer. When the pike has swallowed the bait, it is capital fun-to watch the bladder bobbing up, in spite of the exertions of the very largest fish to keep it down; but there ends the sport, such as it is. Connoiseurs in huxing substitute a live duck for the ox-bladder, and infinitely prefer the splashings and quackings of the one, to the silent bobbings of the other. In the Shannon, in Ireland, the people use geese for this purpose, which are said to kill very large fish.

Trolling is the only mode of pike fishing which is worthy of a sportsman, or which a genuine angler will condescend to practice. It requires considerable skill and patience; a good general knowledge of the habits of the fish; a practised eye for the quality and condition of the water; an aptitude for choosing the most favourable spots—an art which can neither be communicated nor described; firm nerves, and a steady, quiet hand. In favourable weather, when the sky is clouded, the air cool, and, above all, when there is a fine rolling breeze bending the trees and rippling up the surface of the water into mimic waves, it is a most exciting and fascinating amusement. On such occasions, the fish generally run pretty freely, and afford the angler plenty of opportunity for his patience and skill.

The rod for trolling should be about ten or twelve feet long. Some, it is true, prefer a longer rod; and an experienced angler of our acquaintance declares, that a rod of eighteen or twenty feet is preferable to any. For our own part, no matter what the kind of fishing, we maintain that a rod can never be too light and manageable, consistently with the necessary strength. Rods which require the occasional use of both hands, are, in our opinion, a cumbrous and uncalled for addition to an angler's difficulties. In fishing for the lordly and riotous salmon, it is often absolutely necessary to carry such a weapon; but we have never yet seen the fresh water fish which could not be killed with a rod easily manageable by one hand, supposing the angler to possess ordinary patience, and a certain degree of skill.

The trolling rod should be tolerably stiff, and the fewer rings it has on the better, care being taken that they are sufficiently large, especially at the end of the rod, which should be a fixture, and much thicker than the others.

The trolling line should at least be fifty yards in length; and we have found even this, with large fish in broad water, quite little enough. This line should be wound on a reel or winch fixed to the bottom joint of the rod. Some prefer wooden reels or pirns, apparently without sufficient reason. One of the very best trollers we ever knew used something of the sort, and let his line trail on the ground as he fished along. We employ ourselves the winch, as handy and convenient, but do not much relish a multiplier, because it winds up too fast and noisily, and pays out too stiffly. This, however, is a mere matter of taste.

Everybody has some theory about a line. For ourselves, we prefer a good one of pure horse-hair to every other. In the first place it is not so liable to chafe, if properly attended to, as some other lines; and, in the next, it holds no water, dries quickly, springs well, and never becomes dabby and sticky. This latter quality is, we apprehend, so valuable to the angler, that it must necessarily overbalance every other consideration. What troller has not experienced the miseries which arise from wet flabby lines, which hang about his clothes and feet like spider's web, and ruffle about among the grass like a skein of crumpled silk. It is true, a genuine, unadulterated, horse-hair line of the requisite length and strength for trolling, is rather an expensive article; but then it will last a man's lifetime, with care and good luck. Silk is not good for trolling-lines; and silk and hair do not make the best compound in the world.

The hook used in trolling, is the common double hook, fixed on a brass wire shank, with a loop at the end to receive the gimp bottom, which it is necessary should be employed in this mode of fishing. This hook should not be large. The wire shank must be loaded with lead, about two inches in length from the very bottom of the hook, tapering nicely up towards the other end. This lead should be as large as it can be, to go easily into the mouth and throat of the bait, because we are persuaded that the bait generally sinks through the water too slowly. Between the gimp bottom attached to the hook—which should be moveable at pleasure— and the line, you may insert a sort of gimp trace, furnished with three or four swivels, which many trollers recommend, and which most of the tackle-shops will supply you with; but we confess we do not think the swivels possess the advantages commonly attributed to them. They very often break, they do not always work freely, and they are liable to rust and to corrode the gimp. We never fish with swivels ourselves; we merely fasten our line with a simple slip-knot to the gimp bottom; but, perhaps, a very strong one, which can be readily removed at pleasure, may not be disadvantageous in strong running water. If, however, the general custom influence the angler, he can easily obtain the required tackle at any fishing shop.

To bait this gorge-hook, it is necessary to have a *flat* brass needle, somewhat longer than the fish you bait with. We need not give specific dimensions, because some trollers prefer larger baits than others. A friend of ours, who is the very soul of *nattiness*, has his needle graduated, so that by simply laying his bait along the needle, he sees at a glance what sized hook will best suit his purpose.

Fix the loop of the gimp bottom, or trace, to the little hook at the but-end of the needle. Push the point of the needle in at the mouth of the bait, drive it straight through the entire body, and bring it out *exactly* between the forks of the tail. There is a stiff membrane encircling the tail, which will hold the gimp firm, and prevent the necessity of tying a thread round the tail—the clum- siest of all contrivances, unless, perchance, the water be bunged up with weeds, and then it may be excusable. The arming-wire attached to the hook should never protrude beyond the tail, but remain concealed in the bait.

When all is ready, throw your bait lightly into the water, and let it sink very nearly to the bottom. Draw it up again at a moderate pace, in any direction you choose, taking care to give it a slight curving motion. Practice will soon make perfect in this respect. Experience alone can guide the angler to the most favourable spots for his casts. The water in likely places cannot be fished too closely and carefully. Fish are very easily missed; and therefore, in favourable water, almost every square inch should be worked over. Weeds will give the troller but little trouble, if he be careful to lay the barbs of the hook close to the cheeks of his bait, and to turn the points downwards. Keep your bait clean, and preserve it from being bruised, if possible, as the pike, with all his voracity, is occasionally very particular. If fishing in a pond or lake, you may make your casts as far and wide as you please; although we do not believe your chance of success will be greater on that account. Take care that the bait falls gently on the water, except in windy weather, and then it does not signify how great a splash you make—perhaps the greater the better. But if you are fishing in a navigable river, up and down which boats are perpetually passing, you cannot fish too close to the side. Eighteen inches or two feet from the bank, provided the water be not too shallow, is quite far enough out in such waters. We have seen this proved to demonstration over and over again. A French officer, quartered in Calais in the summer of 1844, a very skilful troller—an accomplishment, by the way, somewhat unusual in a Frenchman—never fished more than two feet from the side in navigable waters, however broad; and he was generally very successful. His tackle was peculiar: his lines and hooks were remarkably small; and his rod was very light indeed, very little removed from the make and pliancy of a fly rod, bending and springing when he hooked a large fish like a switch. Notwithstanding this tackle, which we would not take upon us to recommend, Captain Guilluame understood the art of trolling right well, and was a most skilful brother of the craft.

When you feel a run, which the pike generally takes care shall be no doubtful matter, pay out your line and let him rove where he likes. Do not let him run it off the winch himself, but slack it out for him, for if he feel the slightest resistance, he will suspect all is not right, and perhaps refuse to gorge. If, when he has taken the bait, he merely intends to play with it, he will keep swimming about from place to place, and your chance of getting him is in such a case very small; but if he be in earnest, he will move off to his haunt at once; and when he has remained there perfectly still precisely ten minutes—more time is often necessary—you may draw in your line with the left hand, and begin your contest. Striking him smartly under these circumstances, as some anglers recommend, is not advisable. During the ten minutes you have allowed him, he has gorged the hook, and all the striking in the world will make it no faster; although, if the fish be very large, the indiscreet performance may possibly snap your rod or line. If the fish move off before ten minutes be expired, let him alone, and he will, perhaps, soon stop again; if not, *then* jerk him smartly, and make the best of it; you will most probably capture him.

It is, however, impossible to give directions which can meet every contingency that may arise. Experience alone can enable the angler to deal successfully with every difficulty; but no art, no combination of power of words, can convey to others the practical skill and ready *tactique* resulting from that experience. General rules and leading principles may be laid down, but the art of applying these rules and principles in all their singular variations and diversities, can be obtained, or even comprehended, by experience alone.

When the last struggles of the pike are over, lift him gently out of the water. Some recommend landing nets, gaffs, &c., &c., for this purpose. For our own part, we are not passionate admirers of these supplementary aids, and have always found our gimp strong enough to effect this object when the fish is fairly done up. Some anglers put their fingers in the pike's eyes; and others, which is, perhaps, after all the best way, play him to some shallow place, and run him up the shelving side. Whatever you do, however, never put your hand near his mouth. His teeth are formidable weapons, and he bites like a crocodile. Let him go, sooner than let him hold your finger.

It is sometimes advisable to bait a few gorge-hooks previously to starting, as they will save trouble on an emergency, and probably be sufficient for the day's sport. Put them, when baited, into a little bran, and they will keep stiff and fresh until you want them.

There are various opinions about the sort of bait which is best adapted for the pike. Some recommend frogs, some roach, dace, gudgeon, bleak, minnows, and even perch, with the back fin cut off. Some, again, maintain that mice, birds, bats, &c., are accepted as dainties; whilst others have affirmed that eels cut up into small bits are perfectly irresistible.

"Who shall decide when doctors disagree?" All these opinions are most probably the result of observation, and are founded on fact; but the observations may not have been sufficiently strict, and the facts may have been too hastily generalized. The truth, perhaps, is, the pike-fisher goes out on some particular day, unprovided with his accustomed favourite bait, whatever that may be. The day turns out to be highly promising, and the fish are eagerly on the feed. In his destitution, he baits with anything he can get—frog, eel, or mouse—the first that comes to hand. He has an excellent day's sport, and goes away under the full persuasion that he is indebted to the bait for all his good luck. No such thing. The day was favourable—the fish were ravenously hungry—

and, in all probability, any other bait in the catalogue would have
done just as well. The best bait must surely be that which will
most universally attract the fish under all circumstances. That
bait, we apprehend—and we think most old trollers will agree wit
us—is a fresh, dark-backed, red-finned roach, with bright shinin
sides. Taking all waters and weathers and moods of the pike int
consideration, this bait cannot be beaten; and the angler wh
sticks to it will, in the long run, outdo all his more fanciful con
petitors. To say that a pike will run eagerly at frogs, &c., i
nothing. We know a troller once took several fish with the fresh
red gills, which, for lack of bait, he had cut out of one previously
caught; but who would pretend to argue that these are therefore
a good general bait? A large pike was once dragged out of a
river in an eastern county, by putting a snap hook very neatly on
the back of a sparrow, and letting the bird flap upon the top of the
water. Where is the angler who would deduce from this solitary
incident that a sparrow is the best bait for a large fish? A friend
of ours has more than once had good sport with a fresh *herring* for
his bait; but we never heard him contend that it was the best bait
in the world.

The fact is, when the pike are very hungry, they will run at
almost anything; but a good roach will often tempt them when
they are not hungry, and seem disposed to run at nothing. This
is the true test; and, in our humble opinion, the roach will bear it
better than any other kind of bait which has ever been recommended.

Some trollers take live roach with them in a fish-kettle, this is
not necessary. Put a fine fresh caught roach, into clean, sweet
bran with care, and by the time you arrive at the water side, they
will be firm and stiff. Do not wash them before you bait, because
you are very likely to rub off some scales in the process. As soon
as the hook is thrown into the water, off goes the bran, and the
fish sparkles and glitters with his skin unblemished.

Another way of catching pike is with the snap. The spring snap
is sold at all the tackle-shops, and, as it is easily adjusted to
any part of the bait by means of the smaller hook, it is a very
good weapon for the purpose. There is also a double-hooked
snap sometimes used, for managing which directions are given in
some fishing books; but it seems at best but a roundabout troublesome process, scarcely worth comprehending or adopting. We
have in our possession a singularly formidable sort of hook, or
rather bundle of hooks, used, and we believe invented, by a game-
keeper of Lord Yarborough's. It consists of two strong treble-
hooks, one double hook, and a single one, laying in succession
along a very strong gimp trace, with a good swivel in the middle
of it. One of the barbs in the first treble hook is thrust upwards
from under the mouth through the head of the bait, the second
treble hook crosses over the shoulders, and has one of its barbs
pushed under the back fin; the double hook is run in near the tail,

F

and the single hook hangs loose behind. If the pike venture to touch this bait so armed, he must get the hooks into his mouth, and a smart jerk will fix them immoveably.

This is unquestionably a killing affair; and, in the hands of a keeper, or an unfair fisher, is a powerful and valuable weapon; but the genuine angler will be somewhat reluctant to adopt methods like these. They destroy the great charm of the art. He may assuredly obtain fish; but where are the suspense, uncertainty, dexterity, skill, and patience, which constitute the purest luxuries of the fisherman's amusement?

Some people spin the minnow for pike. This is but a sorry business; but those who are disposed to practise it, will find it fully described under the instructions for catching trout. In this mode, as with the snap, the casts are made much in the same manner as in trolling.

The pike is sometimes shot by those who have a fancy for such sport. A light charge is put into the gun; and all the art displayed in the performance, consists in making due allowance for the refraction of the water, according to the depth and distance of the fish. It often happens that the fish is very much mutilated by this process.

September and October are fine months for pike-fishing; but if the angler can stand the weather, the winter months are decidedly the best for large fish. Thorough pike-fishers always insist that they catch the finest fish on sharp frosty days, when there is a thin film of ice spread over the surface of the water; and we have ourselves taken good fish, after having had to break ice an inch thick to get our bait into the water.

CHAPTER VI.

THE GREYLING.

THE Greyling is a fish bearing considerable resemblance to the trout, and chiefly abounds in the rivers of Derbyshire and Yorkshire; in the Teme, near Ludlow; and in the Lugg, and other streams in the vicinity of Leominster. Its general shape is rather longer, and more slender than the trout, particularly towards the tail; the head is small, and the eyes very protuberant. The sides of the fish are of a beautiful silvery gray, with numerous dark stripes of a longitudinal shape. He is a keen and ready feeder, and rises readily at the fly, and is partial to worms and maggots. Indeed, all kinds of water insects afford him sustenance, as well as

Greyling, p. 66.

Perch, p 68.

Carp. p. 71.

the roe of other kinds of fish. Walton says, "Of grubs for greyling, the ash-grub, which is plump, milk-white, bent round from
head to tail, and exceedingly tender, with a round head; or the
dock-worm, or grub of a pale yellow, longer, lanker, and tougher
than the other, with rows of feet all down his belly, and a red head
also, are the best—I say for greyling, because although a trout will
take both these, and the ash-grub especially, yet he does not do it
so freely as the other, and I have usually taken ten greylings for
one trout with that bait; though if a trout come, I have observed
that he is commonly a very good one."

The best months for angling for greyling are September, October, and November. The larger kinds of this fish are partial to
deep water, into which there is a gentle stream running. The
smaller ones, which frequent the shallows and streams, may be
readily taken with the fly, but those in deep pools are easier caught
with the worm or maggot. The bait should lie close to the ground;
and when a fish is hooked, great care must be taken in killing him,
for he has a very tender mouth from which he often slips his hold.
Some anglers, in fishing for the greyling in still water, throw in a
few maggots before commencing, with a view of drawing the fish
together. Cabbage-grubs, grasshoppers, and lob-baits, are all suitable to the tastes of the greyling.

The following dialogue on this fish, by Walton, is very charac-
teristic of both the fisher and the fish.

"Pisc. Why, then, by what you say, I dare venture to assure you
it is a greyling, who is one of the deadest-hearted fish in the world,
and the bigger he is, the more easily taken. Look you, now you
see him plain; I told you what he was; bring hither that landing-
net, boy; and now, sir, he is your own; and, believe me, a good
one, sixteen inches long I warrant him; I have taken none such
this year.

"Viat. I never saw a greyling before look so black.

"Pisc. Did you not? why, then, let me tell you that you never
saw one before in right season; for then a greyling is very black
about his head, gills, and down his back, and has his belly of a
dark gray, dappled with very black spots, as you see this is; and I
am apt to conclude that from thence he derives his name of
Umber. Though, I must tell you, this fish is past his prime, and
begins to decline, and was in better season at Christmas than he is
now. But move on, for it grows towards dinner-time; and there
is a very great and fine stream below, where we are almost sure of
a good fish.

"Viat. Let him come, I'll try a fall with him; but I had thought
that the greyling had been always in season with the trout, and
had come in and gone out with him.

"Pisc. Oh no! assure yourselves, a greyling is a winter fish, but
such a one as would deceive any but such as do know him very
well indeed; for his flesh, even in his worst season, is so firm, and
will so easily carve, that, in plain truth, he is very good meat at all

times; but in his perfect season, which, by the way, none but an overgrown greyling will ever be, I think him so good a fish as to be little inferior to the best trout that I ever tasted in my life."

CHAPTER VII.

THE PERCH.

The Perch is a handsome, noble looking fish; a bold, dashing biter, and a courageous fellow when hooked, never yielding as long as he has any strength remaining, but fighting bravely to the last. He is extremely voracious when hungry, and will spring at anything that comes in his way. Indeed, he will often follow a smaller one of his own species when hooked, and make every effort to devour it. In short, he is altogether, when large, one of the best fish for sport which the fresh waters contain.

The perch is gregarious, and in the matter of taking bait, remarkably imitative; so that when you have caught one, you should invariably remain some time in the same place, as there is every probability you will ultimately get all there are. This is so commonly understood among anglers, that it is quite a proverbial matter, known to every schoolboy, and invariably acted upon by all the lovers of the gentle craft.

In March or April, and perhaps in May, according to the season, the perch cast their spawn, so that they should be suffered to remain unmolested at least till July or August. In May and June they are out of condition, are then of a pale, lead colour, and most execrable flavour; very different from the deep, bright hues which make them like bars of gold in the water, and the sweet firm flesh which distinguishes them in September and October.

The perch is very prolific. Picot, of Geneva, opened a fish of a pound weight, the ovarium of which weighed a quarter of a pound, and contained 992,000 eggs. Their increase, in favourable situations, must consequently be enormous.

This fish reaches a considerable size. Some authors affirm that he has occasionally attained a weight of nine or ten pounds. Perch have sometimes been caught at Whittlesea-mere of six pounds; and we have ourselves taken them of three and four pounds. But, speaking generally, an angler must consider himself somewhat fortunate if he succeed in killing perch, whose average weight shall reach a pound or a pound and a half. Excellent sport is to be obtained with fish much below these weights; for, as he is a fearless dashing fellow, he will always afford the sportsman more amusement than any other fish twice his size, with the exception of the trout and salmon, whose magnificent leaps and rushes, none who have ever witnessed them can possibly forget.

The perch frequents deep weedy holes, the stone walls about locks and mills, reedy streams, where the water pours freely; and invariably in those places where there is a constant or frequent rapid fall of water. If you can keep your line down, the stronger the stream in which you angle for perch the better; but more will be said on this matter in another place.

Perch are to be met with almost everywhere; there is scarcely a river in England, adapted to his nature and habits, in which he cannot be found. The lakes in the north of England, and many in Scotland, are full of these fish; and private ponds in which jack are preserved generally abound with them; as the jack will not eat the perch unless urged by extremity of hunger, and then he seldom recovers the effects of the perch's sharp and penetrating dorsal fin.

The flesh of the perch was deemed salubrious by the physicians, and they were accustomed to prescribe two little round bones in his head to be dissolved, and taken as a remedy for the "stone." There are various modes of cooking the perch. The best way with which we are acquainted, is to fry him in butter, and then serve him up with rich, hot shrimp sauce. In Scotland, they make what is called a "water-souchie" of him; but this is a flabby, wishy-washy affair altogether; the flavour of the fish is lost in that of the onion, and you wish in vain that you could lose the taste of the onion as easily.

Being a bold biter, and a somewhat unscrupulous fish, the perch is very readily attracted by bait, and very quickly caught. When he bites he requires rather more time than might be imagined from his bold and determined character; but experience will soon convince the angler, that, whenever the perch escapes, it is, generally speaking, because he has not been allowed time enough to get the hook well into his gullet. The perch requires considerable indulgence in this respect, especially when angled for with a gudgeon.

Almost all kinds of tackle, however common and unpretending, will do for catching perch. The rod should be rather stiff, light, and not larger than is necessary to clear the weeds and other obstacles which sometimes line the sides of perch haunts. The line should be of hair, about nine hairs in thickness. The hooks about No. 4, and the bottom gut a yard in length at least. Some anglers use gimp, but there can be no necessity for tackle of such strength; salmon and trout are killed with gut, and why not perch?

Most anglers use a float in perch fishing. This method undoubtedly saves trouble and attention in still water; but in strong streams and boiling eddies, where the best perch fishing is often to be obtained, it is of no use whatever. In this case the line must be kept down with a bullet attached to it, below the bait; or a

paternoster as it is called, well leaded, may be made use of. To
the hooks—and in this mode of angling you may have as many as
you like—small gudgeons or minnows should be fixed by the
nose or the back fin; and when the fish bites in the running
stream, the angler will feel the short, quick jerks which indicate a
perch run under such circumstances. These hooks may also be
baited with worms, if large and red.

In fishing with gudgeon or minnow in tranquil, or in gently
flowing waters, run the hook under the back fin, and put shot
enough, about a foot above the bait, to keep it down well. You
may use a float or not, in this case; but it is more difficult for
young anglers to kill a fish without a float than with one. Some
authors recommend spinning a dead minnow for the perch, on the
curious ground that the rod-fisher may kill a trout or pike. This
chance must be a very remote affair, as we should fancy, for the
angler seldom encounters the two in the same stream.

Several kinds of bait are recommended for the perch; gudgeon,
minnow, worms, gentles, frogs. Undoubtedly this fish will take
all these, and many others of a similar kind. We have seen them,
for instance, killed with slugs, and the stone-loach is thought to be
very persuasive. The common bait, however, for this fish, taking
all things into consideration—season, size of fish, state of water,
weather, &c., &c.—is a fine large red garden worm, commonly
called a lob or dew-worm. These may be gathered by thousands
late in the evening after rain, without any fear of injuring them, as
they are then crawling about above ground; but none but red
worms must be taken, the black being altogether useless, avoided
even by small eels. Fill a large flower-pot, or some other convenient vessel, earthenware being preferable, with a quantity of
long clean moss; press it down hard, put the worms on the top of
it, and drop upon them a very small quantity of pure, sweet milk,
to purge and purify them. If this moss be frequently washed and
turned, and the worms carefully put on the top of it every time,
they will keep a long period, and will become clear, firm, and of
surprising toughness. We do not believe that a better bait than
these worms, so prepared, can be found for perch. Brandlings,
and small red worms, and similar fancy things, are lauded by some
authors; but we feel confident that a little experience will soon
convince the angler there is nothing comparable to a well-prepared
dew-worm. It will often tempt the perch, late in the evening, when
he is roving about shallow places in search of prey; and a large
eel will rush at it greedily.

Perch may be caught nearly all the year round; but perhaps
August, September, and October, are the best months, as the fish
are then in high season, splendid in colour, and full of condition and
vigour. In cloudy weather, this fish will bite all day; but,
generally speaking, early in the morning and late in the day, far
into the evening, are the most favourable periods. The largest
perch we ever saw taken, were caught with a dew-worm, near a

public ferry, where the bottom was gravelly, and the water not too clear. They were caught between three and five in the morning, in August, whilst the thick, heavy dew was on the water, and before it had been disturbed by the usual traffic.

The hooks commonly recommended for perch, are too small. No. 4 will be found the most efficient size; for this fish has a large mouth, out of which a small hook may very easily slip.

As to the float, if he must have one, the angler should be guided by circumstances, such as weight of shot, nature of bait, current, depth, &c., but on no account should it be very large; indeed, as an ordinary rule, every part of an angler's apparatus, which may be seen by the fish, should be as small as the exigencies of the case will permit.

In many countries, the perch is esteemed a very dainty dish. In Italy, Androvandus praises it. Gesner prefers it to the trout. He tells us that the Germans have a proverb, "More wholesome than a perch of the Rhine;" and adds, that the river perch is so wholesome, that physicians allow him to be eaten freely by wounded men, those suffering from dangerous fevers, and by women in child-bed.

CHAPTER VIII.

THE CARP.

THIS is a shy, cunning, and careful fish, very crafty and suspicious and, therefore, very difficult to deceive. All the skill and ingenuity of the angler, are required to entrap him; and his patience—that only virtue which the would-be wise of this world will allow him—will be tried to the uttermost.

The carp is a very handsome fish, and is very highly esteemed, especially among some continental nations, for his edible qualities.

He is to be found in most of the ponds and rivers of Europe; but he chiefly frequents those waters which have a very gentle flow; and in haunts of this kind, his flesh acquires the highest degree of delicacy and *goût* of which it is susceptible. Perhaps, those fish are the best, both in colour and flavour, which are taken out of lakes, and ponds of pure, limpid water, which is continually changed by a placid current perpetually running through them, and the bottoms of which are covered with fine sand or pebbles. If, in addition to these advantages, the water which drains into these ponds or lakes from the surrounding lands, falls over a shingly or gravelly soil, the carp will be of splendid quality, and become a most delicious fish.

The carp will live to a great age; and in favourable situations, will attain a very large size. It is said, that the big old carp which are to be found in the fosse of the chateau at Fontainebleau, in France, were placed there in the time of Francis I. Buffon speaks of carp in the fosse of Portchartrain, which were one hundred and fifty years old, and still possessed all the vivacity and agility of ordinary fish. Others are spoken of by some authors, which had attained the age of two hundred years.

We must, however, take all these stories about the ages of fish, *cum grano salis.* It is extremely difficult to obtain correct information on such a subject, especially as the evidence, from the nature of the case, must necessarily be of a very loose and inadequate description. The weight of fish is a more tangible affair; and on this point we cannot be very far deceived, if proper precautions be adopted. Carp, if only half the statements on record be true, will undoubtedly reach a very large size, especially in the north of Europe, where they seem to be highly prized, and very carefully protected. Pallas says, that the Volga produces carp five feet in length. "In 1711," says Eleazar Bloch, in his splendid work, "a carp was caught near Frankfort, on the Oder, which was more than nine feet long, and three round, and which weighed seventy pounds." In the lake of Zug, in Switzerland, one was taken which weighed ninety pounds. Monsieur Pesson-Maisonneuve seems to think their size varies according to the places they inhabit, and the food they live upon. "In France," says he, "they reach ten or twelve pounds; in Germany, they become monstrous. They are taken in Pomerania, thirty or forty pounds in weight; and in Prussia, fifty pounds is a common size!" For our own part, we should like to see one of these extraordinary fish, but much fear we shall not be so fortunate.

The carp spawn in May, and even in April, when the spring is forward and warm. They seek out quiet places covered with verdure, in which to deposit their eggs; and it is said that two or three males follow each female, in order to swim over and impregnate the deposit. At this season, carp which inhabit rivers and running streams, endeavour to get into more tranquil waters; and if, during their migration, they meet with unexpected obstacles, they are very resolute and determined in their efforts to overcome them; leaping, it is affirmed, after the fashion of the salmon, five or six feet in height, in order to accomplish their purpose.

The carp multiplies prodigiously. A fish of half a pound in weight has been found, on examination, to contain 270,000 eggs; one of a pound-and-a-half weight, 342,000, and one of nine pounds, the enormous number of 621,000 eggs.

The carp are very tenacious of life. Many anecdotes illustrative of this fact are on record. Indeed, in France it is no uncommon thing to transport them to great distances from one lake or river to another, wrapping them in fresh grass, and dipping them every twenty-four hours of the journey into fresh water for

a few minutes to recruit their strength. In this manner they are
made to perform long journeys with comparative security, and
scarcely any risk of loss.

Carp are subject to many diseases. We have seen them often
covered with spots like the small-pox; and some of the large old
ones are frequently nearly white, as if infected with a kind of
leprous disorder.

The flesh of the carp is soft, luscious, well-flavoured and nou-
rishing. In Prussia, the head is preferred on account of its excellent flavour. The intestines are likewise esteemed delicacies
when eaten with pepper, ginger, and salt. In fact, the carp is an
excellent fish when properly cooked; for accomplishing which,
almost any cookery book will furnish a tolerable receipt. The
soft-roed fish are much sought after by professed epicures as a
delicate dish; and, indeed, some writers attribute to them the
property of restoring consumptive persons to perfect health.

The older physicians dabbled with the carp, as well as with most
other fish. His fat has been used as a mollifying unguent to soothe
the nerves when suffering under what is termed "hot rheumatism."
His gall has been applied as a linament for sore eyes. A small
triangular stone, supposed to be discernible in the jaws of the
carp, is said to act as a styptic when ground to a fine powder, and
has been found efficacious in bleedings at the nose; and "above
the eyes," says an old doctor, "two little bones exist, semicir-
cular in shape, which are diligently preserved by noble females
against the lunitical disease." All this seems sufficiently absurd at
the present day.

The baits recommended for carp are very numerous, and many
of them very fanciful. Pastes of all kinds and colours, flavoured
with cheese, sugar, honey, gin, &c.; beans, corn, flies, slugs, gentles, grubs, caterpillars, and worms, are to be found in this singular catalogue. In Germany, where carp abound, grains of
wheat, steeped in water until they swell and split the outer skin,
are considered tempting luxuries. A small grasshopper has occasionally proved successful; but no artificial bait will ever seduce
the carp. Yet, notwithstanding this sumptuous array of dishes
for the epicure, perhaps, after all, a clean tough red-worm, or a big
bluebottle fly, will be found the most generally attractive bait for
this singular fish.

The rod for carp-fishing should have plenty of spring, because
the line must be as thin and fine as possible, consistent with the
size and strength of the fish. Running tackle must be used for
carp, as, indeed, it ought to be for all fish, big or little; and the
line, which should be of horsehair, must be only three hairs thick.
The bottom of the finest gut should be the length of the rod; and
the hook, No. 8, must be covered over with the bait, shank and
all. If, however, you bait with a bluebottle, no matter how small
your hook, but it must be put across the body, just under the
wings.

The float—you are on the whole better without one—should be very small; a bit of quill an inch long will do, and the bait must rest on the ground.

When thus prepared, conceal yourself completely behind a tree or bush: drop your bait as gently as if thistle-down were falling on the water; sum up the whole stock of your patience, and calmly wait the event. As soon as you see the float or line move, let the fish run away a short distance, and then check him very gently. All attempts at striking will be merely ridiculous, as your extremely light tackle will be snapped in a moment. Only give him plenty of line, just keeping pressure enough to stimulate his exertions, and you are sure of your prey. His very strength and vigour will soon tire him, and you may thus draw him out with security.

Carp bite freely from February until June, and may then be caught at all times of the day. From June to September they bite well, morning and evening. After this it is useless to fish for them with a line till February again. In the heats of summer, the night is unquestionably the most favourable season for killing this shy fish. You can see nothing, but then you cannot be seen; and the jerk of the line will infallibly tell you when you have got a fish.

It is also recommended to *ground bait* the spot where you intend to fish, some hours before you commence operations. The following has been often eulogised as a favourite compost. Take a quantity of well-cooked veal, a handful of oatmeal, and a little honey, bruise them in a mortar, and mix them in a thin paste or batter, with new milk, and a few grains of assafœtida. Crush down in a mortar a quantity of worms, gentles, slugs, and some lumps of the most tallowy cheese you can find; thicken the veal batter with this compound, and then roll it up into little balls; these balls must be thrown into a compost of tallow greaves and grains steeped in bullock's blood, and the entire mess sunk in the place you intend to fish, some hours before you commence.

This, we are informed, is a most attractive ground-bait; and, sure we are, it is sufficiently nasty to satisfy the most inflexible advocates of such ground-bait practices.

It is difficult to decide where the favourite haunts of the carp really are, but the angler will always have the best chance of success, who selects the most retired spots, and studiously keeps himself from observation.

Carp, like pike, may be taken with the snare, when they lie basking in the sun. The operator must conceal himself as much as he can, and then no more dexterity is required than in snaring a pike. This is by no means an uncommon practice in France.

Tench, p 75.

Barbel, p 77.

Chub, p 79.

CHAPTER IX.

THE TENCH AND BARBEL.

THE tench is a handsome thick fish, of a greenish yellow colour, with a peculiarly greasy slippery skin. His form and appearance give one the idea of great richness and delicacy; and, indeed, when properly cooked he is really a very delicious fish.

Tench are found in nearly all parts of Europe, but only in lakes, *marais*, ponds, and weedy rivers, where there is little or no current. They prefer stagnant muddy waters to any other; and during the severity of the winter, like eels, they bury themselves in the mud. In the hot days of summer and autumn, they are to be seen basking and floundering about under the large leaves of the water-lily; and in the deep *étangs* in the *marais* in continental countries we have seen them wallowing about in shoals amongst the weeds and lilies, beneath the hot burning sun, apparently regardless of our boat until we could almost touch them.

These fish spawn late in the spring, or early in the summer, according to the lateness or forwardness of the season, and seek the most secluded and weedy places, clogged up, as it were, with vegetation, to deposit their eggs, which are of a greenish colour and very small. They are wondrously prolific, and increase prodigiously if undisturbed. In a female, weighing about three pounds and a half, there were counted more than 297,000 eggs.

When particularly well nurtured, and in a favourable situation, the tench will occasionally attain a weight of seven or eight pounds. This, however, is of rare occurrence, for although the fish grows very fast, he will seldom be found to exceed two or three pounds.

Like carp, tench are extremely tenacious of life, and may be carried very long journeys in wet grass, without the slightest fear of losing them.

Many medicinal properties have been attributed to the tench— but who will vouchsafe for their authority and truth? It has been credited, that when cut into pieces and placed on the soles of the feet, his flesh will overcome the virulence of the plague, and dissipate the heat in the fiercest fevers; that, when applied alive to the brow, he will relieve pains in the head; that, planted on the nape of the neck, he will allay inflammations in the eyes; and that, when held in contact with the lower part of the body, he will effectually cure the jaundice.

The tench has been called the physician of the pike, the latter being supposed to rub himself against its soft mollifying skin when sick or wounded. This notion does not seem to rest upon any sufficient foundation, and yet it is almost universally credited.

The flesh of this fish is rich, luscious, and delicate, although somewhat muddy in its flavour, but the ancients, who have offered some illustrious examples of their familiarity with the gastronomic art, and the appreciation of the delicacies which nature supplies, considered the tench very difficult of digestion, and held him in light estimation. And an old Silesian physician, who seems to have shared these prejudices, says—"The tench is a vile neglected fish, very flabby and glutinous, bad for digestion, a food fit only for paupers and serfs." If he had ever eaten the fish when under the influence of Dr. Kitchener, or Mr. Soyer, he would have smacked his lips, and revoked his opinion.

The tench is by no means a shy fish, but he bites, perhaps, slower than others. He will play with and mumble the bait some time before he will take it, so that he requires a great deal of indulgence, and must be allowed to have his own way for some minutes before the angler can venture to interfere with him.

The baits commonly recommended are the same as those suggested for carp-fishing, and the ground-bait, when required, may be made up from the recipe just given.

Some anglers, and very skilful ones too, have a few pet baits peculiar to themselves, which they pronounce irresistible in angling for this fish. We are acquainted with a clever artist, who never fishes for tench with anything but a large dew worm, and he boasts of his extraordinary success. In France, the small white garden slug is recommended in wet weather, just after showers of rain. But Captain Guillaume affirms that *merac* is the best and most attractive bait for tench—that it is, in fact, perfectly unequalled. We have never submitted this hint to the test of experience, but the captain is a high continental authority, and may be safely relied upon by his brethren of the craft.

As a general rule, perhaps, a clear red worm will be found the most taking and useful bait, especially in the heats of summer. The bait should always touch the ground in any water, and in all seasons.

In rivers, the tench may be caught from April to October, and in still waters from May to September, although we once had a capital day's sport in the middle of November, in a small pond, during fine open weather. These fish bite best in the morning and evening, but in mild showery weather they will feed all the day, and offer good sport.

In fishing for tench the angler must be cautious, circumspect, and still, as the fish, in the event of any noise or alarm, will bury himself in the mud as quickly as possible. If, on being hooked, he endeavours to rush into the mud, hold him firm, but without pulling; this will keep his mouth open, and prevent him rooting his nose into the mire. After being held in this way for a short time he will bolt off, and try the same dodge in another place. These efforts the skilful angler will defeat, until the fish is exhausted by his own exertions.

THE BARBEL

Is a well made, handsome, and powerful fish, very active and vigorous, quite the sort of fellow to try the strength of the angler's tackle, and the dexterity of his hand. He is very fond of rapid waters, which run over stony bottoms, and will lie for a long time in a boiling current under shelving banks, near old stone walls and piles, or about sunken trees or old timber. In these sort of places the larger fish are generally to be found, and as the barbel dreads alike the fiery heats or extreme cold, he commonly lies near the bottom, and haunts the deepest parts of the stream.

The barbel is gregarious, and is to be found in many of the rivers in England; but the Trent and the Thames are perhaps better supplied with this fish than any other British streams.

Stories have been told of the barbel having attained a weight of fifteen or twenty pounds; but these are instances of very rare occurrence, as he seldom exceeds eight or ten pounds, and even this is deemed a very large size; and by no means usual. These fish spawn early in June. Walton says in April; but perhaps they vary according to seasons and situations. Some authors suppose he never casts spawn until his fifth or sixth year.

The barbel is a long-lived fish. His flesh is white and delicate in appearance; and, when cooked according to the receipt for stewing tench and carp, he is not altogether the most despicable of all fish, and might perhaps be eaten by a very hungry man.

The fish will live four or five hours after he has been taken out of the water. The barbel is supposed to possess the peculiar power of causing the water to bubble up on the surface above his head when he makes his respirations. The eel is also believed to exhibit the same faculty; but as these air bubbles may be accounted for in a more satisfactory manner, we may be allowed to call in question the truth of these notions altogether.

The barbel takes its name from the beard or wattles which hang about his mouth; and when he is young and very small, he is called in France "Barbillon." "With these beards or wattles," says Walton, "he is able to take such a hold of weeds and moss, that the sharpest floods cannot move him from his position. He seems to have the power of rooting into the mud, and pig-like, wallowing in the mire and weeds at the bottom of deep holes, and under overhanging banks."

This fish feeds on flies, bees, bugs, wasps, maggots, worms, slugs, snails, and similar kinds of bait; but anglers have invented or adopted various other baits to entrap this wary, shy-biting fish, which we shall soon notice.

The eggs of the barbel are supposed to be injurious; and an opinion once prevailed in the north of Europe, that they who partook of them copiously would "shrink up in great danger of life."

The barbel is a strong and powerful fish, and strong and powerful tackle is commonly recommended in angling for him. This is not necessary. The same tackle that will kill the salmon, will, in skilful hands, bring the most powerful barbel to the creel; and, therefore, the angler who uses light tackle with this cautious fish, has a much better chance of deceiving him, than one who employs a coarser sort. The fishing materials suggested for carp and tench will be found, under all circumstances, the best adapted for this description of fish.

The baits recommended are worms, tallow greaves, slugs, gentles, grubs, and bits of cheese. To these the French anglers add maggots found in dead rats, leeches, meat, cheese used in cooking maccaroni, called *la gruyère*, and the yoke of eggs, all mixed up together to a proper consistency. The common red worm, when clean and tough, is as good a bait as any of these mentioned, and will be most effective if allowed to trail on the ground; indeed, in barbel-fishing, the bait should always touch the bottom.

Running water is preferable to any other for the sport, and a large shot, cased in sand-coloured leather, a foot or two above the hook, will keep it down without being perceived by the fish. Leather is to be preferred to clay, which is commonly used, because the latter will soon wash off, and, owing to the constant kneadings required, assists in wearing the fine gut bottom. The angler is better without a float.

The night is the best time for catching barbel. Evening and morning are likewise favourable periods; but he will not bite well in the full day, nor in bright moonlight nights. The barbel requires time when he takes the bait, and a single short jerk is necessary to fix the hook well in his leathery jaws. When hooked he affords good sport with light tackle, because he is very strong and active; but when you have exhausted his vigour and got him out, the best thing you can do, in the opinion of many rod-fishers, is to throw him in again for another bout, as he is not worth his salt in a culinary point of view.

The receipt for ground-bait, without which there is little profit in angling for this fish, is recorded in the instructions for carp-fishing, and will serve for all fish which require such inducements.

Barbel-fishing is not much sought after by regular and thorough-going anglers. The fish is seldom to be caught unless the ground-bait has been previously thrown in; and even then, success is far from being certain. Many London anglers are, however, fond of the sport, and are remarkably skilful in it; and, as the Thames abounds in many localities with these fish, there is opened out a wide field for this branch of piscatory recreation. Walton, who was partial to this species of sport, says of the barbel, "he is curious for his baits that they may be clean and sweet; that is to say, to have your worms well scoured, and not kept in sour and musty moss, for he is a curious feeder; but at a well-scoured lob-worm he will bite as boldly as at any bait, and especially if, the night or two before you fish for him, you shall bait the places where you intend to fish for him with big worms cut into pieces; and note that none did over-bait the place, or fish too early or too late for a barbel. And the barbel will bite also at gentles, which not being too much scoured, but green, are a choice bait for him; and so is cheese, which is not to be too hard, but kept a day or two in wet linen cloth to make it tough; with this you may also bait the water a day or two before you fish for the barbel, and be much the likelier to catch fish."

CHAPTER X.

THE CHUB, THE BREAM, AND THE ROACH.

THE *chub* is a strong, compact, but rather clumsily built fish, well adapted to afford capital sport to the angler, but is a very miserable affair in the hands of the cook. Walton gives a receipt which he says will make him eatable, but who will be at the trouble of trying it? The French, who understand this department of cookery as well as, or better perhaps, than any other people under the sun, pronounce him a villanous fish; and they are most certainly right. His flesh his woolly and watery, and has a nasty sweetness about it which is absolutely nauseous. Perhaps the best mode of serving up the chub, would be to imitate the Irish manager's method of performing Hamlet—send up the richest receipt you can get, hot and piquante, *omitting the fish*.

The chub spawns about the time of Easter, and is probably very prolific. His eggs, which are yellow, and about the size of a grain of poppy seed, are deposited on the gravel, in very shallow water. The operation is supposed to occupy a period of about eight days.

Most of the rivers of England contain chub. He haunts deep, quiet holes, under overhanging banks, frequents the bottoms of old walls, and deep retired nooks, where piles and old posts stick up out of the bottom, and yet he likes occasionally to fight against strong rushing streams, and to contend with the most rapid waters. The chub of the river is far finer, and more active than his brother of the pond or lake; indeed, he is not often found in the latter,

except it communicates easily and freely with some river, or
constantly open current.

The fish attains a considerable size. It is said he will sometimes
weigh six or seven pounds; and in some continental waters, he has
been known to reach the weight of ten pounds. Fish of this size,
however, must be very scarce; as few sportsmen can boast of
having seen them so large. A chub was caught in the Thames, in
the month of May, 1844, which weighed four pounds. He was a
very strong, active fish, shot across the river like an arrow on
feeling himself hooked, and fought well for a full hour, before he
could be got out of the water. He was caught with a common
gut-line; and, therefore, required considerable indulgence before
he could be overcome. This was a remarkable fish in the estimation of many who saw him.

Chub are gregarious, and in hot weather may be seen basking on
the surface of the water, over some deep hole, in considerable
numbers. The moment they become sensible that they are
observed, they sink down in an instant, being perhaps, with
scarcely an exception, the shyest of all fish.

The chub requires adroit management when first hooked. But
clumsy and strong as he is, and thick-headed as he looks, we
would nevertheless recommend the same tackle as that suggested
for the carp. The lighter the tackle, the easier it is to deceive the
fish, and the greater the merit of overcoming him.

The baits generally recommended for chub-fishing, are red
worms, gentles, grubs, bits of cheese, insects, &c.; but as the
fish is a gross feeder, he prefers large baits to small ones,
invariably. A lobworm will tempt him, while a smaller one would
be unheeded; and a cockchafer will attract him, when a lesser
insect will excite no attention whatever. The best summer bait,
is a large bumble-bee. If the angler will pass his hook under the
fore legs of the bee, without injuring him, and, concealing himself
behind a tree, or any other shelter which may overhang the
haunt of the chub, will dibble the insect on the surface of the
water, allowing him to burr and spin, and produce little rippling
circles all about him, he will soon see the chub rise leisurely out
of the deep, and gently suck the bee into his mouth, as a city
alderman laps up his callipee. In this manner, precisely, the large
one just recorded was caught in the river Thames.

Occasionally, a chub will take a minnow or frog; but this
happens very seldom, and only at the close of the spring. Baits
have been recommended for different sections of the season, for
chub-fishing; but many of them are fanciful, and some very nasty.
Flies and worms will capture him at all times; and he is scarcely
worth being very nice about. Grasshoppers are fine bait whenever
you can get them; and little pills made of tallow and cheese,
flavoured with musk, are said to be peculiarly tempting. The
French fish for him with cherries; but many of the anglers in
France consider the bait of more value than the fish, and seldom
give themselves any trouble about him.

Bream and Gudgeon, p 81.

Roach and Dace, p. 85.

Eel, p. 88.

The chub requires ground-bait in a general way, which may be made according to the receipt already given.

As this fish will rise at a fly, those who like it may whip away for him at the end of summer, when there is nothing better to be done.

The best season of the year for chub-fishing, is from June to the end of August; but he may be caught all the year round. Evening and morning are the best parts of the day, as he seldom feeds when the sun is high. The angler must be cautious and still, for the chub is a shy, suspicious fish; and if two or three are taken in rapid succession out of the hole where they are assembled, they will grow fearful, and change their haunts for some time.

The chub is soon killed in a general way; but when he is large, he is exceedingly difficult to manage, and is a very troublesome customer with delicate tackle. Perseverance and patience, however, are sure to beat him; and if devoid of these qualities, the angler had better break his rod, and renounce the craft for ever.

THE BREAM

is a great, flat, coarse, ugly fish, strong in the water, but utterly detestable on the table. The French, it is true, are of a somewhat different opinion, and hold him in some degree of estimation.

This fish frequents still places in deep, placid waters; but prefers the retirement of ponds and lakes, where the water is still, the locality undisturbed, and the bottom weedy and muddy.

The bream is to be found in most of the slow, still rivers of England, and sometimes attains a very large size; he is then very much like a pair of bellows in shape, and much the same in flavour. In the north of Europe, this fish has been known to reach the weight of twenty pounds; and, in 1749, there were taken at a single draught, out of a large lake in Sweden, five thousand bream; the aggregate weight of which was eighteen thousand pounds. We have ourselves caught them four or five pounds in weight, and have heard of other people catching them still larger; but this size is by no means general.

The bream spawn late in June or early in July, and at that season seek out the level shelving sides, or the muddy bottoms of rivers well stocked with weeds. Each female is accompanied with three or four males. They multiply very rapidly; and, indeed, 137,000 eggs have been counted in the ovarium of a single female. During the season, it is said the males are covered with tubercles like the small-pox. " At this season," says a French writer, "they make a great noise as they swim in numerous flocks; and yet they distinguish the sound of bells or the tambour, or any other analogous tones, which sometimes frighten them, retard their movements, or drive them into the nets of the fisherman." Surely all this must be purely fanciful! Our author gives no authority for

G

the statements, neither does he say that he ever heard these sounds in his life.

The bream grows very fast, and is remarkably tenacious of life when taken out of the water during cold weather. He can then bear transporting alive to a great distance, providing he be carefully wrapped up in snow, with a morsel of bread steeped in alcohol placed in his mouth. This is a plan successfully adopted in many parts of the continent.

There are said to be three or four varieties of the bream in some of the rivers in France, particularly in the Seine. The fisherman in this river give the name of "Henriots" to the young fry, and that of "Brêmotes" to the middle-sized fish.

Bloch says, "the bream is little esteemed; and still less when he has been taken out of muddy waters, which give him a most detestable flavour."

This fish when large will afford the angler some sport; but his gastronomic imperfections are a great bar to him. Carp-tackle and carp-baits are all good for him, and will kill him as well or better than any other.

The best season of the year for bream fishing is from June till October, when he often disappoints the perch fisher by nibbling at his clear, tough dew-worm—a sort of bite which is often mistaken for the gentle suckings of a small eel. The bream will perhaps take this bait in preference to any other, although the gentle has a powerful effect upon his fancy.

The bait should be very near the bottom; in fact, it should just touch the ground. As soon as the fish nibbles he must be dealt with on the instant, for, singular as it may seem, the larger he is, the more light and delicate his bite. If of large size—something like a big pair of bellows—he will require some care and dexterity, as, the moment he is hooked, he makes away for the weeds at once, and if he succeed in getting into them you are done for; and it will prove a very difficult matter to dislodge him.

When you have succeeded in getting him out of the water, be careful not to handle him, as he possesses a most filthy hide; but get the hook out of his mouth in the quickest and best way you can.

The bream requires ground bait; or at least it seems to be the custom to use it in his case. The recipe already given for other kinds of bottom fish will answer very well for him.

The fish is very timid, shy, and crafty. He hides himself in deep holes, and requires caution and silence, being easily frightened from his haunts by the slightest disturbance of the water.

These fish bite early in the morning and late in the evening, when the glare of day is off the waters, and all is calm and still. It is well for young anglers to practise their hand with large bream, as they require considerable management, and will call into requisition their patience and skill. Perhaps a slight float is absolutely necessary in fishing for bream, as his bite is extremely delicate, and he must be attacked on the instant.

THE ROACH

is supposed to be so called on account of the redness of his fins. He is a poor mean fish so far as eating goes, but he is handsome and strong, and will afford the angler capital sport when he rises at the fly, which he commonly does about the months of August and September, both boldly and freely.

Roach are gregarious. They love limpid and clear waters, and yet are to be found in still and muddy rivers, ponds, and lakes. They frequent almost all the rivers and lakes in Europe, and in places are inconceivably numerous. Many of the rivers and ponds of England are full of them; and in France they are abundant everywhere, particularly in the neighbourhood of Paris. In the *marais* of the Pas-de-Calais, and about Peronne, there are millions of them. In some countries of the North of Europe, and especially on the banks of the Oder, they are so plentiful that they are commonly used for manuring the land; and Bloch assures us that, before the *marais* on the Oder were drained, such enormous quan-tities were constantly caught that they supplied the neighbouring villages with abundance of provender on which to fatten their pigs.

Roach spawn about June, and they may be fished for two or three weeks after this process is consummated. They cast their spawn in narrow, weedy, grassy places, and are very prolific. In the ovarium of an ordinary sized roach were counted 125,000 eggs.

At a certain season—the spawning season—roach have been observed to migrate like the salmon, the trout, &c. &c. "In the spring," says a French author, "the roach mount up the rivers in a very singular order. The males and females separate them-selves so as to form distinct troops. One troop of males takes the lead, a troop of females follows without mingling with the other, and at last a second troop of males closes the march. They go very close together; and if any accident separates them on their route, they quickly form their battalions, and resume their march when the danger is passed." We never noticed this habit ourselves; we never heard of any sportsman who did; and we never before saw any account of it in any book; it may, however, be true, although it savours something of the fanciful.

The roach attains a large size. They are said to have been killed in England of the weight of two pounds; but in many con-tinental waters they reach a larger size than this, and give the angler a good deal of trouble, as they require delicate tackle to deceive them. The roach is by no means the stupid reckless fish some represent him to be; on the contrary, he demands a fair amount of skill and caution, and affords very respectable sport when of good size and in full season.

Walton calls this fish the "water-sheep," on account of his simplicity and foolishness. However this may be applicable to the small fry of roach during the summer, and in turbid and thick waters, the larger fish are unquestionably timid, shy, cunning fellows, undeserving the reproach cast upon them by so high an authority. It is, indeed, very difficult to catch a large roach in bright water, unless you use very fine tackle, and carefully keep yourself out of sight.

The rod for this fish should be light, supple, and handy. The line as fine as you please. A line of three hairs, with a fine gut bottom, is perhaps the best that can be used in all waters, and under all circumstances. In fact, when the water is very clear and limpid, your tackle can scarcely be too fine.

The gentle is a very excellent bait during the finer parts of the year; and in August, if the hooks on which are rigged the artificial house-fly, be tipped with live gentles, the roach will dash at them like fury.

In the months of June and July we have seen very large ones taken with the common yellow fly, which is to be found in abundance on fresh dropped cow-dung. These are easily caught, and may be placed in a dry phial-bottle. The angler should use a long rod, say twenty or two-and-twenty feet, with running tackle of the finest kind. About two yards of gut should hang from the end of the rod; and on a small hook, say No. 12, one of the yellow flies should be placed; and then, keeping out of sight as much as possible, the bait should be dibbled lightly on the surface of the water. It is curious to witness how eagerly and fiercely the large roach will come out of their deep and secluded holes, and sail and sail around the fly, indicating great caution and fear. But the temptation is generally irresistible in the end; and a splash, like a dog thrown into the water, announces that the fish is hooked. In autumn, the same mode of fishing may be adopted by the use of the grasshopper, which proves a very seductive bait. Large roach may be taken in this way, when they are utterly unapproachable in any other way.

Another bait, strongly recommended for roach, especially in the early part of the summer, is a gentle that has been kept in bran until it has changed and turned red. In this state, it is called by the French l'épine-vinette, and is highly prized by them. We have tried it frequently, and certainly must admit it to be a successful bait; but it is an extremely difficult job to keep it on the hook; and, after all, it is not comparable to the yellow fly already mentioned.

In roach fishing, when a float is used, it should be a very small one; a bit of quill an inch long is quite sufficient. One small shot, No. 7, will sink the gut without drawing down the float, and this timid fish will be unable to distinguish it from a straw on the surface of the water.

Morning and evening are the best parts of the day for roach-fishing in the ordinary way; but the angler who uses flies, alive, or dead, or artificial, will find all hours of the day pretty much alike. The Londoners angle for this fish with tackle of the finest possible description—even with lines made of a single horsehair; and many of them are very clever and successful performers with this frail material. But where is the good of it? Gut is *fine enough*, and the roach that breaks it, when in the hands of a skilful rod-fisher, must be of extraordinary dimensions.

Ground bait is recommended for this fish; but when fishing for him with flies or insects of any kind, this is entirely unnecessary.

There is a fish of the roach species called in England the RUDD, which is very numerous in many continental waters. It is called in France the ROACH-CARP. Walton is inclined to think the rudd lies between the roach and the bream. Other writers consider it to be a distinct fish altogether; but the probability is, that it is a true cross between the roach and the carp. In France, this fish attains to a great size. He is mostly found in the fosses round fortified towns. He may be angled for in precisely the same manner as for the roach.

CHAPTER XI.

THE GUDGEON, THE DACE, AND THE EEL.

THE GUDGEON.

THIS is a very handsome, active, and well-shaped little fish; most delicious in flavour, when properly cooked, and deservedly considered very *recherché* by most continental gastronomers.

This fish is to be found in almost all the rivers of England, and, indeed, of Europe. He prefers running waters and rapid curling streams, which flow over a pebbly and sandy bottom, although he will live and thrive in lakes and ponds through which a gentle draw of water continually passes.

The gudgeon is supposed to spawn about the month of May. Walton maintains that they breed two or three times a year. This does not appear to be very clearly established; but the prodigious rate at which these fish increase, would seem to lend a certain degree of probability to the notion. A French writer says, "They pass their winter in the lakes and large ponds, and in the spring remount the rivers, where they deposit their spawn on pebbles and stones. This operation is with the gudgeon a very laborious affair, and the fish is frequently occupied an entire month in the difficult process. Towards the autumn, the gudgeons gain the lakes." This does not appear to be the general opinion, neither do we acquiesce in it; but other grave angling authorities seem to entertain some such notions as to the migratory habits of this fish, although their language is, for the most part, somewhat vague and uncertain.

Gudgeons undoubtedly multiply prodigiously, and in certain favourable situations are to be found in immense quantities. They are used in some parts of France to stock lakes, ponds, and rapid streams, as food for pike, eels, and trout.

Gudgeons may be caught all the year round, but August and September are the best months. In favourable weather they will keep the angler well employed, and he may fill his basket in a very short time.

The rod used in gudgeon-fishing should be an extremely light one, made of cane, and without much spring in it. The line should be all gut, or, at any rate, not more than three hairs thick, if of horse-hair, with very small hook, say No. 13. A float is sometimes used, but we think it better dispensed with. The best mode is to fix a small bullet to the end of the line, fasten one hook below the lead, so as to let it drag on the bottom, and suspend two or three others at short intervals above it. The bullet is dropped into a likely part of the stream, and the hooks, baited with a very small red worm, or gentle, or grub (the worm is the best), are suffered to lie on the bottom, or work about in the running water. When the gudgeon takes the bait, he will make little short jerks, which are easily perceptible if the line be held tight, and the angler be careful not to be too quick for him.

The best general baits for gudgeons are small red worms, grubs, and gentles. The very small grubs to be found sometimes under antique cow-manure, in company with an admirable red worm, are very tempting bait, which we have seen the gudgeons take with great rapidity. When the red worm is used, it should but just fit the hook, like a tight glove; to accomplish this, it is often necessary to bait only with the shining red head of the worm. If the bait hang loose, the gudgeons will bother you like eels, and you will hardly ever succeed in hooking them.

Some amateurs recommend baskets containing the leaves of marsh-mallows, with a paste made of hemp-seed, to be sunk in the water previous to angling for gudgeons, as a kind of ground-bait; and others again suggest the propriety of raking the bottom of the water, under the notion that when it is thus muddled, the gudgeons imagine they are about to obtain a copious supply of food. The latter plan is frequently attended with some degree of success in tranquil waters, but in streams it is of course useless.

When the gudgeon is well cleaned, and wiped perfectly dry, rub over with egg and bread-crumbs, fried *crisp* in butter, and served up with *hot* melted butter, along with well-buttered hot household bread, he is a very delicious fish. At the breakfast table, when in this condition, he is inimitable. The French have many modes of cooking him, but few better than this.

THE DACE.

The DACE is a well-made fish, of a bright silvery hue. He frequents clear, rapid waters, and is very often found in the same streams with the trout. It makes but little difference to him whether the water be deep or shallow, provided it be bright and tolerably rapid.

These fish are gregarious; and, in favourable waters and well-adapted positions, are to be found in very large shoals. They are numerous in all suitable waters in every section of Europe.

Early in the summer the dace casts its spawn, and is very prolific. He multiplies with surprising rapidity; and the rather so, that he is enabled to avoid numerous enemies, both on land and in the water, from the great swiftness with which he scuds through the streams. The eggs of the fish are of a dirty whitish colour. He feeds freely on worms, gnats, and flies; but other bait will tempt him, as we shall soon show.

The angler may enjoy first-rate sport with the dace, because he is bold and dashing, and, for his size, a very strong fish. He fights hard, and dies game. The cook, perhaps, would rather not be troubled with him; but as he does not seem to be in much request —no, not even with bream-eaters—recipes for cooking him are scarcely necessary, and yet, when fresh, and fried nicely in butter, he is a capital addition to the breakfast table.

In the spring, and late in summer, he bites freely. The tackle employed in roach-fishing is well fitted for the dace; and if he happen to be of a good size, he will afford the rod-fisher very respectable sport.

Many kinds of bait are in use for this fish, but the best, in our opinion, are red worms and flies. The French very frequently use a small water-worm, which is found in little narrow straws, like quills, and which floats on the water : they call them *porte-bois*. We never tried this bait, but have been often assured that dace are very fond of it. It is like our caddis-worm.

The common black gnat is a good bait; and if the point of the hook on which the fly is wrapped be tipped with a live gentle, as in roach-fishing, the dace may be killed with surprising ease and rapidity, particularly when he is rising at the natural flies on a fine summer evening.

The dace must be sought for in running waters; and it is by no means an uncommon circumstance to meet with them in trout-streams which abound with deep holes, and where even the waters are not constantly bright and sparkling. A brilliant red worm, covering a small hook, shank and all, with a shot a foot above it to sink the line, will catch them readily in such localities.

The dace is a very strong fish for his size, and when hooked resembles the trout in his exertions to escape. When numerous, they furnish great amusement, and are well fitted for practising the young artist for his more difficult task of capturing the salmon and trout.

THE EEL.

Few fish are better known than the eel. He is associated in our minds with many of our youthful exploits and troubles in our upward progress to piscatory fame. He frequents all the rivers and waters of Europe, where the cold is not too severe; and he is to be met with on the most sumptuous as well as on the most frugal tables—food alike for the London alderman and the poor houseless man in the streets.

The haunts of this fish are familiar to every angler. He inhabits all kinds of waters, ponds, lakes, ditches, trout-streams, rivers. No water is too dirty for him, nor too pure. He thrives in the muddiest holes, and grows fat and sleek among the stones of the mountain torrent. A fresh water fish in all his habits, yet if he gets into the salt water he shows little anxiety to leave it again; and though it evidently affects his colour, he grows prodigiously in it, and gets as fat as a porpoise. No matter where he may be fishing with a sunk bait, the experienced angler is never surprised when he pulls out an eel. In short, this fish is almost universal, and his attachment to one place rather than another is very problematical. Wherever he can get food, there he is; nay, indeed, he has been sometimes found in situations where, to all appearance, he could get none.

Various have been the opinions about the mode in which eels are generated. Writers on fishing, one after the other, recapitulate the old opinions, and nearly in the same words. Some of these opinions are very diverting and curious. We are told that one ancient author supposed they were born of the mud; another, from little bits scraped off the bodies of large eels, when they rubbed themselves against stones; another, from the putrid flesh of dead animals thrown into the water; another, from the dews which cover the earth in May; another, from the water alone; and an old and deep-rooted notion entertained in the north of England at this hour is, that eels are generated from horse-hairs thrown into the water.

The following statement wears a reasonable appearance, and will account for the story from Bowlker, quoted in "The Angler's Sure Guide."

"The eel proceeds from an egg. The egg is hatched in the body of the female, as in fish of the *ray* species. A slight pressure on the lower part of the body of the female facilitates the egress of the young ones. But, in order that the eggs may be capable of being hatched, there must be some intercourse with the male fish. This takes place, it is conjectured, in the same manner as among the snake tribe. The eggs are, of course, more or less numerous in different fish. It sometimes happens that the female eels disembarrass themselves of their eggs before they are hatched; but this must occur very seldom, because it has never yet been clearly ascertained where, in such cases, the eels deposit them."

Now this, which is an abridgment of the more elaborate account of a French author, seems to be a plain and rational account of the matter, and is, in all probability, not far from the truth.*

Eels increase in numbers most prodigiously; they will also reach a very large size. In Italy—a magnificent country for the angler —they are taken, it is said, of the weight of twenty pounds. In Albania, they are stated to be occasionally as thick as a man's thigh; and some writers have affirmed that in Prussia they have been sometimes caught ten or twelve feet in length. We have ourselves often seen them in France of five and six pounds.

The eel is a fish of very slow growth; but, as a set-off against this, he seems to be endowed with the gift of very long life. Writers on fishing commonly limit him to a period of five or six years; but a French author, who speaks with the greatest confidence on the subject, says, "Experience has proved that the eel will live for a century. How otherwise can the prodigious increase of these animals be explained, since it can be demonstrated that the females do not breed before they are twelve years old? The eel increases until his ninety-fourth year. Each female, therefore, can produce during a period of eighty-two years; and this satisfactorily accounts for the enormous quantity of eels to be found in the waters which are adapted for them."

The eel is exceedingly voracious, and a most indiscriminate feeder. Nothing can be too delicate, and few things too nasty, for his ravenous appetite. Many instances of their voracity have been recorded from time to time; and many wonderful stories told about the size, migrations, and miraculous powers of the fish.

This fish is no great favourite with the angler. On the table he is delicious, but not a very pleasant affair to take off a hook.

Those who like angling for eels must use strong tackle. A stiff rod, a strong line, and a large hook, are indispensable: a large red dew-worm will complete the equipment.

The eel requires considerable indulgence when he bites; but, as everybody who can brandish a rod knows how to fish for him, we have only to suggest that as soon as he is pulled out of the water, whether big or little, the angler should stamp his foot across his body, hold his line tight with one hand, and with the other cut off its head. This is the only way to prevent the slippery rascal from tying the line full of knots, and twisting it inextricably round his body.

* The late Bishop of Norwich, Dr. Kay, read a paper to a scientific society not long ago on this subject. He had noticed little eels in the thatch of a cottage; and the ce inferred that the spawn had been deposited on the reeds before they had been cut, and vivified into life by the sun's rays.

CHAPTER XII.

THE CHAR, BLEAK, LAMPREY, LOACH, MINNOW, RUFF, &c.

THESE are the small fry of the angler, and not worth much notice. The CHAR is confined to lakes in the North of England, Scotland, and to some parts of Wales. It is not very familiar to anglers generally. It is a handsome fish, spotted like a trout, and attains a very respectable size, say fifteen or sixteen inches in length. The habits and natural history of the fish are but imperfectly known. Epicures attach a high value to the fish, and "potted char" is constantly advertised as a standard delicacy. How it is made is another matter; but as few things in England can escape adulteration, most probably the char undergoes the profitable process.

THE BLEAK.

This little fish abounds in nearly all the rivers and fresh waters in Europe. It is found in prodigious quantities in the Caspian sea, from whence, according to some authors, they were originally introduced to other parts of the world.

This fish is very handsome and active, and when first taken out of the water shines like a bar of silver. His sparkling scales are used by artists to give to mock pearls the beauty and brilliancy of those of the East.

The bleak spawn in May or June, and multiply rapidly. In fine weather they are constantly playing on the surface of the water, but they prefer rushing and powerful streams—in the middle or on the borders of which they are to be caught in the greatest quantities.

The baits used in bleak-fishing are flies, gentles, and small grubs. At these, in the proper season, and in proper waters, the fish will bite with the utmost avidity, and keep the angler fully employed. The tackle should be as light as possible, the rod not too supple, and the hooks small.

In places where bleak abound the angler should take his stand near a very rapid run of water—some sluice or staunch. Close to the side of the current he should throw his line, baited with fresh gentles. The fish in such spots will run at the bait most furiously, and the sportsman will have little to do but to pull out his cap-

lives—sometimes half-a-dozen together, if he have as many hooks on his line.

Artificial flies, tipped with a minute bit of white leather, taken from a white kid glove, will answer very well when gentles are not to be procured. A float, about an inch long, made of the end of a pen, with one little girdle of quill round it to hold the gut, is often used in bleak fishing, and when the water is still it very much improves the efficiency of the tackle. In a strong stream a float is useless.

Bleak-fishing is very improving to young anglers, and often amusing to older ones. The little fish yields more real sport than many other kinds of fish of much greater magnitude.

THE LAMPREY.

The LAMPREY is exactly like the eel in form and colour, but he possesses some attributes peculiar to himself. Close to each eye he has two ranges of small orifices, four on one side and five on the other, and, independent of these, behind each eye he has seven more, through which he effect his respirations. He is slippery, like the common eel, and swims with great force and activity. He possesses the power of attaching himself to stones, &c., by means of his mouth, which, from the elasticity of his lips, and the strength of his crooked teeth, acts as a kind of sucker, and enables him to hold fast to many substances with singular tenacity. A lamprey of three pounds has been known to lift a weight of twelve pounds.

We shall not enter into any detailed account of the methods of fishing for the loach, minnow, and ruff. These are known to most schoolboys of ten or twelve years of age in every section of the kingdom.

CHAPTER XIII.

LAWS AND REGULATIONS FOR TAKING FISH.

In the act called the Black Act, it is enacted that any person being armed and disguised, and who shall steal, or unlawfully take away any fish out of a river or pond, or maliciously break down and destroy the mound or head of any river, whereby the fish shall be lost or destroyed, or shall rescue any person in custody for such

ANGLING.

offence, or procure another to assist him therein, shall be found
guilty of felony, without benefit of clergy.

For destroying or killing fish in enclosed ground, being private
property, a penalty of five pounds, or imprisonment in the House
of Correction for not exceeding six months.

For breaking into an enclosed or private ground, and stealing or
destroying the fish, transportation for seven years, and receivers
the like punishment.

No persons may have in possession, or keep, any net, angle
piche, or other engine for taking fish, but the makers and sellers
thereof, and the owner or renter of a river fishery, except fishermen
and their apprentices, legally authorised in navigable rivers; and
the owner or occupier of the said river may seize, and keep, and
convert to his own use, every net, &c., which he shall discover laid
or used, or in the possession of any person thus fishing without his
consent.

Damaging or intruding, by using nettrices, fish-hooks, or other
engines to catch fish, without consent of the owner or occupier,
must pay any amount the magistrate or justice orders, provided it
exceeds not treble the damages, and be fined, not exceeding ten
shillings, for the use of the poor of the parish, or imprisonment in
the House of Correction, not exceeding one calendar month,
unless he enters into a bond, with one surety, in a sum not exceeding 10l. not to offend again, and the justice may cut or destroy
the nets, &c.

If any person unlawfully or maliciously cut, break down, or
destroy any head or dam of a fish-pond, or unlawfully fish therein,
he shall, at the prosecution of the king, or the owner, be im-
prisoned three months, or pay treble damages, and after such
imprisonment, shall find sureties for seven years for his good
behaviour, or remain in prison till he doth.

To prevent the fish in the Thames from being improperly destroyed, the 30th of George the Second enacts, that no person shall
fish, or endeavour to take fish, in the said river, between London-
bridge and Richmond-bridge, with other than lawful nets.

For salmon, not less than six inches in the mesh;

For pike, jack, perch, roach, chub, and barbel, with a flew or
stream net, of not less than three inches in the mesh throughout,
with a facing of seven inches, and not more than sixteen fathom
long;

For shads, not less than two inches and a half in the mesh;

For flounders, not less than two inches and a half in the mesh,
and not more than sixteen fathom long;

For dace, with a single blay-net, of not less than two inches in
the mesh, and not more than thirteen fathom long, to be worked
by floating only, with a boat and a buoy;

For smelts, with a net of not less than one inch and a quarter in
the mesh, and not of greater length than sixteen fathom, to be
worked by floating only, with a boat and a buoy;

Under the penalty of paying and forfeiting the sum of five pounds for every such offence.

No fish of any of the sort hereinafter mentioned may be caught in the Thames or Medway, or sold, or exposed to or for sale, if caught in the Thames or Medway—

No salmon of less weight than six pounds,

No trout of less weight than one pound,

No pike or jack under twelve inches long, from the eye to the ength of the tail.

No perch under eight inches long,

No flounder under seven inches long,

No sole under seven inches long,

No plaice or dab under seven inches long,

No roach under eight inches long,

No dace under six inches long,

No smelt under six inches long,

No gudgeon under five inches long,

No whiting under eight inches long,

No barbel under twelve inches long,

No chub under nine inches long,

Under pain to forfeit five pounds for every such offence.

Salmon and trout may be taken only from January 25th to September 10th.

Pike, jack, perch, roach, dace, chub, barbel, and gudgeon, may be taken between July 1st and March 1st.

Bottom-fishing is prohibited in the river Thames, as far as the Corporation of London has jurisdiction, from the 1st of March to the 1st of June.

The right of fishing in the sea, and in all rivers where the tide ebbs and flows, is a right common to all the king's subjects.

Any person or persons considering themselves wronged or aggrieved by any decision against them by the magistrate or justice, may appeal against it at the quarter sessions.

PROTECTION OF PRESERVES.

"That no person shall fish with any sort of net, weel, night-hook, or any other device, except by angling in, or make use of any net, engine, or device to drive the fish out of any place which shall be staked by order of the Lord Mayor of the City of London for the time being, as conservator aforesaid, for the preservation of the fishery, and whereof notice shall be stuck up in some public place of the town or village, next adjoining to the place or places so ordered to be staked; and that no person shall take up or remove any stake, burr, boat, or any other thing which shall have been driven down or sunk in any such place as aforesaid, upon pain to forfeit and pay, from time to time, the sum of five pounds for every offence or breach of any part of this order."—*City Ordinances,* Item 44.

PART II.—WHERE TO GO.

INTRODUCTORY REMARKS.

THIRTY or forty years ago, it would have been a comparatively brief and easy task to inform the angler *where to go* to enjoy his amusement; for he would not have ventured to diverge to any great distance from his own home, or the county in which he resided. Now, however, the case is somewhat different. The application of steam to maritime purposes, and the construction of railroads, have altered the entire position of the angler's craft. They have opened out to him a new world of recreation and adventure, and stimulated his ambition to the highest pitch. At a comparatively trifling cost of money and of time, he can be transported into the finest fishing districts in the most remote and unfrequented parts of the kingdom, or out of it, if he chooses; and can pace the wild heath and barren mountains in search of the lordly salmon, and the huge lake-trout; objects that were in his younger days seldom seen, and never placed within the range of his rod and tackle. All this has made the duty comprehended in the simple directions *where to go*, of a more onerous and comprehensive character than it has ever been before in the history of the "gentle craft."

The recommendations involved in our "Where to go," will be divided into four parts; namely, England and Wales, Scotland, Ireland, and Continental states.

CHAPTER I.

ENGLAND AND WALES.

ANGLING in England and Wales, is to be viewed in a somewhat different light from angling in Scotland and Ireland. In reference to England in particular, anglers may fairly enough be divided into two distinct classes; the one pursuing the bottom-fishing, and the other, making the salmon, trout, and pike, their chief source of amusement; the one class principally confined to the metropolis and its extensive suburbs, and the other located on the banks of the various rivers and estuaries at the more distant parts of the kingdom. These two orders of rod-fishers are very distinct and well defined. They have little or nothing in common, save the rod and line, and the enthusiastic ardour for their respective branches of amusement and recreation.

The London anglers are a very numerous body; much more so than most people would imagine. It is only necessary to go to some of the usual places of fishing resort near the city on holiday times, and witness the numerous groups of piscatorians huddled together on perhaps a few acres of ground, young and old, rich and poor, enjoying their pursuits with real gusto, to be convinced of the very general predilection of the mass of the people for rod-fishing. We have not the slightest doubt but that if the entire number of metropolitan anglers were mustered—those, we mean, whose chief or only aim is to excel in bottom-fishing—they would amount to full as many as all the other English anglers in the mere rural districts put together. Indeed, few people have any just conception of the prevalence of angling habits and ideas in London, unless some degree of attention has been paid to the subject.

The range of waters to which the London anglers are chiefly confined, and which suit their ideas and modes of fishing, is but very limited, though, on the whole, abounding with sport, and a great variety of fish. The Thames, and its tributaries, with the various canals and docks, form the staple resources of this numerous and enthusiastic class of piscatorians. We shall proceed to enumerate the various localities where the angler may find pleasure in, and scope for the exercise of his art.

THE THAMES.

" Glide gently, thus for ever glide,
O Thames! that anglers all may see
As lovely visions by thy side,
As now, fair river, come to me.
Oh, glide, fair stream, for ever so,
Thy quiet soul on all bestowing,
Till all our minds for ever flow
As thy deep waters now are flowing."

The Thames is a most magnificent river, both for the extent of its range and the immense variety and number of its fish. It springs out of Gloucestershire, and for some distance goes under the name of the Churne, and it has an entire run of upwards of three hundred miles. The angling stations upon it are very numerous, and greatly diversified in their angling capabilities; and we shall now proceed to point out some of the chief of them, as fully as our limits will permit.

BATTERSEA BRIDGE used a few years ago to be a somewhat favourite locality for the perch, barbel, chub, eel, lamprey, roach, dace, blank, and ruff; but now chiefly, perhaps, from the increased steamboat traffic, the fishing is not considered so good. Both salmon and trout have been taken here with the rod, and of great weight and delicious flavour; but these captures are but very rare. The fishing becomes a little improved between this spot and PUTNEY BRIDGE, where the assistance of boats can be procured at a shilling an hour, and sixpence for each succeeding hour. Large quantities of bottom fish are often taken here with the rod; but the state of the weather, and the condition of the river and its tidal movements, exercise a great influence over the feeding of numerous kinds of fish in these ranges of water. We have known an angler, in the space of an hour, take perch to the weight of sixty pounds, while, at another time, he has fished two entire days consecutively, and not seen a single fish of any kind.

At BRENTFORD there is often fair sport to be obtained off a place called the Aits. There have been trout occasionally taken here with the minnow, but they are scarce. Perch, barbel, dace, and gudgeons, are tolerably plentiful.

RICHMOND is a good and favourite locality for the rod-fisher and there are many expert piscatorians in this district, who know every inch of the water and every hour of the day when it is probable that certain fish can be obtained. There is a favourite stretch of water of considerable depth above the bridge, extending for about two hundred yards, where barbel are sometimes taken of great weight and numbers. August and October are the chief months for complete success in this locality. At the *wier*, dace are taken in great quantities, and so likewise are gudgeons. It is requisite to notice here that the preserved waters extend six hundred and eighty-three yards from the wier eastward, to the east end pile of the breakwater. The inns at Richmond are numerous; but the chief resort of anglers is at the King's Head, near the bridge; the Pigeons, near the Duke of Buccleuch's; the White Cross, the Greyhound, the Roebuck. The fishermen, who will give all manner of assistance to the angler, are George Platt, John Platt, Brown, Howard, Carter, and Styles.

If the angler who visits Richmond wishes to employ his time to the best advantage, he must pay great attention to the state of the waters. Some sections of them are very good in clear water that are of no use when flooded, and *vice versa;* and the state of the *tide* has likewise a very marked influence on the movements and feeding hours of the fish. The *neap* tide should be chosen. For example, when it is high water at London Bridge, say at six o'clock in the morning, it will then be high water at Richmond between eight and nine, and with but a faint flow of water. The angler may, under these circumstances, commence at nine, and he may continue his amusement till seven in the evening, when it will be flood again. This is the only method which can give any reasonable chance of success. And the same remarks apply to all the parts of the river which lie between this place and Tedding-ton Lock, where the tide movement terminates. Particular fish lie in particular sections of the river; and this must also be noticed by the rod-fisher. On the towing-path above the bridge, on the Richmond side, dace and barbel are plentiful, and there is a good stretch of fly-fishing water from the west end of the Duke of Buccleuch's garden to Twickenham Ferry.

TWICKENHAM.—This is a celebrated spot in literary history, having been the place of residence of Pope. It is much frequented by anglers from the metropolis. There is a long *deep* in which dace and barbel abound; but the preserved waters extend four hundred and ten yards from the western extremity of Pope's Villa to the Ait. This circumscribes the movements of the general angler considerably. All the resident anglers in this vicinity affirm that the angling has greatly improved here within the last few years, and that the best months for fishing these deep pools are September and October. The early portion of the season is not favourable for sport.

TEDDINGTON LOCK is a noted place, and forms a well-known and pointed landmark between the fresh and the salt water. It is a mile and a half beyond Twickenham. Plenty of barbel, of large size, are to be found here. There are more fish of every kind about the waters in this locality than almost any other on the Thames, and chiefly from this cause: when the season proves a dry one, and the stream becomes shallow, the fish cannot ascend above the lock, and consequently have to take shelter below it. This has rendered Teddington a great favourite with metropolitan sportsmen. Many of them have achieved great things here, killing their forty, fifty, and sixty barbel a-day. Gudgeons are likewise taken here in great quantities when the water is in good order. Teddington Lock has likewise the honour of being considered, in the popular creed, as a commencing or starting point in the Thames for real trout fishing. Whatever are taken of this enviable fish further down the river, are only considered as mere accidents, or exceptions to a general rule. Very large trout have been from time to time taken out of the water below the Weir—three or four within the last few years, weighing fourteen and fifteen pounds. In the meadows above the lock, and below the village, there are some stretches of good fishing water, and here jack are occasionally taken of fair size and most excellent quality. The inns are the King's Head, and the George; and the fishermen Redgate, Coxon, Harris, and Chamberlain.

KINGSTON is considered by many Thames rod-fishers to be as good a spot as Teddington for barbel, perch, and dace. There is, however, a general notion abroad that the fishing has been impaired since the old bridge was removed. This removal interfered with

H

many choice old spots that yielded shelter for fish, and where they could at all times be found by the rod-fisher. The prime portion of the season for gudgeon-fishing is from June till August. There is a portion of the water preserved here, extending seventy yards eastward, and thirty yards westward of the bridge. The inns commonly frequented by angling parties here are the White Hart, the Swan, and the Anglers; and the fishermen are William Bolton, Robert Brown, and William Clarke.

THAMES DITTON, opposite Hampton Court, is a locality enjoying a high reputation among anglers for almost all kinds of fish with which the river abounds. The rod-fisher's movements are considerably hampered here, from a large section of the water being very strictly preserved. The range of deep water opposite Lord St. Leonards' house, to the extent of five hundred and twelve yards, is in this predicament; and likewise the deep, reaching two hundred and fifty yards from Keene's wharf. The inns are the Swan, and the Crown and Anchor; and the fishermen William and Henry Tagg.

HAMPTON COURT contains a fine reach of angling water, under preservation, and extends, according to official authority, two hundred and seventy yards from Weir Moulsey Lock to Lower Head Pile. This range of water can be fished either from the banks, or in a punt. It contains a number of fine perch and barbel, and some trout of considerable size have been taken out of it of late years. The inns are the Castle, and the Mitre; and the fishermen, William Wisdom, and Thomas Davis.

HAMPTON is about a mile from the last station, and is a very interesting village. There is good fishing water here, and barbel and roach are plentiful; there is a fair sprinkling of gudgeons, and some odd trout. According to authority, the preserved waters extend nine hundred and sixty yards from the west end of Garrick's Lawn to the Tumbling Bay. This village used formerly to be a very favourite locality for anglers. It was here that we have upon record a remarkable instance of piscatory enthusiasm and patience. Sir John Hawkins, who was himself a great angler, and edited a fine edition of Walton's works, relates an anecdote of a gentleman who came to reside here for the facility of enjoying his fishing sports. Sir John says, "Living some years ago in a village on the banks of the Thames, I was used in the summer months to be much out in a boat on the river. It chanced that at Hampton, where I had been for a few days, I frequently passed an elderly gentleman in his boat, who appeared to be fishing at different stations for barbel. After a few salutations had passed between us, and we were become a little better acquainted, I took the occasion to inquire of him what diversion he had met with. "Sir," said he, "I have had but bad luck to-day, for I fish for barbel, and you know they are not to be caught like gudgeons." "It is very true," answered I, "but what you want in tale you make up in weight." "Why, sir," said he, "that is just as it happens. It is true, I like the sport, and like to catch fish, but my great delight is going after them. I'll tell you what," continued he, "I am a man in years, and have been used to the sea all my life (he had been a London captain), but I mean to go no more; and I have bought that little house which you see there, for the sake of fishing. I get into this boat (which he was then mopping) on a Monday morning, and fish on till Saturday night for barbel, as I told you, for that is my delight; and this I have done for a month together, and in all that while I have not had a single bite."

The best months for fishing in this locality are September, October, and November, and the water should be full, and not too clear. The inns for refreshment are the Red Lion, and the Bell; and the fishermen are the families of the Milbournes, and the Benns, Will. Chambers, and J. Snell.

SUNBURY is situated on the Middlesex side of the river, and there are often very fine trout taken in the waters of the vicinity, particularly near the weir. Gudgeons are plentiful, and afford the angler considerable amusement. The preserved district extends six hundred and eighty-three yards from the weir, eastward, to the east end pile of the breakwater. The inns are the Flower Pot, the Magpie, and the Castle; and the fishermen are Goddard, Fulcher, and Johnson.

WALTON is another fishing station, situated on the Surrey side of the Thames, and is eighteen miles from London. There is some fine deep stretches of water here, but part of it is preserved. Large barbel are caught, and there is a good stock of dace, roach, and chub. Trout are scarce, but when they have been taken, have generally been of very heavy weight. The inn is the Duke's Head; and the fishermen Thomas and George Rogerson.

SHEPPERTON has some extensive ranges of deep water, full of fine perch, chub, and jack. Both sides of the river can be pleasantly fished from the banks. There are three districts or sections of preserved water here. There is good accommodation for travellers, and steady and obliging fishermen.

WEYBRIDGE is about twenty miles from the metropolis, and is an excellent locality for genuine fishing purposes. Trout are often pretty plentiful. At the time we are penning these lines we have seen a capture of this fish made, on an angling excursion, by Mr. Alfred, jun., of 54, Moorgate Street, City, which is a splendid specimen of Thames trout-fishing. His creel contained thirteen fish in all; one was *twelve and a half pounds*, one *seven*, and one *five* pounds; and the residue were of more than average size. These were caught by an artificial bait (an imitation of a small gudgeon, manufactured by himself), by trolling. Two of these fine fish are now preserved, and may be seen at the above fishing-tackle establishment. Such an exploit as this shows that the trout must have now become pretty numerous in the river, and that the late regulations respecting poaching and netting have operated beneficially for the interests of the fair angler.

The inns in this place frequented by rod-fishers, are the King's Arms, the Ship, and the Lincoln Arms; and the fishermen are Harris, Keen, Purdue, and Milbourn.

CHERTSEY BRIDGE is a fair station for the rod. There are some good trout, and a considerable number of perch, jack, and chub. The official list gives four hundred and forty yards of preserved water, extending from the weir to eighty yards eastward of the bridge. The inns are the Cricketers, the Crown, and the Swan; and the fishermen Upjohn and Galloway.

LALEHAM AND PENTON HOOK are places where good fly-fishing can be obtained. The trout are, on some favourable occasions, taken here in considerable numbers, and some of large size. The waters are preserved for the distance of eleven hundred and fifty yards. The inn is the Horse Shoe; and the fishermen the Messrs. Harris.

STAINES is now a favourite station for the London sportsman on the Thames. Trout-fishing has greatly improved here of late years. The preserved waters extend two hundred and ten yards east of the bridge. Barbel, roach, chub, and a fair portion of gudgeons, are to be caught in this locality. The inns are the Bush, the Angel, and the Swan; and the fishermen, whom we have invariably found very civil and obliging, are Flitcher, Vears, Amos, and Chambers.

WINDSOR has now become a very fair trout station; some fine large fish have recently been taken in its waters, both with fly, and with natural and artificial minnows. Eton and Surley Hall weirs are favourite spots for good fish. The bridge at Windsor is an excellent place for barbel; and about Datchet this kind of fish are always more than usually abundant. There are numerous shoals of gudgeons about the Windsor and Eton waters, which we have seen taken in large quantities.

The angling stations of MAIDENHEAD, COOKHAM, HENLEY, WARGRAVE, READING, PANGBOURNE BURN, and STREETLY, come all within the reach of the London anglers, and are looked upon as suburban waters for their especial recreation. We refrain from enumerating their individual properties and facilities for piscatory labours; they all bear a strong family likeness. These angling stations just mentioned are all easily accessible by railway conveyance; and speaking generally, the further the angler ascends up the river—the greater distance he travels towards the higher waters—the better will he find this famous stream for the ordinary purposes of trout, and especially of fly-fishing.

Our limits would not permit us, as we have hastily run over these angling stations on the Thames, to dwell upon the numerous sources of interest embodied in all of them to the rod-fisher of taste and refinement. There are spots of superlative scenic beauty, and also great literary and historical interest, interspersed in every direction, which are calculated to awaken in the mind of all imbued with a love and reverence of what is great and interesting, the most thrilling and lively associations. We can scarcely imagine a person fond of the gentle art, and who prosecutes it with a fair share of ardour, who could pass through such interesting localities —connected with some of the most stirring incidents of our national history as a people—and not feel his bosom glow with delight at what every way surrounds him. We believe that fisher- men have a large store of this love of excellence; and sure we are that nothing can so vitally augment the simple pleasures of their craft, as to cherish and cultivate it with assiduity and care.

OF THE TRIBUTARY STREAMS OF THE THAMES, NEAR THE METROPOLIS.

There are several tributary waters which flow into the Thames, in the neighbourhood of London, where the city anglers can procure a day's pleasant sport, at a very small cost of time and money. The rivers *Colne* and *Lea* are in the county of Middlesex. The first springs out of Hertfordshire, and has many fishing stations on its banks, some of which are, however, very rigidly preserved. The mills and chemical works situated on its banks, have greatly marred the angling. Pike of good size are to be met with, but trout are somewhat scarce. Denham is considered the best trout- ing spot upon it.

The *Lea* rises out of the county of Bedford, and is the most fre- quented stream by anglers in the immediate neighbourhood of London. It contains a great variety of fish, and some of them of great weight. It flows through a flat district, and it runs slug- gishly; these circumstances are against its ranking among the first- rate trout streams. There are many fishing stations on its banks, some of which we shall enumerate.

The first from the Thames is TEMPLE MILLS. This is free water, and many large barbel, roach, and chub, are caught here through the season. Gudgeons are likewise in immense numbers. Trout are scarce.

The WHITE HOUSE, Hackney Marsh, is a locality much frequented. The liberty of fishing here is let out, either by the year, or by the day. The subscription for the season is ten shillings and sixpence; this includes the right of trolling for trout or jack. One shilling is the charge for a day's sport, including fly-fishing and bottom- fishing, but not trolling. There are great numbers of fish here; and some capital sport is occasionally obtained.

The HORSE AND GROOM, at Lea Bridge, is a very old angling station, having been used as such for upwards of a century. The angler has here the liberty of two miles of water on each side of the house; and the terms are precisely the same as at the White House. The fish are commonly more numerous here than on any other portion of the river, chiefly on account of the locks being here, and the fish can ascend no further unless a passage be opened out for them. Sometimes the fish may be seen in immense shoals about the vicinity of the locks, and may readily be taken by even lowering naked hooks among them. Trout of twelve, pike of twenty-five, barbel of nine, and chub of four pounds, have been taken out of the Lea in this locality.

A portion of the river above Lea Bridge is free to the angler, but the sport is very indifferent.

TOTTENHAM MILLS is situated five miles from the city, and about a mile further up the stream is the subscription water of the BLUE HOUSE. The terms are half a guinea for bottom-fishing, and a guinea for trolling.

BLEAK HALL is a favourite station. There is an abundance of fish; and some trout of good size may occasionally be hooked; chiefly, however, by trolling. The subscription is two guineas per annum for both the waters of Bleak Hall, and those of CHINGFORD.

WALTHAM ABBEY is an interesting station; but the chief portion of the river is in the hands of the Government, and permission must be obtained from some of the public servants in the ordnance department, before angling is allowed. The waters are well supplied with all kinds of fish; and trout have been taken with both fly and minnow, of considerable magnitude.

BROXBOURNE, PAGE'S WATER, and the RYE HOUSE, are all good stations for bottom-fishing; but a mere sprinkling of trout can only be expected under the most favourable circumstances.

The NEW RIVER is pretty well stocked with roach, dace, and gudgeons, and is commonly open to anglers from the *Sluice House*, situated about two miles from Islington. On holiday times it is often amusing to see the scores of young anglers gathered together on the banks of the stream, trying their *prentice* hand on the gentle art. To have the privilege of fishing the reservoirs of the New River Company, tickets must be obtained from some of the officials.

FISHING IN THE DOCKS AND PRIVATE WATERS.

The Docks about London are to the bottom-fishers in its various localities, what the banks of Newfoundland are to the regular trading fishmongers—a constant and reliable source of supply. The quantities of fish in these shipping reservoirs, estuaries, and canals, is surprisingly great; and the number of rod-fishers who frequent them exceeds all credibility. The majority of the London anglers who make it a point to visit these dead and still waters, obtain a sort of tact or intuitive knowledge of their own, which enables them to gain success in their amusement under the most untoward and discouraging circumstances; and the zeal, the untiring enthusiasm, the labour, and personal privation, that are witnessed among them every fishing season, would scarcely be credited by anglers in the rural districts of the kingdom, where the sport is so easily and readily obtained and enjoyed.

The docks in and about London are so large and numerous, that they contain immense quantities of fish of all kinds, but particularly such as suit the bottom-fisher. They are likewise at a commandable and limited distance, and can consequently be visited without any serious loss of time or money. All these considerations weigh with the rod-fisher, and naturally induce him to consider these still waters to be a valuable adjunct to the general stock of piscatory recreation.

A day at the Docks, to many a tradesman in London, is what a stag-hunt, or the Derby Day, is to the aristocratic loungers of St. James's. The piscatory citizen talks of it for weeks before, and the pleasure from anticipation is, doubtless, were we in a state to make a fair comparison, greater than from actual realization. But this is something like his usual mode of procedure. He leaves his business for a day, and betakes himself to the New River, or some other spot, to obtain a stock of gudgeons for live-bait. These he places in a proper vessel for careful preservation. He is very anxious his bait should preserve all their native vitality and sprightliness; and he manifests the most sedulous care to supply them, at regular intervals, with fresh water. When he arrives at his home, he is generally tired and worn out; but still his family must be immediately summoned to look at the finny strangers, ere they take their departure to the wars at an early hour of the morning. The sight is cheering, and full of novelty. The angler pays his gudgeons a visit before he steps into bed, and concludes that the water will keep fresh and invigorating till the appointed hour of rising. His slumbers are broken from the thought of having to rise at such an early hour. He jumps out of bed to see his bait. Perchance some of them seem rather dull and sickly. He tries to procure them another supply of fresh water, but fails. He throws his clothes loosely about him, and off he sets to the street pump in the neighbourhood, and revives the drooping energies of his captives. He starts at three o'clock in a fine June morning, and walks hurriedly to the scene of action at the East or West India Docks. He gets himself prepared, looks at his live gudgeons, which seem pert and lively, and then he throws in his first bait. In a short time he succeeds in killing some perch of great weight; and then some jack, and bream. If he has fair luck, he will have, in the course of a couple of hours, fifty or sixty pounds weight of fish, of one kind and another. He now takes his breath, and dines; sometimes in a sportsman's fashion, and sometimes he goes to a convenient place of refreshment, and leisurely enjoys himself. He comes home delighted, and all his family are delighted too; and thus ends one of the long-looked for and joyous days of his city life.

Now all this is very healthful, pleasant, and socially improving.

To his brother craftsman in the country, the London bottom-fisher may possibly seem a somewhat grotesque personage; but we should remember that in angling, as well as in everything else, a large margin is allowed for different tastes, opinions, and habits, which are really in almost all cases the result of external circumstances, rather than from sheer choice. The love of out-door sport and amusement is such a powerful and impulsive feeling in human nature, that to suppress it is altogether impossible; and when men are placed in certain unfavourable positions for its full and healthful exercise, we should express neither surprise nor censoriousness if they deviate a little in the modes of gratifying this instinctive love of external recreation.

There are a few general observations or rules which relate to dock-fishing, which we shall take the liberty to state, because they will, we are persuaded, prove useful. In cold east or north-east winds, it is of little use trying for fish in these localities. The finny tribes seem under such an atmosphere to lie dormant or powerless. The *spring tides* must also be attended to. When fresh supplies of water rush into the docks from the main body of the river, fish will not feed freely for some days after. West and south-west winds are always favourable to the rod-fisher, and generally guarantee him some share of sport. Even if the wind in any of the quarters be high and boisterous, it will all be in his favour. Shot should be used for perch-fishing, and placed about a couple of feet below the float, and about eight or ten inches from the hook. To know the precise localities where fish frequent in these dock-waters, is half the game in successfully fishing them. Some anglers have great skill in this matter, and can form very excellent *guesses* where fish frequent. Close to the shore, or about a couple of feet from it, you are almost sure to meet with fish; and about the edges or sides of logs of timber, or about the sides of ships that have been long in dock, are likewise excellent spots of water. It is of little use to remain long at one place; if not successful after a short time, shift your position, and try a fresh piece of water. Shrimps are very excellent bait for perch in the dock-waters—few baits equal them. The hook should be a regular perch-hook, and the shrimp should be placed upon it in such a manner that it may swim well in the water.

Some dock-fishers use two hooks; the one whipped on the line, three inches or so from the lower hook, the contrary way, that is, the hook towards the float. Two separate kinds of bait can in this case be used—sometimes a worm and minnow, and sometimes a shrimp with either. It must be observed that in fishing some parts of the docks, the waters are so deep, that it is difficult, and indeed useless, to fish with a float.

The East and West India Docks are excellent places for the bottom-fisher. A ticket from some of the directors is required; but this is not difficult to obtain. In some of the other docks nearer the city there are quantities of fish, but they are not so easily taken, on account of the obstacles arising from the number of ships in these still waters. The Commercial Docks, at Rotherhithe, where large stocks of timber are kept in the water for years, is a good neighbourhood for rod-fishing. The depth of these docks varies from six to nine feet, and the line of the angler should be adjusted accordingly. Many sportsmen recommend fishing here, and, indeed, in all the dock-waters, with a roach rod, and a running line of plaited silk, not much thicker than a good thread, and a very small float. Take stale bread, and soak it in water; then squeeze the water out as well as you can with the hand. This must be carefully and cleanly kneaded into soft paste to form a bait, which should be put upon a small roach-hook, and should not exceed in size a common pea. Some anglers chew a little bread, and throw in it for ground bait, before commencing operations. This is considered as a successful enticement. At the slightest motion of the float, the angler must give a gentle strike; if the fish is not secured, he must let the bait drop again into the same place.

The striking of fish in these waters should be very gently performed; for the tackle being very light, and the fish sometimes large, breakage is the natural result of anything like vigorous rashness. When a fish is hooked, the line should be kept straight, for if it be slackened, the fish will probably get off. When there is considerable resistance from the weight of the fish, a little play must be used; for if you keep him rigidly by the head, his hold will likely give way, and he will be once more at liberty. The adroit management of the line is a great matter, and the proper application of the angler's strength and power to the exigencies of the case, constitutes the entire art of bottom-fishing, so far as the mere killing of the fish goes. That part of the art which consists of a knowledge of the localities of various kinds of fish, their habits, their hours of feeding, and the favourable condition of the waters, can only be thoroughly understood by continued practice, and careful and systematic observation.

There are several private waters, let out by subscription, in the immediate vicinity of London, where bottom-fishing can be obtained. The cost of a day's fishing here is trifling. These localities are very much frequented by such sportsmen as have little time to spare, and who just want a little run out to dissipate the nervous excitement which a close application to city business and duties necessarily produces on many constitutions. There are three of these private fisheries near the Shepherd's Bush, Bayswater, which lies within a sixpenny ride from the Bank of England. They are fair collections of water, have a tolerable stock of barbel, roach, and dace, and there are accommodations for refreshments. Sometimes rod-fishers succeed in taking away five-and-twenty or thirty pounds weight of fish. The names of these waters are, *Willow Vale Fishery*, *Victoria Fishery*, and the *Star Fishery*. The ordinary charge is one shilling a day.

The *Kingsbury Fishery* is considered a very good one. The subscription is one guinea annually; and the following are some of the chief regulations of the establishment. No day tickets are allowed; no member's ticket is transferable; every member must produce his ticket when demanded; one friend to be introduced by a member; the member to use only two rods, whether alone or accompanied by a friend; the season to commence on the 1st of May, and to end on the last day of February for perch; no live or dead bait to be used before the 1st day of June; jack-fishing from the 1st of June to the last day of February; no member to use a trimmer, peg-line, lay-line, or net, except a landing or keep-net.

We have now entered as fully into a description of those places suitable to the London angler's pursuits, as we have been able. We feel somewhat confident that he will find our remarks and instructions of some use. We must now proceed to more distant localities, and descant upon those fishing waters adapted for another class of anglers—those who aim at the capture of the salmon, the trout, and the pike.

It is requisite to premise, that in directing the rod-fisher *where to go* over the varied extent of fishing waters in England and Wales, our observations and descriptions must necessarily be of a very general cast. We cannot descant at any length on many interesting sections of river scenery, admirably fitted to impart to the intellectual angler the most lively and delicate pleasures. So far, however, as the higher branches of the angling art are concerned, we shall make a point of dwelling, with as much minuteness as possible, upon those places where really good fly-fishing may be readily obtained, and where the sportsman will find pleasure and improvement in passing through them. Large districts of monotonous scenery, and of sluggish waters, must be hastily passed over.

Taking London as our point of departure, and the great leading railways as our diverging lines of travelling, we shall direct the angler's attention to the class or series of rivers which are intersected, or nearly approached, by the Eastern Counties Railway, and the Dover and Brighton lines. This will comprehend a large proportion of the eastern and north-eastern sections of England.

The travelling angler must always bear in mind, that the greater the distance from the metropolis, the better will the fly-fishing be, and the less restriction will be laid upon his movements, by means of preserved waters. The very best angling streams are those at the extremities of the kingdom.

This is not a first-rate trouting district; nor, indeed, second-rate either. The class of waters in this direction, including rivers canals, and estuaries, are better adapted for bottom-fishing than anything else. They contain a great number of perch, chub, roach, pike, eels, and gudgeons; but the hooking of salmon and trout is like angels' visits—few and far between. For this kind of ground angling those eastern and north-eastern localities have long been

celebrated; and many zealous and good anglers contrive to eke
out of them a fair modicum of sport, in spite of all the dis-
advantages under which they labour.

If the angler sets out from any of the rivers that the Dover and
Brighton Railways cross or run near to, he will find some share of
sport. The county of Surrey has a few trout streams, though not
of the first-rate description. The *Wey* has some fish in it, both of
good size and rich flavour. It runs by Farnham, Godalming, and
Guildford, and falls into the Thames at Weybridge. We have
found light-coloured flies more successful in this river than any
other. There are some fine carp in certain spots of the stream.
The Wandle is a clear and interesting water; it springs from the
vicinity of Carshalton, which is twelve miles from the metropolis,
and enters the Thames at Wandsworth. It is preserved in many
sections of its waters, but trout of twelve pounds have occasionally
been captured in this stream. The *Cray* enters the Thames between
Woolwich and Dartford, and is of little importance. The *Mole*
contains but a small number of trout, but a good sprinkling of
pike, and some of very large size. A few years ago one was taken
near Bletchworth Castle which weighed twenty-five pounds.

The county of Kent has but few streams worthy of general
notice; neither would we advise a fly-fisher to undertake a journey
with the rod into either Essex or Sussex. There is plenty of
bottom-fishing, but nothing that could satisfy a man who knows
anything about fly-fishing, and who relishes the sport.

The Eastern Counties Railway extends now over a wide range
of country, but there is not much fine fishing water within its reach.
In the several counties of Suffolk, Huntingdonshire, Cambridge-
shire, Norfolk, and Northamptonshire, we can scarcely find any
waters but such as suit the bottom-fisher. There are some excellent localities for his kind of sport.

The best tour we should recommend, within a reasonable distance
of London, is the Derbyshire district. Here we get in among the
mountains, which impart such a peculiar feature to all excursions,
and produce those clear, rapid, and sparkling waters in which trout
delight to swim. This tour would prove a great treat to all who
have not hitherto been made familiar with the rugged and bold
features of nature; and now, the expense of time and money to
accomplish it is very trifling to what it used to be a few years since.
The river *Trent* flows through a portion of Derbyshire, but of it we
do not purpose to say anything at present: we shall deal with the
smaller streams. The *Erewash* is a pleasant water. It rises near to
the town of Mansfield, and divides the counties of Derby and Nottingham. Fly-fishing in its upper waters is very good, but the fish are
somewhat small, and are proverbially fickle in their hours of feeding.
We have known many anglers get completely out of humour with this
locality, chiefly from this reason. The flies to be used in this river
should be rather small, with lightish coloured wings; and the tackle
should be of the most delicate cast. The stream flows through many

delightful localities, which cannot fail to inspire the contemplative
angler with the most lively emotions. When this stream has been
flooded by rains, we have seen large trout taken out of it with minnows.
The river *Dove* is the great object of attraction among anglers
who visit this part of the kingdom. Its beautiful scenery and fishing
capabilities make it a stream of more than usual interest. It was
here that Walton and Cotton used to sojourn, when they now and
then left the smoke and turmoil of London and its suburban localities for their northern travels. To go to Derbyshire two hundred
years ago, was no small or insignificant enterprise. These well-
known anglers of past times have celebrated the Dove in the
following lines :—

"Such streams Rome's yellow Tiber cannot show,
The Iberian Tagus, or Ligurian Po;
The Meuse, the Danube, and the Rhine,
Are puddle-waters all, compared with thine.
The Loire's pure streams yet too polluted are,
With thine much purer to compare;
The rapid Garonne and the winding Scine
    Are both too mean,
    Beloved Dove, with thee
    To vie priority.
Nay, Tame and Isis, when conjoined, submit,
And lay their trophies at thy silver feet."

The Dove springs out of the mountain-range in the north-western
border of the county of Derby; and from its rise to where it falls
into the Trent, it forms the boundary line between this county and
Staffordshire. The fishing in the Dove is first-rate; not that the
trout are very large, but they are commonly of a fair size, and the
sport is of that even and exhilarating character that most anglers
enjoy it much. Everything about the locality inspires pleasure.
The tackle required must be of the finest kind; for the waters run
clear, and the high banks on each side screen the streams from the
influence of the wind.
Dove Dale has been, from time immemorial, a subject of admiration and eulogy among all classes of tourists. "If we enter the
Dale by the north of Thorpe Cloud,—a lofty hill, with an interest-
ing-looking village at its base—we shall obtain some delightful
views of the county. There is a singular character of wild sim
plicity about it which makes a deep impression on the feelings, and
brings up to the surface the contemplative and reflective powers
—those vague and shadowy abstractions which most men have of
vacuity and chaos. We stand and gaze, almost without the faculty
of either utterance or active thought. After, however, the first
sensations have passed away, we begin to scan the landscape as if
it were by piecemeal, and to detect and define the individual
beauties of which the whole is composed. The eye fixes itself upon

patches of furze and aged thorns, scattered over the edges of the Dale, and then traces out the glassy stream as it meanders through the naked and desolate-looking scene. As we move forward, the Dale assumes a deeper and more concentrated aspect, and appears completely hemmed in near a locality called Sharplow, which rises very abruptly from the edge of the waters. Here the stream becomes extremely imposing."

The river *Blyth* is a stream worthy of the angler's attention: it falls into the Trent at King's Bromley. It has two feeders, the Soar and the Peak, in both of which trout are to be had, especially with worm, after a summer's rain. The river *Tame* comes from the vicinity of Coleshill, and has many fine rippling streams, which an angler's eyes delight to look upon. The minnow, especially after a flooded state of the waters, does great execution. We have witnessed fine baskets of fish taken at such times.

The *Derwent* is a first-rate river: the chief angling stations upon it are Baslow, Rowsley Bridge, and Matlock. The stream below the last-named place is not so fruitful of sport as the several localities above it.

The whole course of the river is about sixty miles. "In the space of forty miles," says a writer, "which includes the whole course of the river from the highest and wildest parts of the Peak to the town of Derby, scenery more richly diversified with beauty can hardly anywhere be found. Generally, its banks are luxuriantly wooded; the oak, the elm, the alder, and the ash, flourish abundantly along its course, beneath the shade of whose united branches the Derwent is sometimes secluded from the eye of the traveller, and becomes a companion for the ear alone; then, suddenly emerging into day, spreads through a more open valley, or winding round some huge mountain or rocky precipice, reflects their dark sides as it glides beneath. Sometimes, this ever-varying and ever-pleasing stream precipitates its foaming waters over the rugged projections and rocky fragments that interrupt its way; again the ruffled waves subside, and the current steals smoothly and gently through the vale, clear and almost imperceptible in motion."

The rivers *Manifold* and *Wye* are likewise good Derbyshire waters. In fact, this entire district is calculated to give the angling tourist every degree of satisfaction. The streams are all such as to please, both by their fishing capabilities, as well as by the lovely and interesting scenery which adorns their banks in every locality. These range of waters can be reached from the metropolis in a few hours by railway, and the means of transit from one section of them to another can readily be obtained at a trifling cost.

Should the angler wish to extend his journey further north, there is a fine tour lying before him from Derbyshire, embracing the counties of York, Durham, and Northumberland. Here there is fine fishing; and we shall endeavour to point out, as briefly as we can, the chief spots in this wide range of waters which are fitted to yield a fair chance of good sport.

First of Yorkshire. This is an extensive county, and embraces many rivers, some of which are good fishing streams, and some of no use in this respect whatever. Wherever manufactures are extensively carried on, the streams are of little use to the angler. The waters become turbid, variable, and unhealthy for the support of piscatory existence. There is a considerable portion of the waters in this part of England well fitted for bottom-fishing. There are dull and torpid running waters that fall into that great estuary called the Humber, where there are plenty of fish of a certain kind always to be had; such as pike, the perch, eels, and the like. But the salmon and trout fishing in such spots is scarcely worth mentioning; and certainly not of such a character as to induce anglers to visit them from any great distance.

To fish the best portion of the trout streams in Yorkshire, the angler should not throw a line till he gets north of the city-of York. He may, in the early portion of the season, obtain a few trout in the upper waters of the *Derwent*, above Malton; in the *Dove*, the *Hodgebeck*, the *Costin*, the *Rical*, and the *Black River;* but he cannot, with any certainty calculate on success. In fact, these streams are more fitted for bait-fishing, than for fly; but whatever trout are obtained from them, are often both of good size and rich flavour. Small flies must in general be used, and fine tackle likewise.

The higher waters of the *Ribble*, the *Swale*, and the *Wharfe*, afford the best trout fishing. The first river enters the sea in the Solway Firth at Preston, in Lancashire, but in its course through Yorkshire, it is a fine trout stream, and where both the salmon and salmon-trout can be occasionally taken with the fly. Indeed, the waters have great local celebrity; as the following song, which we believe has never been published at any great distance from its birthplace, does in some measure testify:—

ON THE RIVER RIBBLE, IN LANCASHIRE.

" By Ribble's stream I'll pass my days,
    If wishes aught avail;
For all that anglers want or praise
    Is found in Ribblesdale.

" Here, heath-clad hills and caverned dells,
    And rocks and rills prevail,
And sylvan glens and fairy cells,
    Abound in Ribblesdale.

" Impetuous gushing waterfalls
    The startling ear assail,
While each impending crag appals
    The eye in Ribblesdale.

"The meads are decked by Flora's hand,
  Her gifts perfume the gale,
And Bacchus dyes with magic wand
  The floods of Ribblesdale.

"The sweet though fatal power of love,
  Which sighing swains bewail,
No witching beauties ere could prove
  Like those of Ribblesdale.

"T'was here the gallant feats befell
  Which fill the poet's tale;
For all the deeds romances tell
  Were done in Ribblesdale.

"Be court or city other's lot
  While angling scenes I hail;
Be mine, in some sequestered spot,
  The charms of Ribblesdale."

The most highly esteemed spots of the Ribble for comfortable trout-fishing, are from Clitheroe to the town of Settle. The county is open and pleasant.

There are fine streams for fly, in the higher sections of the Wharfe; and the minnow after a flood is a deadly bait. This river rises out of the mountainous parts of the county near Mardale Moor, and enters the Ouse a short distance above Selby. For several miles after it leaves its first springs, the streams are very fine and numerous, and are beautifully constructed by the hand of nature herself, for the facilities of easy and comfortable fly-fishing. Large trout are occasionally met with; but the general run of the Wharfdale fish are below the average of the trout commonly obtained in many of the rivers of the south of England. Care should be taken not to fish with flies of too large a size; and anglers will find that the palmers, both red and black, are well suited to these waters.

The *Swale* is a good stream. It springs from lofty hills in the vicinity of Kirby-Stephen, in Westmoreland. Catterick Bridge is an excellent fishing station on the river; where everything that can render travelling comfortable can be readily and reasonably obtained. Ten or twelve dozen of fish are no uncommon day's work, when the waters are in full trim in this neighbourhood. The same kinds of flies that answer for the Wharfe, will do here.

There are only two rivers in the county of Durham of any great fishing repute, the *Tees*, and the *Wear*. The first enters the sea at Stockton, and the latter at Sunderland. They each have a range of fly-fishing water of full forty miles. The Tees, in its higher sections, flows through a moorish and wild district called

Teesdale; a portion of the country which is now more accessible than it was a few years ago, and is becoming daily better known and more frequently visited by angling tourists. It is a free and open country, delightfully suited to the unfettered movements of the pedestrian rod-fisher. The trout are good, but not large; and when in the taking mood, anything in the shape of a fly will suit their taste. Ten or twelve dozen of fish may be taken in the course of a few hours; but the salmon and salmon-trout are very scarce. Like most rivers that have a hilly origin, the further we descend the stream towards the sea, the larger and better fed are the fish. This is the case with the Tees. A few miles above Stockton, fine trout of four or five pounds weight are sometimes taken, both with fly and minnow. But for fly-fishing, the higher up the river the better. After heavy rains, when the water has turned to a sort of ale colour, and considerably subsided, flies of a lightish hue are found more killing here than any other. Palmers are also favourites.

The Wear rises out of a range of high mountains in Cumberland, and flows for some miles after it leaves its parent springs, through a singularly wild and interesting locality. An angler coming direct from the level and richly cultivated counties of the South of England, to the waters of Wear Dale, will experience a singular class of sensations. Nothing can be more impressive than a range along their banks for full twenty or five-and-twenty miles. The town of Bishop-Auckland is an excellent spot to go to, and from this to fish the water upwards. The sportsman will find the main river increased by several small tributaries or feeders, namely, *Lyn Burn, Red Burn, Wascrop Burn,* the *Shittlehope,* the *Stanhope, Horsley Burn,* the *Westhope,* the *Swinhope,* the *Middlehope,* and the *Bookhope.* There is good angling with the worm in all these waters, but the fish run small. The main river is always to be preferred, except the angler enjoys a ramble up the smaller waters for the sake of their wild and romantic scenery. All kinds of flies are used here, and with success. The minnow, after rain, does great execution, particularly in the summer season. Though the country is wild, and a good part of it entirely moorland, yet the tourist finds plenty of places for refreshments and lodging. The habits of the people in this part are simple and hospitable, and most cheerfully do all they can to administer to the comforts of their guests.

The Tees and the Wear are of ready access from London, or, indeed, from any section of the kingdom, by railway conveyance. An angler leaving the metropolis in the morning, can be upon the banks of either of the rivers in the evening. There are other smaller rivulets and streams in the county of Durham, but they are not worth any formal enumeration.

Two or three streams in Northumberland are of first-rate angling note. The *Coquet,* the *North Tyne,* the *Aln,* and the *Till,* are places much frequented by rod-fishing tourists at particular seasons of the year. They are all accessible by railway communication. The Coquet is the most celebrated, and has for more than a century been a stream enjoying aristocratic and fashionable notoriety as an angling locality. In former years, before the fashion ran so strongly for distant Scottish rivers, the Coquet used to be the annual *rendezvous* of all our London literary, scientific, and political rod-fishers; and even now there are more anglers on its streams, and more fish taken out of them, including the salmon-trout, than in any other half a dozen of chief rivers in the northern counties of England.

The river springs out of the south-western range of the Cheviot. Mountains, and has a range of nearly forty miles, all of which is open water for the angler, with the exception of three or four small sections of it; and these, even, are not very rigidly preserved. This freedom from constraint of every kind is a pleasurable element in piscatory recreations. The salmon fishery at the mouth of the river belongs to the Duke of Northumberland, and is let for a considerable yearly rent; but we have never known any angler called to account for capturing the salmon with the rod and line, wherever he might be perambulating on the Coquet. There are no artificial or natural obstructions for the free passage of the fish from the sea to its highest waters, so that this noble fish can always be found, in more or less abundance, in every section of its waters.

The river Coquet is a remarkably clear one, and often requires fine tackle. Its trout are likewise very capricious and uncertain; some days you can get nothing, and on another twelve or fifteen dozen may fall to your share. The trout here run small, and they are likewise of very indifferent quality. But for real sport, the river, take it all in all, has few to equal it in England.

The Newcastle-upon-Tyne and Berwick railway crosses it near Warkworth, and the angler has then thirty miles of fine angling streams before him; this is a great facility. All kinds of flies are used on the Coquet, but care should be taken as to the size of the hook. This, however, depends much upon the state of the waters, and the season of the year. Trolling has become quite the rage of late years on this water; and unquestionably the finest and largest trout are taken by this means.

The North Tyne is a first-rate water; it joins the South Tyne a little west of the town of Hexham. This southern branch is nearly denuded of trout, from the effects of the lead mines situated on its higher waters. There are none of these establishments on North Tyne. The river is preserved in some few spots, but there are large stretches of fine water open to all rod-fishers. Trolling has here, too, become quite fashionable. All kinds of lightish winged flies are suitable for summer fishing in this stream.

The *Aln* passes Alnwick, the county town; and there is a range of about five miles of water open for all rod anglers. The Newcastle and Berwick railway crosses it near *Bilton* station, where the sportsman may place himself on the banks of the stream by a five minutes' walk. It is very prolific of trout, of a better size and quality than the Coquet fish, but the salmon-trout are scarce.

The river Till is approached by way of Berwick. The railway from that place to Kelso crosses the Till. It is a slow and languid running stream, very deep in certain localities, but contains very rich and fine trout, with a small sprinkling of pike, though not of large size. Till is not a good fly-river, but is admirable for trolling. It runs into the Tweed, and is well stocked from this splendid reservoir. There is an old rhyme, among the people in the neighbourhood, in reference to the comparative swiftness of the two rivers.

> "Tweed said to Till,
>   'What gars ye rin sae still?'
> Till said to Tweed,
>   'Though ye rin wi' speed,
>   And I rin slaw,
> Yet where ye drown ae man,
>   I drown twa.'"

In the rivers *Reed*, *Wansbeck*, and *Blyth*, all rivers of Northumberland, there are fine trout, but they can only be properly angled for by persons who have a very accurate knowledge of the peculiarities of each stream. For general tourists they are not well fitted.

We come now to enumerate at some length another batch of rivers and lakes, all full of interest, and abounding with fish of all kinds—namely, the rivers and lakes of Cumberland, Westmoreland, and Lancashire. Here, an angling traveller can have a ramble among rivers of all sizes, and in sections of the country diversified by every kind of landscape. We know no place in England where a man of any mind at all can be more highly gratified, with a fishing-rod in his hand, than in a tour embracing the entire waters in these several counties; and the best way of really enjoying the sports of the angle, after getting to the locality by railway, is to walk from river to river and from lake to lake. A great part of the country is wild—astonishingly wild and lonely—but full of grandeur and picturesque beauty; and there are now plenty of places where refreshments can be readily obtained, and every civility met with.

Supposing the angler leaves London by the London and North Western, at Euston-square, for Lancashire, he will be there in a few hours, and the next day may enter upon his amusement. Part of the rivers in this county are rendered unfit for general piscatory movements, by reason of the manufactures established upon their banks. The *Lune*, which springs from the high and mountainous parts of Westmoreland, and enters the sea below Lancaster, is a good stream, both for salmon and trout. The best districts on the river are those which lie between Kirby Lonsdale and Hornby, near which the small stream of the *Wenning* enters it. There are often very fine baskets of trout taken in this direction. We have seen both large trout and salmon captured within a very short distance of the town of Lancaster. There are many *favourite* flies for this river; and if you inquire of any of the regular frequenters of the river, each will have his pet bait, and strenuously insist upon its superiority to every other.

When the rod-fisher has got a footing at Lancaster, he has the railway right through to Carlisle, to the borders of Scotland, and which goes by, or rather cuts at right angles, many of the rod-fishing streams in Westmoreland and Cumberland. This is a great convenience; because the tourist can choose any direction he likes, without loss of time or waste of money. On the left, on the route to Carlisle, all the lake district waters lie; but there is good fishing by ascending the higher springs of some of the rivers which are to be met with up the country on the right hand.

Assuming that the rod-fisher starts from the town of Preston, where the *Ribble*, out of Yorkshire, flows into the sea, or from the town of Lancaster, and bends his way to the lake district, he will find the lakes *Coniston-water* and *Windermere* excellent fishing localities. The first-named sheet of water is seven miles long, and averages about three-quarters of a mile in breadth. The scenery around it is captivating in a high degree, and the angling really good. The village of Coniston is a convenient place for refreshment and lodging. There are trout, pike, and perch, in the lake, and all of good size.

Windermere is a more extensive stretch of water than the one just named. Its extent is full eighteen miles, by one in breadth: its greatest depth is 200 feet. The angler will find *char* here, as well as trout, pike, and perch.

Crummock-water, Lows-water, Over-water, and *Bassenthwaite-water,* are all situated near the north-western extremity of the range of mountains which range beyond and near to Mellbreak. These several lakes are but small in extent; but they abound with various kinds of fish, and are calculated to afford a fair portion of sport to the rod-fisher. Their several banks are romantically surrounded by rocky promontories and jutting capes and headlands, which impart to all the scenery around and about them peculiar features of sublimity and grandeur.

Derwent-water and *Ulls-water* abound with fish of nearly all kinds. Angling is practised on these waters with fly, by trolling, and by worm and other kinds of ground bait. There can be no lack of sport to any rod-fisher who is acquainted with even the rudiments of his art. But, to our taste, the lake district and the lake angling are not so heart-stirring and so engrossing as the river fly-fishing; and in the two counties of Cumberland and Westmoreland, there are rivers of first-rate excellence for the latter mode of following the gentle craft. Indeed, the rivers here are full of fine trout, and sport of the best sort is to be had in every direction. And the most effective, and really the most amusing, method of traversing these waters is by walking *just as the crow flies*. Let a rod-fisher take some provender with him, not neglecting a little *spirit* for medicine's sake; and, relying upon his own resources, make the best of his way over mountain and valley, and there can be no doubt but he will fill both his basket with capital fish, and his heart with exhilarating gladness. This is the true and only method of angling in these wild and secluded tracts of country. To afford him a little guidance, we shall just dot down, from our own personal recollections and experience, a few general observations on the various rivers connected with this interesting range of piscatory waters.

The chief river in Cumberland is the *Eden*. It is an imposing and magnificent stream, and abounds with trout and salmon of the finest quality. It springs out of the high grounds—all moorlands of the wildest kind—close upon the western section of Yorkshire, and has a run of forty miles and upwards. It enters the county of Cumberland near its junction with the *Eamont*, and flows on, through most interesting sections of the county, to the city of Carlisle, and enters the Solway Firth near Rockcliff March. The angler has a ready access to Carlisle, either by the Lancaster Railway, or the Carlisle and Newcastle line; so that he can be brought into immediate proximity with the finest range of angling streams in the kingdom.

One of the very best fishing stations on the Eden is that of Penrith. It is about five miles from the river; but, by a walk to it, we are placed at once on some of its choicest streams. These run so clear and sparkling over the rocky bed of the river, and are broken into such a succession of rippling currents, that the eye of the most experienced rod-fisher cannot but be fascinated with their appearance, and the number of trout which are taken here is often surprisingly great. We have known ten and twelve dozen taken in three or four hours; and when the waters have been in first-rate order after a summer's rain, and the minnow been employed, the heavy fish we have seen captured have more than once been so great to our own knowledge, that the angler had to leave them behind him. The trout of the Eden, on such occasions, take any kind of fly very greedily; but when the waters are very much reduced from a long continuance of dry weather, and become very clear, then the finest tackle and small-sized flies are indispensably requisite.

The salmon becomes tolerably plentiful as the angler approaches to the city of Carlisle. In the stretches of water that encircle it, consisting of long and deep pools, there are always a great number of fish to be found; and a good curl on the surface, with a suitable fly, will scarcely ever fail of bringing some of them to the bank. There are a number of very skilful anglers in this town; and it is an excellent place to obtain such kind of flies as are most in request, not only in the Eden, but in other neighbouring streams. The manufacture of these artificial flies is grounded on long observation and experience, and a constant habit of paying attention to every phase of fly-fishing. On this account, any purchase of flies, either for salmon or trout, may be safely depended upon as likely to answer the end desired.

The other angling streams worthy of attention are the *Eamont*, the *Duddon*, the *Ehen*, the *Derwent*, the *Greata*, the *Cocker*, the *Ellen*, the *Weaver*, the *Wampool*, the *Caldew*, the *Peterel*, the *Esk*, the *Liddal*, the *Line*, or *Leven*, the *Irthing*, and the *Geet*.

The Eamont springs out of Ulls-water Lake, near to Pooley Bridge, and falls into the Eden near to Carlton. If the angler should be in the vicinity of the town of Penrith, he can readily make his way to some of the best fishing-streams of the Eamont. Its trout are both numerous and of good size, and excellent sport may be obtained during the whole of the fishing season.

The Duddon constitutes the boundary line between a part of the counties of Cumberland and Lancashire. It has fine salmon and trout, and is a particularly pleasant stream to fish with the fly.

The Ehen rises out of the mountain range in the neighbourhood of Borrowdale, and is about twenty miles in length. It forms *Ennerdale Lake*, and then flows on, passes Egremont, and reaches the waters of the Solway Firth. Trolling is now very generally adopted by anglers who frequent this stream. The flies that will suit the Eden, will answer very well for this river.

The Derwent springs from the vicinity of the hills near Borrowdale, and after winding through some rugged and sublime mountain districts, full of wild grandeur and impressive desolation, it forms the lake that bears its name, at the mouth of which stands the town of Keswick. This is a good starting point for the angler, inasmuch as it commands a ready access to many fine trouting waters. The river runs past the town of Cockermouth, and falls into the Irish Sea near the small town of Workington. The whole of its range will be fully thirty miles. The fishing in the Derwent is often very uncertain. The finny tribes seem to take capricious fits of abstinence, for nothing in the shape of bait will induce them to move. We cannot account for these odd humours, nor have we ever heard or read of any one that could.

The Greata is formed by two small rivulets, which spring out of the lofty district of Saddleworth. These united waters pass Keswick, and fall into the Derwent. In the early part of the season, and during the summer, after rains, there is capital trouting in the Greata, and very fine trout they are. The palmer flies seem to be great favourites with the local anglers of these streams.

The Cocker has a mountain source; and, after rains, comes down with great impetuosity, sweeping everything before it. It flows through the lakes of Buttermere and Crummock, dividing the beautiful vale of Lorton. The trout run generally small, but occasionally there are some taken of more than average size.

The Ellen springs out of Coldbeck Fells, and has several small tributaries in which tourists often fish with the worm, and are very successful even in clear bright weather. The small but deep whirling eddies of these rivulets are very favourable for this mode of fishing. The river .passes Udale and Ireby, and flowing in a western direction through a very lovely vale, falls into the sea at the town of Maryport.

The Weaver and the Wampool are not of much interest to the travelling rod-fisher; but the Caldew is a good stream, and will afford good sport for a few days. It springs out of a wild and savage looking district, in the vicinity of Skiddaw, one of the loftiest peaks in England. It has several small feeders well stocked with trout, and worm-fishing, even in the clearest days, may be very successfully followed in the rippling and gurgling eddies of these mountain waters. The bait is beautifully carried down the streams, and proves a very deceptive bait indeed.

The Peterel joins the Eden near Carlisle, and abounds with small trout; but the waters require to be in a certain condition to insure anything like good sport.

If the rod-fisher prosecutes his journey a few miles north of Carlisle, he will fall in with several streams where excellent angling can be obtained. The Esk is one of these waters.

" Majestic o'er the steeps, with murmuring roar,
  See winding Esk his rapid current pour,
  And on the bright wave the sportive salmon play,
  And bound and glisten in the noon-tide ray."

This river rises in the high grounds between Hawick, in Scotland, and Carlisle. It is a singularly beautiful piece of running water. It is particularly adapted, by the short deep contraction of its streams, for trolling; and large fish are taken out of it by this process. The salmon run up it for a considerable distance. The Caledonian Railway from Carlisle to Glasgow crosses the Esk, so that the angler has every facility in reaching its pure and rippling waters.

The Liddal is another river of Scottish origin; it falls into the Esk not far from the English border. The trout-fishing in the Liddal is generally good, except when its waters become very low from long continued dry weather; even then we have seen good fishing in it by baiting with fine small red worms, and using fine tackle.

The Leven springs out of a wild moorish tract, near Nichol Forest and Bewcastle. It has two principal springs, and after flowing a few miles, it receives the waters of two or three other feeders. It then becomes a good fly-fishing stream, and forms a junction with the Esk a few miles down the Solway Firth. All kinds of flies, if not too large, seem to be readily taken here when the fish are on the feed.

The Irthing—some call it the *Irving*—comes out of some remarkably bleak and desolate looking tracts of high land, which divides Cumberland from Northumberland. After receiving some feeders, in which there are many small trout, readily caught with good red worms, it falls into the Eden near Newby. The Irthing is a good river for the fly, and likewise for trolling after rain in summer.

The Gelt springs from Croglin Fell, and after receiving the waters of some small rivulets, falls into the Irthing near Edmon Castle. It is a pretty fair trouting stream in the early portion of the season, or towards the autumnal months. The angling is frequently seriously damaged in this, as well as in other similar streams in this part of England, by fishing in the autumn with the salmon roe.

We have been somewhat minute in our notice of the various rivers and still waters of this division of England; and our sole reason is, that we know of no range of country to which a rod-fisher, who has a few days or weeks to spend in his favourite amusement, could repair with so fair a chance of being gratified, than the one now noticed. It is full of interest to both the mere angler, and to the man of contemplative and intellectual habits. We can form no conception of what a person can be made of, who, with rod in hand, could wander among these hilly districts, without receiving some signal moral benefit, and without bringing back with him a stock of ideas which he never had before. Indeed, we scarcely believe there could be such a specimen of humanity in this country, who could be proof against the influence of such external objects of grandeur and beauty as here surround him on every side.

The only sure mode, however, by which we shall be able to reap the full benefit from such an angling tour as we now recommend and point out, is to travel as much as possible on foot. Nearly every principal section of this lake district is now approachable by railway, and this is a great convenience; but the rod-fisher should only make it a means to an end. If he wishes to do any good in the way of his amusement, he must leave the beaten tracts of mere visitors and loungers, and betake himself to wild and distant sections of the country, where he may possibly wander by a river side for a whole day, and never see a human being. This is the kind of rod-fishing which is really delightful and improving, inasmuch as it is not only conducive to health, but it awakens and sustains the dormant powers of inward reflection, which are too apt to become deadened by the long and continued tension of a town life. Angling should invariably be considered only as a means to an end; that end the improvement of the man, mentally and physically. It is beautifully and eloquently said by an author, who travelled over this tract of country nearly a century ago, "If travellers and anglers would frequent this country, with a view to examine its grandeur and beauty, or to explore its varied and curious regions with the eye of philosophy; or to adore the Creator in his sublimer works; if in their passage through it, they could be content with such fare as the country produces; if, instead of corrupting the manners of an innocent people, they would learn to amend their own, by observing in how narrow a compass the wants of human life may be compressed; a journey, either with or without a rod, through these wild scenes, might be attended with more improvement to the traveller, than the tour of Europe."

What is a great inducement to take a piscatory ramble among the Cumberland and Westmoreland waters, is the kind and hospitable attention of the country people. This is very strikingly displayed in almost every locality the angler can frequent. Everything bespeaks real kindliness, cleanliness, and comfort. There are certainly no fashionable elegances, no parade of ceremonies; but the tourist is sure to receive a true welcome, which is far superior to the customary formalities, in which the heart has seldom any part. It is a pleasant thing, after a long day's fagging at the river's side, through a lonely country, to meet a friendly expression of countenance, and a cordial welcome. This finds the way to the heart, and tells you, in the language of the affections, to consider yourself no longer a stranger, but at home. Under such circumstances, the exquisite lines of Catullus have often been recalled to our mind:

> "Oh quid est solutis beatius curis!
> Cum meus onus reponit, ac peregrino
> Fessi labore venimus larem ad sacrum."

How delightful to wander through these solitudes of nature! How full of interest to the human soul. We never seem to appreciate the quick animating principle of our being, until we are fairly engulfed in these deep recesses, where the foot of man seldom treads, and his voice is seldom heard. In those inward breathings of the soul which such localities inspire, how often have we thought of the lines of Byron:

> "There is a pleasure in the pathless woods,
> There is a pleasure on the lonely shore,
> There is society where none intrudes,
> By the deep sea, and music in its roar:
> I love not man the less, but nature more,
> For these our interviews, in which I steal
> From all I may be, or have been before,
> To mingle with the universe, and feel
> What I can ne'er express, yet cannot all conceal."

We must now turn for a short period to another class of waters, in which there is a considerable range of sporting displayed, though of a somewhat different order from that which we have just been noticing over the wild and unfrequented mountain districts in the north-western section of England. There are two large rivers in the heart of this country, the *Trent* and the *Severn*, on the banks of which there are constantly anglers to be met with; fishing both for the trout, as well as for the vast number of bottom-fish which are to be found in their streams.

The Trent takes its rise from the north-west part of the county of Staffordshire, about ten miles north of Newcastle-under-Line. At first it takes a circular turn towards the south-east, bending to the south as far as within ten miles of Tamworth, where it receives the *Tame*, flowing through that town. Afterwards the Trent runs north-east, towards Burton-upon-Trent, a little beyond which it is enlarged by the waters of the Dove, which flow from a north-west direction. After this the Trent receives the Derwent, which descends from the mountainous parts of Derbyshire; and the whole of these waters collectively flow towards the north by Nottingham and Newark, to the Humber. The Trent has an entire course of two hundred and fifty miles. It is navigable for one hundred and seventy miles from the Humber; and by means of canals, has a communication with many of the most important rivers of the kingdom.

In many sections of this long river, there is good angling; we do not mean first-rate fly-fishing; but trout are taken in it with the fly, and a still greater number by trolling. This species of fish likewise attain a good size in the Trent, and are of rich flavour. There is a fair proportion of pike, perch, roach, dace, bream, eels, &c.; and we would say that a great mass of the angling on its extended waters, is purely of a bottom-fishing kind, in which there is considerable skill displayed by numerous zealous anglers who reside in towns lying near its route throughout the heart of England. The Trent is certainly not a river we should think of recommending to a first-rate angler; but still there is a good deal of angling on its waters, though of a mixed and subordinate cast.

And the Severn is a river of nearly the same nature, both in its navigable character and angling capabilities. It has long been celebrated for the number and variety of its fish. Michael Drayton, nearly two centuries and a half ago, sung its praises in this respect Hear what he says:

" I throw my crystal arms along the flowery valleys,
  Which, lying sleek and smooth as any garden alleys,
  Do give me leave to play, whilst they do court my stream,
  And crown my winding banks with many an anadem;
  My silver-scaléd sculls about my streams do sweep,
  Now in the shallow fords, now in the falling deep:
  So that of every kind, the new spawned numerous fry
  Seem in me as the sands that on my shore do lie.
  The barbel, than which fish a braver doth not swim,
  Nor greater for the ford within my spacious brim,
  Nor (newly taken) more the curious taste doth please
  The grayling, whose great spawn is big as any pease;

The perch with pricking fins, against the pike prepared,
As nature had thereon bestowed this stronger guard,
His daintiness to keep (each curoius palate's proof)
From his vile ravenous foe: next him I name the ruff,
His very near ally, and both for scale and fin,
In taste, and for his bait (indeed) his next of kin,
The pretty slender dare, of many called the dace,
Within my liquid glass, when Phœbus looks his face,
Oft swiftly as he swims, his silver belly shows,
But with such nimble flight, that ere ye can disclose
His shape, out of your sight like lightning he is shot;
The trout by nature marked with many a crimson spot,
As though she curious were in him above the rest,
And, of fresh-water fish, did note him for the best;
The roach, whose common kind to every flood doth fall;
The chub (whose neater name which some a chevin call),
Food to the tyrant pike (most being in his power),
Who for their numerous store he most doth them devour;
The lusty salmon then, from Neptune's watery realm,
When as his season serves, stemming my tideful stream,
Then being in his kind, in me his pleasure takes
(For whom the fisher then all other game forsakes),
Which, bending of himself to the fashion of a ring,
Above the forced wears, himself doth nimbly fling,
And often when the net hath dragged him safe to land,
Is seen by natural force to 'scape his murderer's hand;
Whose grain doth rise in flakes, with fatness interlarded,
Of many a liquorish lip, that highly is regarded.
And Humber, to whose waste I pay my watery store,
Me of her sturgeons sends, that I thereby the more
Should have my beauties graced with something from him sent:
Not Ancum's silvered eel excelleth that of Trent;
Though the sweet-smelling smelt be more in Thames than me,
The lamprey, and his lesse, in Severn general be;
The flounder smooth and flat, in other rivers caught,
Perhaps in greater store, yet better are not thought:
The dainty gudgeon, loche, the minnow, and the bleak,
Since they but little are, I little need to speak
Of them, nor doth it fit me much of those to reck,
Which everywhere are found in every little beck;
Nor of the crayfish here, which creeps amongst my stones,
From all the rest alone, whose shell is all his bones:
For carp, the tench, and bream, my other stores among,
To lakes and standing pools that chiefly do belong,
Here scouring in my fords, feed in my waters clear,
Are muddy fish, in ponds, to that which they are here."

But great as the praise is, which is justly due to the waters of Severn,
we would not think of recommending a metropolitan angler to pay it

an express visit. The river—and a noble one it is, especially for commercial and navigable purposes—is unquestionably interesting to the rod-fishers in the several localities on its banks, as it flows through Shropshire, Staffordshire, and Worcestershire to the ocean; but it does not possess those peculiarly interesting attributes which a purely fly-fishing river should have. Bottom-fishing, in all its forms and richness, is undoubtedly its staple angling commodity; although there are many spots upon its waters where the fly can be thrown with a fair chance of success.

Trout have been taken in the Severn of great weight; one we know of late years, by trolling, of twelve and a half pounds. The salmon are likewise very excellent in quality. Anglers on these waters recommend dark coloured flies, with gold tinselled bodies, as the most effective in these waters, more especially in the early sections of the fishing season. Trolling is more successful than the fly.

The Severn has a Welsh origin. It springs out of the vicinity of Mount Plinlimmon, and its primary feeders all unite at Llanidloes; from thence it pursues a very circuitous course to Shrewsbury. In this distance it runs for nearly one hundred miles, and here its waters are by far the best for rod-fishing. It likewise receives the waters of several tributaries. From Shrewsbury it continues its winding course, and receives the Tern at the foot of the Wrekin, about which it describes a semicircle; then curving repeatedly, it flows towards Colebrook Dale, from which it flows in a north-west direction to Tewkesbury. Within this section, besides inferior streams, the Severn receives the Teme at Worcester from the west; and the waters of the Avon, from the north-east, run into it at Tewkesbury. These several accessory waters augment its volume considerably. After turning to the south-west, it winds its way to the British Channel, receiving at its mouth the Wye from the north, and the Avon from the south-east. The entire course of the Severn is about three hundred and twenty miles; and for upwards of two hundred and thirty it is navigable.

The best bottom-fishing for carp, perch, roach, chub, and eels, is within those portions of the river appropriated to navigation. Grayling are to be met with in many parts of the Severn.

The tributaries of the river are to be preferred for fly-fishing. Many of them are excellent. The *Elun*, which passes Ludlow, is a great favourite with anglers in this part of England. So likewise are the *Wevel* and the *Carne*.

An angling tour to the Dee, in Cheshire, is generally a very pleasant and successful one. There is excellent fly-fishing for both trout and salmon in the river; and the town of Chester itself may be made one of its angling stations. It is better, however, to move upward. All the tributaries of the Dee are good trout streams. Fine baskets of fish are here taken every season; but much depends upon the state of both waters and weather. Trolling is practised to a considerable extent in the Dee; and flies of

every varied hue are used by the rod-fishers of the district, many
of whom are first-rate piscatorians. The higher waters of the
Dee belong to Denbighshire and Flintshire.

The *Weaver* runs through the chief districts of the county of
Cheshire, and has a number of feeders, in which there are both
salmon and trout. The principal of these are the *Peover*, the
Croke, and the *Walvarn*. The entire district of the Dee waters
contains a great number of skilful and enthusiastic anglers, who
are generally very ready to give a stranger any useful information
he may require. It is likewise a district readily accessible, and there
is every requisite accommodation for lodging and refreshments.

Turning our attention now to the west and south-west of
England, there are some admirable districts for fly-fishing. They
all lie more or less near some of the chief railway lines which
traverse the country in this direction. This affords the rod-fisher
the facility of choosing where to commence his amusement without much loss of time. The Great Western and the Southampton
Railways constitute the chief trunks of communication which
lead to most of these fishing waters.

In Buckinghamshire we have the *Thames*, the *Ouse*, the *Coln*, and
the *Wick*, in all of which there are trout of good size. The most
eligible station on the Ouse is about three miles above Bucking-
ham; and Bilbury and Barnsby are convenient spots for reaching
the Coln, in which there are fine trout. The Wick springs out of
the high grounds in the vicinity of West Wycombe, flows by High
Wycombe, and enters the Thames at Marlow. All these waters
in the summer season require fine tackle and light fishing. There
are large trout taken occasionally in the Wick. The waters are
preserved in several districts.

Passing on to Berkshire, we meet with the *Kennet*, the *Loddon*,
and the *Lamborne*. The first stream has its rise in the county of
Wilts, and enters the Thames at the town of Reading. It is
considered by many anglers as a very fine rod-fishing stream both
for the fly and for trolling. Hungerford is one of the stations on
its banks, which is sixty-five miles from London. Many of its
sections are preserved, and it requires interest and money to gain
access to them. The higher you ascend the Kennet the better is
the fly-fishing, and less restricted are its streams. After rains,
trolling is very successful.

The Loddon is of little repute, except for bottom fishing; and
the Lamborne has only a small sprinkling of trout.

A trip to Herefordshire will secure a fair share of sport. The
chief rivers are the *Wye*, the *Lug*, the *Monow*, the *Arrow*, the
Frome, and the *Teme*. The first named stream is abundantly
stocked with almost all kinds of fish. Beautiful salmon, salmon-
pinks, trout, grayling, and a few pike, perch, and dace. There are
many angling stations on its banks; but the best fly districts of
the stream lie between Hay and Builth. Some of the anglers who
frequent the river affirm that they have occasionally taken with

the rod one hundred pounds weight of salmon with the fly, exclusive of a fair proportion of good trout. But these exploits are not always to be implicitly relied on. Unquestionably the Wye stands high in piscatory repute; and an excursion along its banks cannot fail to prove a rich treat to any rod-fisher. The scenery in some parts of the river is beautiful.

The other rivers of the county we have just enumerated, partake very much of the same character with the Wye and tributaries to it. The rod-fishing is good, but some considerable sections of these waters are preserved, a circumstance which greatly impedes the movements and sours the temper of the tourist, when he has come from a distance on a random sort of visit.

The fishable rivers in Oxfordshire are the *Thames*, the *Isis*, the *Windrush*, the *Evenlode*, and the *Cherwell*. Father Thames becomes in this locality a more manageable stream for the rod, and he yields capital sport when the waters are in full order. The Isis, which forms an integral part of this famous river, springs out of the parish of Coates in Gloucestershire. It is of little repute for the scientific angler. Bottom-fishing is the staple commodity of the Oxfordshire craft.

The *Axe*, in Dorsetshire, is one of the finest of the rivers in this part of England for trout-fishing. It rises near Axeknoller, Beaminster, in this county, and flowing by the towns of Axminster and Colyton, falls into the Channel on the east coast of Devonshire. As a fishing stream it cannot be surpassed, either for the beauty of its scenery or the rippling pleasantness of its waters. There is a constant succession of fine streams and deep pools, and its gravelly bed is admirably fitted for the trout and salmon. There are likewise dace and eels in considerable numbers. Its waters are open to all anglers, and the absence of anything like troublesome brushwood adds greatly to the facility and ease of the rod-fisher's movements. It has suffered considerably from a lawless and reckless system of poaching, but this has been in some degree checked by an angling association formed at Crewkerne; by the rules of which the season commences on the 1st March, and ends on the 1st of October. This is a wise regulation. We have often thought and felt the force of the truth ourselves—that English rod-fishers should be very sparing of their trout-fishing even in the month of September; but, at any rate, the 1st of October is late enough. This, with other stringent regulations on the Axe, have made its waters once more a place where a good day's sport can be obtained by the honest and fair angler. The trout do not run very large, averaging about six to eight ounces; still this is no insignificant magnitude. The two principal fishing stations are Crewkerne for the higher sections of the water, and Axminster for the central and lower. But there is abundance of accommodation in every direction along the banks of this really beautiful and interesting stream.

The other rivers that run more less in this county, are the *Charr*

the *Eype*, the *Wey*, the *Froome*, and the *Stour*. There is fair fishing
with fly in most of them. The Stour is the largest stream, but is
navigable for two-thirds of its length, which is sixty-five miles;
and this, to our taste, spoils a river for comfortable rod-fishing with
the artificial fly. Commercial traffic and rippling and sparkling
streams are two incompatible things. Altogether, however, the
London angler will find Dorsetshire a most delightful locality for
his amusement; and the beauty of the scenery in the immediate
vicinity of its rivers, and the antiquarian remains to be found in
many directions, are great inducements at all times to an enlightened angler.

The county of Devonshire is calculated to afford the angling
tourist considerable sport. It has many first-rate waters, for both
salmon and trout, and is, in many other respects, one of the most
interesting localities in England. We have the *Tamer*, the *Plym*,
the *Yealme*, the *Avon*, the *Dart*, the *Ex*, the *Otter*, the *Syd*, the
Teign, the *Taw*, and the *Tarridge*. All these waters possess similar
angling capabilities. They all abound with rippling and purling
streams—such streams, in fact, as a rod-fisher feels a pleasure in
throwing a line upon. They all flow through a fine country, with
scenery rich and beautiful, and which fills the mind with gladness
and delight. There is a large portion of these waters of Devonshire free and open, and the preserved localities are only studded
here and there in the angler's path. The railway to Plymouth runs
through a considerable part of the county; but the rod-fishing
traveller will find it more to his advantage and comfort to depend
upon his pedestrian powers, for he then possesses a much greater
facility of moving from one river to another, and to fish the finest
of their streams, at the lowest cost of time and labour.

There are many kinds of flies which have a local reputation
among anglers in these waters, which are worthy of a stranger's
attention. These predilections are often founded upon fanciful
notions, and inaccurate observations; but it is not always advisable
to treat them with lightness or indifference. Men who fish particular waters have always a great advantage over one who pays
them but an occasional visit. As far as our own observation goes,
and from what we have gathered from other frequenters of these
Devonshire rivers, we are of opinion, that generally small sized flies
are required, and likewise fine tackle. The colour and make of the
fly is not so essential as its size. Trolling, in particular states of
the waters, is very successfully followed by the brethren of the
angle in this part of England.

Should the angler bend his steps towards the southern point of
the island, and visit the county of Cornwall, he will fall in with
fair streams. The chief of these are the *Tamer* (noticed under
Devonshire), the *Fowey*, the *Camel*, the *Fal*, and the *Looe*. There
are good salmon and trout in all these waters. The drake and
woodcock wings are very suitable here; and after May, the palmer-
flies. The country and scenery about this part of England is

exceedingly fine, and adds greatly to pleasures which a ramble with the rod is fitted to produce. The metropolitan traveller has now a ready access by railway through the heart of this county, so that he can branch off at any section of it to suit his convenience and fancy.

Monmouthshire has fair claims to the angler's notice. The chief rivers are the *Wye*, the *Monow*, the *Lug*, the *Usk*, the *Trothy*, and the *Gavenny*. We have alluded to the three first; the remaining three abound with a fair portion of salmon and trout, and are pleasant streams to perambulate. The flies commonly used here, are small, and the tackle must also be fine.

The Hampshire waters afford an agreeable ramble for the rod-fisher; both for their trouting qualities, and from their proximity to the metropolis. The chief streams of the county are the *Avon*, the *Anton*, the *Test*, and the *Itchin*.

The Avon springs out of moorish land several miles from Salisbury, and flowing past that town, Fordingbridge, and Ringwood, enters the sea at Christchurch. The rod-fishing in it is of high repute; but anglers have of late complained of its waters having suffered considerably from the ravages of the pike. What truth there may be in this, we have no means of ascertaining.

The Anton takes its origin about ten miles north-east of Andover. It is a favourite place for smallish trout, though occasionally, some of considerable weight have been taken out of its waters.

The Test rises out of the north-western section of the county, and falls into the Southampton water. It is a first-rate river of its class. Whitchurch, fifty-eight miles from London, is one of the chief fishing stations upon it for London sportsmen, Leave to fish has to be obtained, either from the person who keeps the inn, or from some of the neighbouring gentry. Stockbridge is another place of rendezvous for the anglers of this water. The streams of the Test are remarkably clear, and they require the finest tackle that can be obtained, and the lightest hand in throwing the fly. Unless these matters are religiously attended to, the rod-fisher need not visit the Test.

The Itchin, in many of its sections, is a good trout stream, but it demands very careful fishing. A style of angling, such as may be very proper, and successful too, in a mountain stream in Wales, or in the highlands of Scotland, will not do here. Great lightness of hand and the finest tackle are indispensable in this stream. Salmon are occasionally taken in it, but the trout is the staple commodity of its waters.

The rivers of Wiltshire will afford a good margin for piscatory sport. A ramble through the country with the rod is both pleasant and improving. Its chief rivers are the *Nadder*, the *Walley*, the *Bourne*, and the *Kennet*. All these waters contain trout, though not of a large size; and the country they flow through is often extremely beautiful and romantic. and leaves agreeable reminis-

cences on the mind of the tourist. Smallish flies and fine tackle
arc required, particularly when the rivers are low, and there is
little wind.   Small spider-flies are, in some streams, great favourites
with the local sportsmen of the district; the only drawback to
their use is, that we lose many of the fish from the very slender
hold such hooks have on their mouth. Some sections of these
waters are preserved.

The various rivers of Somersetshire and Warwickshire afford
good angling both with fly and the minnow. The *Avon* runs
through both counties, and is one hundred miles in length, and
presents to the sportsman a considerable variety of waters—some
for bottom-fishing and some for fly. It has likewise many tributaries : the *Swift,* the *Sow,* the *Leam,* the *Dene,* the *Stour,* and the
Arrow.   In the higher localities of the main river—from Milverton
to Rieton, or Woolston—the fly-fishing, in the early portion of the
season, is very excellent.   There are likewise many fish, though
small, in the feeders just named; and the country by their banks
is often very beautiful and imposing. The Avon is navigable to
Bath ; above this city it receives the waters of the *Frome,* and
Midford Brook, and likewise a stream called *Chew,* at Keynshaw.
There are likewise other small rivers in Somersetshire which afford
trouting sport.   The *Yow,* or *Yeo,* springs out of the slopes of the
Mendip Hills, and has a run of about fourteen miles.   The *Brue*
comes from the chalk-marl hills on the border of the county,
and after flowing through an interesting part of the country for the
distance of thirty miles, enters the estuary of the *Parret.* This
water is full fifty miles in length, and has several feeders in which
there is fair fly-fishing. The *Isle* and the *Cary* are the best reputed
of these; indeed, the numerous waters of these two counties
present a wide field to the rod-fisher, and will be found extensive enough to employ him for some weeks to do all their streams
anything like justice.

ANGLING RIVERS AND LAKES IN WALES.

Having now given as extended an account of the fishing localities
of England as our limits will permit, we shall direct the rod-fisher
to another choice district for the prosecution of his amusement,
namely, WALES. This is a first-rate fly-fishing country, both for
the salmon and trout; and it is now brought, by the modern
facilities of travelling, to within a few hours of the British metropolis.

Wales has been celebrated for hundreds of years for its fishing
resources.   In its history and early literature, we have often direct
allusions made to the subject. We find Taliesin, one of the Welsh
bards, who flourished about the sixth century, mentioning an
incident of his having been found by one of the fugitive princes in
a salmon weir ; and descants at some length on the singularity of

the circumstance. It would appear that the rents of many lands were held, to pay so much *in weight of salmon*. The following lines relate to the subject :—

> " In Gwyddno's *wear* was never seen
> As good as there to-night hath been.
> Fair Elphin, dry thy tearful face,
> No evil hence can sorrow chase :
> Though deeming thou hast had no gain,
> Griefs cannot ease the bosom's pain.
> Doubt not the great Jehovah's power,
> Though frail, I own a gifted dower ;
> From rivers, seas, and mountains high,
> Good to the good will God supply.
>
>   *   *   *   *   *   *
>
> " Though weak and fragile, now I'm found
> With foaming ocean's waves around,
> In retribution's hour I'll be
> Three hundred *salmons'* worth to thee.
> O Elphin ! prince of talents rare,
> My capture without anger bear :
> Though low within my net I rest,
> My tongue with gifted power is blest," &c.*

For many ages after this period, Wales was celebrated, both in prose and verse, for its angling capabilities, and for the number and excellent quality of the fish in its waters. Michael Drayton, in 1612, eulogizes in song the rivers of South Wales. In his descriptive poem of the country, he says,

> " That Remney, when she saw these gallant nymphs of Gwent
> On this appointed match were all so hotly bent,
> Where she of ancient time had parted as a mound,
> The Monumethian fields and Glamorganian ground,
> Intreats the Taff along, as gray as any glass ;
> With whom clear Cunno comes, a lusty Cambrian lass
> Then Elwy, and with her Ewenny holds her way,
> And Ogmore, which would yet be there as soon as they,
> By Avon called in ; when nimbler Neath anon
> (To all the neighbouring nymphs for her rare beauties known ;
> Besides her double head, to help her stream that hath
> Her handmaids, Melta sweet, clear Hepsey and Tragarth)
> From Brecknock forth doth break ; then Dulas, and Cleddaugh,
> By Morgany do drive her through her watery saugh ;
> With Tawy, taking part t' assist the Cambrian power :
> Then Lhu and Logor, given to strengthen them by Gower."

Up to the present hour Wales has maintained its ancient pisca-

---

* Stephen's Literature of the Cymry.

tory renown. Most English anglers who have visited it of recent years, speak highly of it, and contrast it favourably with any other portion of the British Isles.

In placing before the reader's attention a sort of running or statistical account of its rivers and lakes, it is of consequence, to the English tourist especially, that we arrange our remarks under the heads of the separate counties of Wales. The awkwardness of Welsh names, to most English and Scotch ears, renders this plan both requisite and useful. The country designations are familiar, but the town and river districts are not so.

FLINTSHIRE.

On the supposition that the rod-fisher purposes visiting North Wales first, and that he proceeds from England, there are two leading routes open to his choice—by Chester, and by Shrewsbury. Either of these main thoroughfares will bring him to the chief angling waters in this county; but that by Chester is much the nearest.

And here we may be allowed to observe at the outset, that there are two or three matters of some importance to all persons who travel in Wales, and which may require their attention. In the first place, in reference to an angler, if he wishes to fish the country properly, and to enjoy his tour, by cultivating along with his special amusement a love of the sublime and beautiful in scenery and landscape, he will do well to travel on foot. This is by far the most agreeable and independent method of skimming along the course of rivers, and getting through a great portion of fishing water in quick time. It very often happens, particularly in such a country as Wales, that two or more rivers are separated from each other only by a few miles, as the crow flies, but which would require a circuitous route of forty or fifty miles, either by horse or coach, ere they could be visited in succession. This is an important consideration; and the more the rod-fisher gets experienced in countries like Wales, the more will he find it administer to his profit and pleasure to cultivate his pedestrian powers. Walking gives a wonderful facility to angling amusements, by taking us out of beaten tracts, and enabling us to visit unfrequented waters.

The roads are generally good throughout Wales, especially in the northern section of it; and the inns, and places for refreshment, numerous, comfortable, and reasonable. There are mail and day coaches in many parts; as well as post-horses and cars. Guides are likewise to be had—by inquiring at the principal inns throughout the country—who are generally very steady, and rather intelligent men; and are often able to impart to the angler some useful information about the course of particular rivers, and the best localities for fishing them.

The chief fishing rivers in this county of Flintshire, are the *Clwyd*, the *Wheeler*, the *Dee*, the *Levion*, the *Elwy*, and *Allen*.

The river Clwyd enters into the Irish Channel, about twenty miles south of Liverpool. It has its source in Denbighshire, and has several small feeders, in which there is often good fishing in summer with the worm. The trout run larger in those sections of the main river that flow through Flintshire, than in its higher waters; and the salmon are more frequently caught near the ocean, than at any great distance from it. All kinds of flies, if of a suitable size, are eligible for this river.

If the rod-fisher has any taste for scenery, he will be highly gratified by the vale of the Clwyd. The entire landscape is very imposing. The space is filled with an agreeable variety of meadows, woods, and cottages; while on the one side we see the ocean, and on the other dark and retiring mountains. It is a mild and placid piece of scenery.

The waters of the Wheeler have a fair angling repute; and the portion of the *Dee* (which we have partially noticed under Cheshire), which runs through this county, is a first-rate locality for trout fishing. What is termed the Vale of the Dee, presents some beautiful landscapes, and is exceedingly interesting to all who are imbued with even the elements of artistic taste.

The streams Levion, Elwy, and Allen, are all fine fishing waters for fly; and their several banks are very romantic and interesting to the tourist.

DENBIGHSHIRE.

"O Denbigh, now appeare, thy turne is next,
I need no glass, nor shade to set thee out;
For if my pen doe follow plainest text;
And passe right way, and goe nothing about.
Thou shalt be knowne, as worthie well thou art,
The noblest soyle, that is in any part:
And for thy seate, and castle do compare,
With any one of Wales, what'ere they are."
The Worthies of Wales, 1852.

This county has no independent streams; what fishing waters are contained in it, of a running cast, are tributaries to other rivers. These dependent waters, though of a short range, contain a great many fish, and there is a fair proportion of sport to be obtained. There are several lakes, which are well stocked with trout, and other kinds of fish. There is the lake called *Llyn Alwen*, which forms the source of the river Allen; *Llwy Alet*, which is encircled by high, barren, and grotesque looking mountains. The lake called *Llyn Moclure*, is situated eight miles from Llanwist, situated on the eastern bank of the river Conway. There is good fishing in this sheet of water. There are likewise lake *Llyn Llymburn*, in the vicinity of Nant Llyn, *Chwth Llyan*, *Llyn Conway*, and *Llyn Serne*. In all these waters trout abound.

CAERNARVONSHIRE.

On account of the peninsular form of this Welsh county, the rivers have but a very limited range. The *Conway* takes its rise out of a large sheet of water, and is soon swelled into a considerable stream, by the accession of several feeders—the *Serw*, the *Clettwr*, and the *Avon Hwch* on the right; and the *Machno*, and the *Sedan* on the left. There is a fall in the river Machno of considerable elevation, which, when its waters are flooded, produces a very grand and romantic effect. There are also several rapids and falls in the Conway and the Sedan. After the junction of the latter stream, the Conway flows in a northern direction, and on its left bank receives the waters of the Llngwy, which spring from a high mountain called Carnedd. In this tributary there are some fine rod-fishing localities; and there are also a number of beautiful and interesting waterfalls, which give a peculiar interest to the scene. The Conway finally falls into the Irish Channel, under the walls of Conway Castle. Its course, in a straight line, is about thirty miles.

The *Glass Llyn* is considered one of the most romantic rivers in Wales; its scenery would of itself amply repay a long journey. There is a fall not any great distance from its source, of nearly three hundred feet, and below this there are many most delightful streams for the fly. The trout are both numerous and of good quality. Anglers have been known to kill in these waters, trout of four and five pounds weight. The river flows through Llyn Gwynan, and Llyn y Dinas, and has a run of about eighteen miles.

The *Gwrfai* springs out of the mountainous lands on the west side of the Great Snowdon. The *Seiante* rises nearly out of the same locality, and after passing through two lakes, empties its waters into the Menai at Caernarvon. This famous mountain gives rise, likewise, to the *Llynfi*, which flows into the Menai at Bangor. The average length of these several streams is about twelve miles. The trouting in them is very good, and their streams are of such a character as to make the angler's progress agreeable and pleasant.

Should the rod-fisher who visits these waters feel disposed, he has a good opportunity of visiting the summit of Snowdon. This is a great feat, and one which imparts a class of pleasurable feelings of their own kind. There are several different routes by which the summit can be reached; but the most convenient is that by Dolbadarn, in the Vale of Llanberis. The path of ascent is so gradual from this point of departure, that the tourist, if mounted on a Welsh pony, may ride to the very top of the mountain.

When the summit is gained, the view that bursts on the vision is magnificent and astounding. It is very extensive. From this point the eye is able to trace, on a bright day, part of the coast with the hills of Scotland; the high mountains of Ingleborough and Penygent, in Yorkshire; beyond these the mountains of Cumberland and Westmoreland; and, on this side, some of the hills of Lancashire. When the atmosphere is in its highest state of transparency, part of the county of Wicklow, in Ireland, becomes distinctly visible. The Isle of Man, and the surrounding mountains of Caernarvonshire and Merionethshire, all seem directly under the eye.

The view is vastly enhanced in scenic interest by many of the vales being exposed to the eye, which, by their freshness and verdure, relieve the dreary scene of wild and barren rocks. The number of lakes or pools within the range of the vision, amounting from thirty to forty, lend also a varied character to the prospect. The summit of this lofty hill—3,571 feet from the level of the sea—is, however, so frequently enveloped in clouds and mists, that, except when the weather is particularly favourable, the traveller may wait some time without meeting with a day sufficiently clear for his enterprise. When the wind is from the west, the summit is almost always completely covered with clouds; and at other times, even when the weather is considered usually fine, the mountain will often become suddenly enveloped with vapour, and will remain in that state for hours. Some tourists, however, seem to think that the prospects are the more interesting, because more varied, when the clouds just cover the summit. The following description of Snowdon, when seen in this state, is very accurate and forcible :—

" Now high and swift flits the thin rock along
Skirted by rainbow dies, now deep below
(While the fierce sun strikes the illumined top)
Slow sails the gloomy storm, and all beneath,
By vapourous exhalations hid, lies lost
In darkness; save at once where drifted mists,
Cut by strong gusts of eddying winds, expose
The transitory scenes.
Now swift on either side the gathered clouds,
As by a sudden touch of magic, wide
Recede, and the fair face of heaven and earth
Appears. Amid the vast horizon's stretch,
In restless gaze the eye of wonder darts
O'er the expanse; mountains on mountains piled,
And winding bays, and promontories huge,
Lakes and meandering rivers, from their source
Traced to the distant ocean."

There are various lakes in Caernarvonshire in which there is first-rate angling for trout, and many kinds of bottom fish. The names of the principal of these are—*Ogwen Lake, Lake of Cwm Idwel,* the *Llanberis Lakes,* the *Lakes of Nantle, Nant Gwynan, Llyn Cwellyn, Llyn Bachlwyd, Llyn Tal y Llyn,* and *Llyn Crafnaut*

Trolling with the minnow, or small trout, is sometimes very successful in capturing large trout, which have been taken sometimes out of these Welsh lakes, fourteen pounds weight. To those who are partial to lake fishing, these waters will afford an abundant source of amusement and sport.

MERIONETHSHIRE.

" And since each one is praised for her peculiar things,
So MERVINIA is rich in mountains, lakes, and springs;
And holds herself as great in her superfluous waste,
As others by their towns and fruitful tillage graced.
And therefore to recount her rivers, from their springs,
Abridging all delays, MERVINIA thus begins."—DRAYTON.

This is a very interesting county for the rod-fishing tourist. Its main streams are the *Dee*, the *Maw*, and the *Dovey*. We now arrive at the higher waters of the first, which we have already noticed, and they are most admirably suited to the fly-fisher. The scenery on its banks is very interesting, both to the artist and the sportsman. Before the Dee reaches Carwen, it receives a number of mountain streams, in all of which there is an abundance of small trout, which can be taken readily with worm in almost any state of the weather. The fish in these spots seem remarkably hungry.

The origin of the Maw lies in the centre of the county. From its first springs, and for a distance of ten miles, it is but a very slender stream. It is then joined by the *Llyn-ianduon*, which is about an equal length with itself. After this junction, the united waters mingle with the *Wnion*, which has a range of about twelve miles, and then the main river flows on to the sea. For fly-fishing, the angling in the Maw is better above the tide-way than below it. Fine large salmon are often captured with the rod, both in the river and its various feeders. There is good accommodation for the angler on its banks in every direction, and at a reasonable cost.

The Dovey is a stream of thirty miles in length, and springs out of the mountain range on the borders of the county. It winds its way through a very interesting and picturesque vale, to Cardigan Bay. It has some excellent fishing tributaries, as the *Trafalay*, the *Afon*, the *Dulas*, and the *Cwmcelle*. There is a wide range of admirable fishing water in this locality.

The Dovey, in the vicinity of Aberystwith, stands in high repute for its salmon-fishing. The best time, in the estimation of many anglers of great skill and experience, for throwing the fly for this fine fish, is after the Michaelmas floods. The heavy fish are said to take the fly greedily here in the month of October. The part of the river between St. John's Pool and Derwent Lassy, is a very favourite spot. One pound is charged for fishing one month, and five pounds for the season. The Coch-y-bondu, and the black and red hackles, are held in much esteem in this section of the Dovey.

The town of Dolgelly is situated on the banks of the river *Avonvawr*, which winds a devious course through a mass of rude and peaked rocks of great altitude. The scenery about this place fills the mind with associations of loneliness and awe. The fishing is good; and many dozens of trout can be readily taken in a few hours. The fish are small.

The travelling rod-fisher should suspend his amusement for a few hours, and pay a visit to the great Cader-Idris, the second mountain, in point of altitude, in Wales. The most convenient place of ascent is from Dolgelley. To the left of the road from this place to Towyn, and at about three miles distance from it, a small gate leads to a narrow lane. This is the starting point. This ascent, to within two hundred yards of the summit, may be made with a pony.

When the full height is attained, the eye will have the range of a circumference of full five hundred miles. On the north-east, the tourist will see Ireland, Snowdon, and the other mountains of Caernarvonshire, the Isle of Man, the town of Chester, Wrexham, and Salop; the painted head of Wrekin, and the undulating tops of the Clee Hills. To the south lie stretched out Clifton, Pembrokeshire, St. David's, and Swansea—on the west the vast prospect of the British Channel. In addition to all those distant objects, we see, lying as it were at our feet, a countless number of mountains, lakes, rivers, harbours, towns, villages, and country-seats, scattered with fascinating effect over the extensive prospect.

There are several important lakes in Merionethshire, from a visit to which the angler will be much gratified. The chief of these are *Bala Lake*, one of the largest sheets of water in Wales, being about four miles in length, by one in breadth. It abounds with pike, trout, eels, perch, and roach. *Tal-y-Llyn*, is a beautiful piece of water; and the scenery about is very romantic. There are still water fishing localities, called *Llyn Bodlyn*, near Barmouth, *Llyn Cwm Howel*, *Llyn Irddin*, *Llyn Raithlyn*, *Llyn Pair*, *Llyn Treweryn*, *Llyn Arenniag*, *Llyn Gewirw*, and several other sheets of water, all fully supplied with trout, pike, and other bottom fish.

MONTGOMERYSHIRE.

' Ever charming, ever new,
When will the landscape tire the view!
· The fountain's fall, the river's flow,
The woody valleys, warm and low,
· The windy summit, wild and high,
Roughly rushing on the sky!
The pleasant seat, the ruined tower,
The naked rock, the shady bower;
The town and village, dome and farm,
Each give each a double charm,
As pearls upon an Ethiop's arm."—DYER.

The principal streams in this Welsh county are the *Severn*, the *Vrynwy*, and the *Tenat*. There are, besides, several other good fishing waters, which, indeed, are excellent in every locality in this county. The Severn, in these its Welsh grounds, has lost its sluggish and puddled appearance, and is now a bright and limpid stream. It is here well stocked with trout, and has fewer of its bottom-fishing occupants.

The Vrynwy springs out of a wild district on the confines of the county, and has a great number of dependent feeders; the principal of which are the *Eunant*, the *Afon*, the *Gedis*, the *Afon Gynnan*, the *Glasgwn*, and the *Cown*. These undoubtedly constitute a considerable range of the waters, and all well adapted for the fly, and some for trolling as well. After the main river receives all these tributaries, it flows a south-easterly course for twenty miles, and then receives the waters of the *Twrch*, which flows a distance of twenty miles, through a very interesting section of the county. This tributary itself has good angling feeders, capable of affording fair sport with the rod. The Vrynwy likewise receives the *Cain*, and, a little further down, the *Tenat*, both of which contain good fish. The Tenat itself is fed by several good streams; as the *Rhaiadr*, the *Afon Harrog*, and the *Ymrch*. Here there is good fly-fishing. All these waters, large and small, are bright, sparkling, and flowing; and have that peculiar form of stream which indicates good sport.

As to the colour of the fly requisite in these mountain streams, little need be said. In fact, when the fish are in humour, and they are not here capricious, they seem to snatch at anything in the shape of an insect. Very large flies will not, however, answer well.

The lakes in this county are *Llyn y Bugail*, long celebrated for its fine and large trout, some having been taken out of it of late years, full fourteen pounds in weight; *Llyn-y-Grinwydden*, which contains only eels and carp; *Llyn Cudwiw*, a good trolling water for both trout and pike; and *Glass-Llyn*, which contains an abundance of red and common trout.

We have hitherto been sketching the chief angling streams in North Wales, we shall now direct attention to those in the southern side of the country, and shall take our point of departure from the south-west section of England.

CAERMARTHENSHIRE.

Passing then from the English border, we enter this county, and among its angling streams of note, are the *Towy*, the *Tave*, the *Great Gwendraeth*, the *Llynougher*, and the *Teivi*. This is a comparatively level county, but the scenery in it is very grand and imposing. A ramble through it with the rod, is a great treat.

The river Towy springs out of some wild and morass districts at one extremity of the county. As the river flows southward it receives the waters of several feeders, which are all fishable, and several of them yield no small portion of sport, especially to the worm-fisher. When the Towy reaches Llandovery, it receives the waters of the *Braen*, and *Gwydderig*, in which there is good trouting, both with the fly, and by trolling. As the main river winds its course through the mountain defiles, the eye of the tourist will fall upon many spots of great beauty and sublimity. He may, perchance, see the glen—called by the Welsh *Cwm*—of an awful depth, whose edges and rugged descents are luxuriantly clothed with fine timber, that starts with a kind of wild disorder from the crevices of the rocks, where a scanty covering of soil has afforded it sufficient nourishment. This wooded tissue spreads its expansive branches over the chasm, and casts a sullen, dark, and dismal gloom upon the recess below. It is in vain that the eye attempts to trace out the current of the stream with any degree of distinctness; it raves and howls among the rocks at the bottom, but cannot be recognized. At every step its ceaseless repercussions swell more loudly upon the ear, still its waters are hidden; the thickets overspread them, save only at some faint openings where their whitened foam emerges for a moment to the open day, and then passes on and is lost; shrinking in hollow tumult among the rocks and trees that lie scattered in the depths of the terrific chasm. Such scenes as these are constantly to be met with in this land of wilds and mountains.

The river Tave takes its origin from Pembrokeshire, in a district east of the Percelly Mountain. Its banks in many places are most beautifully wooded. It receives several tributary waters, and when it reaches the picturesque village of St. Clears, it is augmented by the streams of the *Cathgenny* and *Cowin*, which spring out of the mountainous grounds in the north of the county. There is good trout-fishing here at all seasons when fish of any kind can be taken by the rod. The main river is navigable to St. Clears, and flows into Caermarthen Bay, a little below the town of Langharne, after running a course of twenty-eight miles.

The stream called the *Great Gwendraeth* is about fifteen miles in length: it springs out of the hilly districts which divide the county from Glamorganshire. There is fair sport—not of first-rate character—in this water at particular seasons of the year.

What are called the Black Mountains give rise to the *Llougher*. It is a rapid stream, and has several feeders, in which there are numbers of small and rather poor trout. It has a course of thirty miles, and falls into the bay of Caermarthen.

The *Llynvan* lake is a place of repute: it is situated at the base of the loftiest section of the Black Mountain, designated the *Van*, or *Beacon*. This sheet of water is about a mile in length, and has fine trout and a large quantity of eels. The scenery about its margins is solitary, naked, and dreary, but still interesting, when contrasted with the highly cultivated districts seen in the distance. The most eligible roads for ascending this singular mountain are from Llandovery and Devynock, near Brecknock.

RADNORSHIRE.

"Oh, sylvan Wye! thou wanderer through the woods,
How often has my spirit turned to thee!
Once again I see these hedgerows, hardly hedgerows now,
Little lines of sportive wood run wild; these pastoral forms,
Green to the very door; and wreaths of smoke,
Sent up in silence from among the trees.
With some uncertain notice, as might seem
Of vagrant dwellers in the houseless woods,
Or of some hermit's cave, where, by his fire,
The hermit sits alone."—WORDSWORTH.

This is a favourite county for the angling sportsman. It has many waters of great repute; among these the *Wye* stands predominant. It rises from Plymlimmon; and after a run of eighteen miles, enters Radnorshire on the north-west. It forms the boundary between this county and Breconshire, and at the village of Rydspence is the line of separation between Radnorshire and Herefordshire. The most romantic route, connected with the angling of the Wye, is in re-crossing the river from Chepstow to Newport, near the Forest of Dean. There is everything here to gratify the lover of fine scenery.

The *Ithon* springs out of Montgomeryshire, and falls into the Wye seven miles above the town of Biulth. This feeder has a run of thirty miles. There are good trout in it, and fly-fishing can be obtained without restriction in almost all its localities.

There are likewise a number of smaller streams in this county, in which there is fair fishing; but the fish run small. The names of these are the *Somergil*, the *Edw*, the *Marteg*, the *Clywedag*, the *Arrow*, and the *Bach-wy*. There is good rod-fishing in all these waters, and on their banks are many spots of great rural loveliness and beauty.

The lakes of this county are *Llyn Gwyn*, near to Rhaider; *Llyn Llanidin*, about a mile in circumference, full of fine trout; *Llyn Bychllin*, near Pauiscastle; *Llyn Gwingy*, on the borders of Cardiganshire; and *Llyn Hardwell*, in the vicinity of Old Radnor. Trout, eels, perch, dace, pike, &c., are the standard commodities in these collections of still water.

CARDIGANSHIRE.

This is a good salmon and trout district. The principal rivers are the *Tyvy*, the *Rydal*, the *Istwith*, the *Towey* (already mentioned), and the *Claerwen*. All these varied waters are open to the angler, and he will find them, in the proper season, calculated to furnish him with ample amusement.

The salmon-leap on the Tyvy has been an object of interest for many centuries. Michael Drayton sings of it 250 years ago:—

" When as the salmon seeks a fresher stream to find,
Which hitherto, from the sea, comes yearly by his kind,
So he in season grows, and stems the watery tract,
Where Tivy falling down doth make a cataract,
Forced by the rising rocks that there her course oppose,
As though within their bands they meant her to inclose.
Here, when the labouring fish doth at the foot arrive,
He finds that by his strength but vainly he doth strive;
His tail takes in his teeth: and, bending like a bow
That's to the compass drawn, aloft himself doth throw;
Then springing at his height, as doth a little wand,
That, bended end to end, and flirted from the hand,
Far off itself doth cast; so doth the salmon vault:
And if at first he fail, a second somersault
He instantly essays; and from his nimble wing
Still gerting, never leaves until himself he fling
Above the streamful top of the surrounding heap."

The Rydal is a stream held in great repute by those anglers who
have frequented its waters. It is, in point of bold scenery, one of
the most interesting streams of the whole country.

There are other smaller stretches of water in which rod-fishing
can be fully enjoyed; but the fish in them are mostly very small.
These are the *Arth*, the *Ayton*, the *Wirrai*, and the *Leri*. Still-
water fishing in this country may be found in the Llyn Teivi, as
well as in some smaller collections of water in its immediate
vicinity. There are also *Lake Maes, Berwyn, Llyn Hir,* and *Llyn
Aeddwear,* all having more or less of red trout.

BRECKNOCKSHIRE.

The chief rivers of this county are the *Usk* and the *Wye;* the
latter we have already noticed. The Usk is a first-rate salmon
and trouting river. More than three centuries ago the salmon of
this river were held in high repute.

" Great store of fish is caught within this flood.
* * * * * * * *

A thing to note, when sammon failes in Wye,
(And season there; goes out as order is)
Than still of course, in Oske doth sammon lye,
And of good fish, in Oske, you shall not mis,
And this seemes straunge, and, doth through Wales appeere
In some one place, are sammons all the yeere.
So fresh, so sweet, so red, so crimp withal,
That man might say, ' Loe! sammon here at call.' "—1555.

The lakes of this country are *Welshpool, Pwll Bixery,* and *Llyn
Vawr.*

PEMBROKESHIRE.

The fishing rivers are but few in number in this county, and of no great note. The *Eastern Cleddy* rises in the mountainous districts, and the *Western Cleddy* from the vicinity of St. Catherine's. The Nezern is a good angling stream. There are likewise the *Gwayn*, and the *Solva*.

GLAMORGANSHIRE.

There are many good waters in this part of Wales. The *Romney*, the *Taff*, and its tributaries, the *Ogmore*, the *Daw*, and the *Avon*, with its feeders, are all well stocked with trout and salmon. The lakes in this part are not worth naming.

CHAPTER VII.

SCOTLAND.

SCOTLAND is a peculiarly interesting section of Britain to the rod-fisher. It is interesting in some essential points. It has almost a boundless range of angling waters; it is an almost entirely free country to move and rove about in with the rod; and it has some of the wildest and most sublime scenery of which this, or perhaps any other country can boast. These are some of the leading features of this piscatory land, calculated to solicit the attention of the rod-fishing tourist, and to induce him to take a ramble through such a district for the full and effective indulgence of his favourite sport. The majority of anglers in England know scarcely anything of the feeling of independence and the hilarity of spirit which glow in the bosom of the Scottish angler, who can go over hundreds of miles, and ramble from the banks of one stream to another, without ever dreaming of any one asking him, "Whither goest thou?"

We regret to have to premise at the outset, that the number of sporting waters is so great, that it is impossible, in our limited space, to do anything like individual justice to them in the way of description. We are compelled to offer a mere rough and general sketch of the principal of them, but which will, we hope, have the good effect of inducing the anglers of England to migrate for a season to Scotland, so that they may be in a position to judge of the country and its fishing resources for themselves. We can assure them they will not be disappointed.

There are various leading routes for reaching some of the main rivers of Scotland. Whether a tourist goes by railway or by sea, makes a considerable difference. The latter mode of travelling is more confined and local. We cannot, however, shape our remarks and instructions so as to meet all circumstances and contingencies; therefore we are under the necessity of treating the subject very generally, and with the chief view of drawing the reader's attention to the best angling localities of the country.

For the sake of arrangement, we shall divide the whole of Scotland into two leading portions: that which lies south of the Forth and the Clyde, or which lies between an imaginary straight line drawn from Edinburgh to Glasgow, and that portion which is situated north of these respective localities. This division will present to us two different classes of fishing waters, and, in many respects, two different orders of rural scenery. We shall call the one the *south division*, and the other the *north division*.

THE SOUTH DIVISION.

Supposing the angler makes his way by the London and North-Western Railway, or by any other route, to the City of Carlisle, he will here find two main trunk lines from this place to Glasgow, each running near to, or right through a wide expanse of fishing waters. The one line takes him by the Clyde and its chief feeders, and the other by some of the main waters of Dumfriesshire. These two routes require separate notices.

If the tourist fixes on the Clyde and its chief dependencies, he will have to go by the Caledonian Railway as far as the *Elvinfoot* station, where he will meet with the river close at hand. There is an inn here for refreshments, and it is a convenient spot to ascend the river to its highest springs. It takes a sudden bend here, and winds its course among a mass of romantic and wild hills and morasses. The waters from Elvinfoot to the primary rivulets of the river, are full of fine trout; and there is a splendid fly-fishing range of many miles in extent. The streams are numerous and rippling, and are beautifully fitted to aid the deceptions of the artificial fly.

The railway runs close by the banks of the river from this station, to within three or four miles of the famous Falls of the Clyde, which commence above the town of Lanark. As there are stations every three or four miles along this route, the rod-fisher has every possible facility for throwing his line upon any section of the stream he may fancy. There is no wood to obstruct his operations, and he will find a succession of fine streams and deep pools in every part of his progress.

The trout found in these portions of the Clyde waters are of very good quality, but they do not run large; though, occasionally, there have been some singularly heavy fish taken, chiefly by trolling, out of streams in the vicinity of the village of Coulter, of full ten pounds weight. The best trout are unquestionably taken with the natural minnow in these waters; and this bait has become of late years quite popular among the mass of Clydesdale rod-fishers. There are no salmon, nor salmon-trout, in these portions of the river. The *Falls* effectually prevent their ascending higher up than a few miles below Lanark. The flies in general use here have light brown wings, and black or red bodies; but the trout are not at all fastidious on this point.

The rod-fishing is interrupted by the *Falls*, which are objects well worthy of a visit from the tourist. Below them, good fishing again commences, and continues down to within three miles of Glasgow Bridge. As the angler descends the river from below the Falls, he will find its bed becoming constantly enlarged, so that he has a difficulty of realizing the breadth of the stream in many directions. To fish this portion of water, *wading* is requisite; but this we do not take upon us to recommend.

There are no tributaries of the Clyde of so much fishing repute as to induce the tourist to turn aside from the main stream. If he fishes it properly from its source to the confines of Glasgow, he will find the range of waters very interesting, and capable of affording him ample sport.

We must now turn aside in another direction, and place the rod-fisher down on the banks of the *Tweed;* one of the noblest fishing streams in Europe.

> Along the silver banks of Tweed,
> 'Tis blythe the mimic fly to lead,
> When to the hook the salmon springs,
> And the line whistles through the rings
> The boiling eddy sees him try,
> Then dashing from the current high;
> Till watchful eye, and cautious hand,
> Have led his wasted strength on land."
>
>   *Glasgow*, 1826.

The Tweed has a fishable range of about sixty miles, and is perfectly free for the fly, or bait, from its source to its mouth at Berwick. It can be approached by several routes; but we should give the preference to any of them that would enable the angler to fish it from its highest waters downwards to the sea. To follow this river with the rod to its full extent, is one of the most delightful tours that any sportsman can take. In accordance with this suggestion, we shall shape our descriptions of its waters, under the impression that this tour will be taken in the way and manner we have pointed out.

The Tweed springs out of the same mountain that gives birth to the Clyde, and the River Annan, which flow into the Western Ocean. And it is worthy of passing remark, that should the angler be upon the Clyde at Elvinfoot, or within a few miles of that station, he may find his way to the higher streams of the Tweed, by a walk of from six to ten miles. Many travelling anglers from the south take this route. They fish the higher waters of the Clyde; and when they wish for a change of scene, strike over the mountain passes, and make their way to the Tweed.

The Tweed becomes fishable at a place called Tweedshaws; the stream, however, runs small here; when it arrives at the Crook Inn, it assumes a broader and fuller appearance, and good fly-fishing may be said to commence at this station. From here, down to the town of Peebles, there is a regular succession of fine streams and stretches of deep water, to which no pen can do anything like justice in the way of description. There are numerous places for temporary refreshment within this distance.

Between the source of the Tweed and Peebles, there are three tributary streams, the *Biggar Water*, the *Lyne*, and the *Manor*. There is good fishing in these when the waters are in fair order.

From Peebles to Kelso the Tweed increases in bulk considerably; and here the salmon, and the salmon trout, are to be met with in much greater quantities than in the higher portions of the water. In this section of the main river there is splendid fishing, and a regular succession of very beautiful landscapes, which cannot fail to gratify the man who has a taste for rural scenery. There are three great tributaries to the Tweed, between Peebles and Kelso, which the angler should visit, because they are not only splendid trouting waters, but they are closely connected with many historical events of the kingdom. These are the *Ettrick*, the *Yarrow*, and the *Teviot*.

To reach the two first streams, the traveller should make his way to the town of Selkirk. This will bring him to the Yarrow at once, and within three or four miles of the Ettrick, which falls into the Yarrow a little above this town. The Ettrick is a fine trouting river, and an extremely interesting one to a contemplative pedestrian who may ramble down its banks. The trout here are very numerous, and readily take any fly when in the humour. There are likewise some lakes in this vicinity in which there are fine large trout, pike, and other bottom fish.

A ramble up the Yarrow from Selkirk is delightful. It flows through St. Mary's Loch, which the tourist should visit. This sheet of water, which is full of fine large trout, is graphically described by Sir Walter Scott, in his " Marmion."

"Lone St. Mary's silent lake.
. . . . . . Nor fen nor sedge
Pollute the pure lake's crystal edge.

Abrupt and sheer the mountains sink
At once upon the level brink;
And just a trace of silver sand
Marks where the waters meet the land,
For in the mirror bright and blue
Each hill's huge outline you may view,
Shaggy with heath but lonely bare;
Nor tree, nor bush, nor brake is there,
Save where of land yon slender line
Bears 'thwart the lake the scattered pine.
Yet even this nakedness has power,
And aids the feelings of the hour;
Nor thicket, dell, nor copse you spy,
Where living thing concealed might lie.
There's nothing left to fancy's guess:
You see that all is loneliness.
And silence aids: though the steep hills
Send to the lake a thousand rills,
In summer-tide so soft they weep
The sound but lulls the ear asleep;
Your horse's hoof-tread sounds too rude,
So stilly is the solitude."

The Teviot is a large river, and runs through almost the entire
extent of Roxburghshire. It is a fine fishing stream, and it has
many tributaries, such as the *Allan*, the *Slitrig*, the *Jed*, and the
Kale, in which there is an abundance of trout. The Teviot enters
the Tweed about a mile above the town of Kelso.

From Kelso to Berwick, a distance of about twenty miles, and
which can now be traversed by railway, there are many splendid
fishing stations, where both salmon and trout can be readily
captured with the fly. The most important feeder to the chief
river, within this distance, is the river *Whitadder*, which enters it
about five miles west of Berwick. This is a much frequented
river by North of England anglers, who find an abundance of sport
in its waters during the whole of the fishing season. The trout
are numerous, though not of very good quality; and there is a fair
sprinkling of salmon during the angling months.

We shall now take our leave of this most interesting river, with
the insertion of the following beautiful lines, written by a lady,
and published in "Blackwood's Magazine," about twenty years
ago :—

"Roll on, bright Tweed, roll on,
    And let thy waters be
A tribute to the many waves
    Of dark and heaving sea!
Many clear, winding streams
    On thy broad bosom meet,

And the sea with gentle murmurings
  Their mingled tides will greet.
Roll on then, Tweed, until they be
Lost in the waves of the deep, dark sea.

"Thy banks are rich and fair,
  Thy woods wave green and wild,
And thou bearest many a roving rill,
  The distant mountain's child.
Roll on then, kingly river,
  By castle, hall, and tower—
By palace proud and lowly cot—
  By greenwood, glen, and bower.
Roll on, roll on, until ye gain
  The wild waves of the restless main.

"As by thy sun-lit waters
  With wandering eyes I stand,
And gaze on all the varied scenes
  Of this fair, pleasant land,
I think—bright flowing river—
  How much has come and gone
While on thy wide and winding path
  Thou hast been rolling on;—
Still rolling on, unchanged and free,
  To the bounding waves of the deep, dark sea.

"How many eyes are closed in death,
  How many hearts are cold,
How many youthful forms have sunk
  Before the gray and old—
How many in these scattered homes
  Have come and passed away,
Fleeting and fair, as the bright sun's beam,
  Or like the meteor's ray—
Whose course through time passed on like thee
  To the billows of eternity!

"Peace be to thy blue waters,
  As with gentle song they flow;
Light be the breath of the whispering winds
  When on thy shores they blow.
May the blue sun's dancing rays
  On thy rippling wavelets gleam,
And gladsome be thy pilgrimage,
  Thou brightly flowing stream!
Roll on in beauty till ye gain
  The white waves of the restless main."

L

If the tourist direct his steps from Berwick towards the Scottish capital, there are few intervening rivers that are worthy of his time and attention. What rivulets there are in this direction are small, and the trouting in them both inferior and uncertain. And the same remarks may be applied to the running streams between Edinburgh and Glasgow. They have all only a local repute, and we need not notice them further.

There is, however, another great batch of fine waters, which lie in the south-western portion of Scotland. These can be approached either by Glasgow or from Carlisle. Should the rod-fisher set out on this tour from the last city, he must make his way to the river Annan, which flows by the town of the same name, and which is a tolerably good river, though not, in our humble opinion, of a first-rate character. To fish its higher streams, the station of Wympray, on the Caledonian railway, is the most convenient. The stream can then be fished down to the town of Annan; where the tourist will find a ready conveyance to take him forward to the river Nith, at Dumfries, an excellent fishing locality. It contains both salmon and trout, and has a range of waters full one hundred miles in extent. It is navigable for small vessels below the town of Dumfries. The vale through which it flows is called Nithdale, and possesses rural scenery of great beauty and magnificence. The highest waters of the stream lie above the town of Sanquhar, which is a good and central situation for the rod-fisher, as he has here the command of several waters that are connected with, and tributary to the main river. The *Crawick Water*, the *Kello Water*, the *Euchan*, the *Ken*, the *Scar*, and the *Cluden Water*, are all feeders of the Nith, and abound with fish of considerable size and good quality. Indeed several of these dependent streams are held in higher piscatory repute than even the principal river itself. There are several lochs in this vicinity which are much frequented by anglers; they contain large trout, pike, bream, roach, perch, chub; and in one called *Castle Loch*, there is a scarce fish, called the *vendace*, which is much sought after. There is a club of anglers in Dumfries who award annual prizes for the taking of this fish. It is said to be known nowhere else, and is of such a delicate organization, that all attempts to transport it to other waters have proved abortive. "It is a beautiful fish, from four to six inches in length, and of a bright silvery appearance, with a slight tendency to a light blue along the back and sides. Upon the top of the head there is a very delicate shape of a heart, covered with a transparent substance of a brownish colour, resembling a thin lamina of mica slate, through which the brain is visible. Nothing to the naked eye is found in the stomach, though a late inquirer has said that their food consists of incredibly minute entromostracea. Overlooking the fact that the vendace dies the moment it is touched or brought to the air, and has hitherto defied transportation, the common people speak of its having been brought by the Jameses from Vendois, in France."

Speaking generally, there cannot be a more agreeable angling tour than along the banks of the Nith and its feeders. There are all kinds of water, and all kinds of scenery. The fishing, on the whole, is excellent. The flies in ordinary use here, are just of the ordinary kind; nor does there seem to be any very special favourites. Trolling is practised to some extent with the natural minnow, and with considerable success. To those sportsmen who like a day or two's bottom-fishing now and then, there is ample room for indulging their fancy. Places of refreshment are to be met with here and there; but in wandering along the higher waters of the Nith, these become both less frequent and of a meaner kind.

When the angler is at Dumfries, there is an extensive and somewhat wild district of fishable grounds lying to the west, and which goes under the general name of Gallowayshire. There is a number of small, but interesting streams issuing out of these mountain passes, which are full of small trout, with a fair sprinkling of salmon. All these running waters empty themselves into the Solway Firth, and have a range of from fifteen to twenty-five miles from the sea. There are no railways in this direction; but there is a mail coach which travels from Dumfries to Port Patrick by the sea-side route—a distance of about one hundred miles. This the tourist can avail himself of if he chooses. But the best method of angling these Gallowayshire waters, is by traversing the country on foot, going from river to river, and from loch to loch. The country is then seen in all its wild freshness and sublimity; and unfrequented waters are met with, where the angling proves very successful, and redolent of genuine sport. The chief rivers in this part of Scotland are the *Urr*, which rises in Kirkcudbright-shire, the *Dee*, the *Cree*, the *Minnick*, the *Fleet*, and the *Stinchar*. These are all prolific streams, and they have each tributary waters, enjoying as great an angling repute as themselves.

The loch-fishing in this vicinity is likewise good. The lochs of *Grannoch, Darnal, Glento*, and *Roan*, contain large trout and pike; and so likewise do *Loch Brack*, and *Barscobe, Honie*, and *Skae*.

When the rod-fisher has finished his Galloway ramble, if he turn the corner of the Peninsula, and direct his steps north towards Glasgow, he will find several rivers of some note in his route. The first is the *Girvan*, which springs partly out of a loch called Spalander, in which there are very large trout. The banks of the Girvan have been long celebrated for their singular beauty. Burns sings of "Girvan's fairy-haunted stream." There is good fly-fishing in it. The *Doon* and its feeders enjoy a high repute for sport. All these waters, and the localities adjoining them, have been rendered famous by the genius of Robert Burns. The lochs in this neighbourhood are full of trout, pike, perch, dace, chub, and the like.

The river *Ayr* springs out of the hills, in the vicinity of Muirkirk, and has a run of thirty miles. There is good fishing in it, as well as in its feeders, the *Garpel,* the *Greenock,* the *Lugar,* and the *Coyle*.

The entire valley of the Ayr is remarkably beautiful and interesting; and the interest which a tourist feels in passing through it is greatly enhanced by the recollection of its being the birth-place of Burns, and where he spent the larger half of his existence. It was at Mauchline, near the river Ayr, that he first saw his "Highland Mary," of whom he beautifully sings—

> "Ye banks, and braes, and streams around
>   The Castle o' Montgomerie,
> Green be your woods and fair your flowers,
>   Your waters never drumlie.
> There summer first unfaulds her robes,
>   And there they langest tarry,
> For there I took my last farewell
>   Of my sweet Highland Mary.

> "How sweetly bloomed the gay green birk,
>   How rich the hawthorn's blossom,
> As underneath the fragrant shade
>   I clasped her to my bosom."

＊　　＊　　＊　　＊　　＊

Proceeding towards the city of Glasgow, the angler will meet with the river *Irvine,* and its feeder, the *Cessnock.* These are not of any moment. The river *Garnock* springs from some high grounds in the neighbourhood of Lochs Kilbirnie and Castlesample, in both of which there are large trout, perch, and pike. This river is augmented by four tributaries; the *Rye,* the *Caaf,* the *Dusk,* and the *Lugton.* There are small trout in all these waters.

In Renfrewshire, we have the *White* and *Black Cart,* and the *Gryf.* There are likewise several lochs in this locality tolerably stocked with trout, pike, perch, bream, eels, &c. The chief of these are *Loch Goin, Brother Loch, Black Loch, Long Loch.* There are char in some of these still sheets of water.

THE NORTH DIVISION.

We have now run over the chief rivers and lochs of the south division of Scotland, and we purpose commencing a like ramble over those of the north division. This, however, is no very easy task, looking at the limited space we have to devote to the matter; for the angling waters are here so numerous, and all so interesting, that an entire volume devoted to the subject could scarce suffice to do them anything like ample justice.

To reach the main fishing waters in the heart of the country, as well as those situated in remote Highland districts, we have both railway and steam-boat conveyances, very conveniently directed to most of the popular and fashionable places of resort for sporting tourists. Edinburgh and Glasgow are both good localities from which to make a start into the "Land o' cakes." Commencing, however, with the great facilities which the Clyde navigation affords to the rod-fisher, and the regular and direct transit which characterises all its ordinary movements, we can place the angler on the banks of some of the charming mountain streams in a very short space of time.

An angler placing himself in one of the Clyde steamers, may reach Dumbarton, or the banks of the river *Leven*, in an hour. This water runs out of Loch Lomond. This stream has been immortalized by Smollet, who was born and educated on its banks, in an ode which is justly considered one of the finest in our language.

> "On Leven's banks, while free to rove,
> And tune the rural pipe to love,
> I envied not the happiest swain
> That ever trod the Arcadian plain.
> Pure stream! in whose transparent wave
> My youthful limbs I wont to lave;
> No torrents strain thy limpid source,
> No rocks impede thy dimpling course,
> That sweetly warbles o'er its bed
> With white, round, polished pebbles spread.
> While lightly poised the scaly brood
> In myriads cleave thy crystal flood:
> The springing trout in speckled pride,
> The salmon, monarch of the tide,
> The ruthless pike, intent on war,
> The silver eel, and mottled par
> Devolving from thy parent lake,
> A charming maze thy waters make,
> By bowers of birch, and groves of pine,
> And edges flowered with eglantine.
> Still on thy banks so gaily green
> May numerous flocks and herds be seen,
> Attentive, then, to this informing lay,
> Read how he dictates as he points the way.
> Trust not at first a quick adventurous pace,
> Six miles its top points gradual from the base.
> Up the high rise with panting haste I passed,
> And gained the long laborious steep at last."

The Leven is about seven miles in extent, and there is generally very fair fishing in it; but it is not a spot to tarry long at. *Loch Lomond*, a celebrated sheet of water, contains many fish, but to angle in it requires a local knowledge of the water, which a stranger has not. It has many tributaries in which there is good trouting; namely, the *Fruin*, the *Gudrick*, the *Douglas*, the *Luss*, the *Finlass*, the *Glenfalloch*, and the *Inveruglass*. The trout in all these feeders run very small, though they are very numerous.

When the angler is at Dumbarton or its neighbourhood, we would advise him to penetrate forthwith into the county of Argyleshire, a district rich in the finest fishing waters, and bold and majestic scenery. The town of Inverary is an excellent fishing station. *Loch Fine* is in the immediate neighbourhood, into which the rivers *Ayr* and *Shira* fall. There is first-rate sport to be had here. The *Douglas Water* runs into Loch Fine, and it is very prolific of fine trout. Dalmally is another fishing station, where a a rod-fisher may spend a week or two with great pleasure. *Loch Awe* is only a short distance from it. There is Port Sonnachan on its banks, another fashionable rendezvous for anglers. The river *Awe* is a first-rate water for fine trout and salmon. There is likewise the *Orchy*, a stream of high repute. About ten miles from Loch Awe, in a north-easterly direction, *Loch Etive* will be found. Both it and the river *Etive* are splendid localities for sport; and the scenery around the waters is the most sublime and impressive that can be imagined. Besides the Etive, the main loch has the following streams flowing into it: the *Kinlas*, the *Noe*, the *Liver*, and the greater and lesser *Esragans*. These, though limited waters, are well stocked with small trout.

From the higher waters of the Etive, *Loch Leven* lies at about fifteen miles distant. *Loch Crenan* is likewise in this vicinity, and has the *Crenan*, the *Brise*, the *Ure*, the *Dergan*, and the *Tendal*, as its feeders. There is good rod-fishing in all these several waters.

But casting an eye to our supposed starting-point at Glasgow, there is a daily steamer for a place called Oban in this county, in the neighbourhood of which there is a great extent of fine fishing waters. Going direct to this town saves a deal of time and trouble, and places the angler besides in the midst of first-rate sport. This district is called the Western Highlands. Near Oban is the *Euchar* and the *Oude*, both springing out of separate lochs. There are ten or a dozen sheets of water within a few miles of Oban, in all of which there is good fishing for trout, and as much bottom-fishing as any man can desire. There is a lake called *Donolly Beg Loch*, in which anglers often capture a peculiar kind of trout—thick, short, very red in the flesh, and generally weighing about half a pound. These are occasionally caught in great quantities. *Loch Nell* is about seven miles in circumference, and is connected with an arm of the sea by means of a small river called the *Clugh*. Salmon are often caught with the rod, of considerable weight. In most of the lochs we have named in this district, the yellow trout, weighing from four to six pounds, are often captured. In what are called the *Black Lakes*, about three miles from Oban, large quantities of sea-trout are often taken with the fly.

There is a large portion of Argyleshire lying to the north-west of *Loch Likune* and *Loch Cil*, which goes under the names of MORVEN, SUNART, ARDNAMURCHAN, ANDGOUR, KNAPDALE, and COWAL, in which there is a very extended range of fishing-waters, full of the finest trout, and having also a considerable portion of salmon and salmon-trout. This section of the Highlands would employ a rod-fisher for two or three weeks, were he to pay a visit to all the leading sheets of water comprehended within its range. All kinds of light and showy flies are used in this district.

On the north of Loch Crenan lies the district of *Appin*, where the angler will find the streams called the *Coinich*, the *Col*, the *Duror*, the *Laroch*, and the *Leven*. These have all a considerable quantity of small trout, with a few salmon and salmon trout. The fishing of them, when the waters are in full trim, affords good sport.

There is another section of this county of Argyleshire, which is of a singular and scattered figure, that lies near to Glasgow. If the angler take a steamboat to Kilmun, he will fall in with the stream called the *Eachar*, which has only a run of four or five miles out of *Loch Eck*, and the *Holy Loch*, but which is very prolific of fine trout, and likewise, at particular seasons, grilse of delicious quality. Loch Eck contains the *powan*, or fresh-water herring. This sheet of water is also reputed to contain the *goldie*—a fish known nowhere else. It is about five inches in length, and is very remarkable for the succession of brilliant colours it displays before it dies.

In that part of this Highland county which stretches away to the south, called Cantyre, capital fishing-streams will be found. They are but very limited in their range: the chief of them are *Torisdale, Caradale, Saddell, Crosaig, Sunadale, Claonaig*, and *Skipness*. All flies should be of a smallish size for these waters. There are numerous small lochs in this neighbourhood which contain good trout, pike, roach, and other fish.

In the island of Bute, *Loch Fad* and *Loch Asgog*, there is good fishing for pike and perch. The *Grenan Loch* has trout of considerable size. Salmon are taken out of *Loch Gorsa*, in the isle of Arran, and good trout out of *Loch Tanna*.

If the tourist prosecute his journey north into Inverness-shire, he will find himself among a prolific series of waters, fitted for all kinds of angling. The main rivers here are the *Oich*, the *Ness*, the *Dundreggan*, the *Foyers*, the *Beauly*, and the *Clannie*. Many of these waters have of late years become fashionable places of resort for English anglers, where the romantic scenery and the abundance of fine fishing operate as powerful stimulants to such yearly migrations from the south. There are very good accommodations in the neighbourhood.

Some of these rivers are of great length, and have many large tributaries, which are themselves important fishing localities. The Beauly has three feeders—the *Farrar*, the *Glass*, and the *Cannich*. These are all connected, more or less, with lakes, in which there

arc both trout and bottom fish of all kinds.   One of these, *Loch
Bruiach*, has an abundance of char, and no less than seven distinct
species of the trout.

In the southern sections of Inverness-shire, there are many
lochs and streams where the angler may fish for weeks, and never
feel anything like lassitude or uneasiness.   The principal of these
inland lakes are *Loch Quoich, Loch Arkoss, Loch Chinie, Loch Shiel,
Loch Eylt, Loch Duich, Loch Hourn,* &c.

Penetrating into Ross-shire, we have again a great extent of
waters before us, all admirably fitted for angling sport of the most
exciting kind.   The river *Conan* has a run of thirty miles.   It springs
out of a lake in one of the most wild and desolate-looking districts
of this mountainous country.   This stream is joined by the *Meig*.
Loch Ledgowan, in this vicinity, abounds with large trout, which
are commonly caught by trolling.   The Conan flows through *Loch
Luichart*, a sheet of water of six miles in extent, in which there is
capital fishing sport.   The river *Orrin* enters the Conan three
miles from Coutin.   Here, likewise, there is good trouting.

In the western division of the county there are fine sheets of
water, well stocked with trout, pike, and a fair portion of salmon.
The chief of these are *Loch Ling, Loch Carron*, into which the river
Carron runs, *Loch Taniff, Loch Maree*, and *Loch Broom*.   There are
good accommodations in the neighbourhood.

Still pressing northward, the county of Sutherland presents an
imposing piscatory ramble, of nearly seventy miles in length by
fifty in extreme breadth.   Here, an angler may spend an entire
fishing season most delightfully.   All kinds of fish are to be had;
and the sublime scenery in the vicinity of many of the lakes and
rivers has such an effect upon the mind of the tourist, that it leaves
an impression which lasts to the end of his days.

The *Oikel* has a run of thirty miles, and is an excellent river for
trouting, more especially in its higher streams.   This river springs
out of a wilderness that seems like chaos itself.   There is a good
turnpike road by its side for full twenty miles; and in this part of
Scotland this is by no means a very common sight.   In the vicinity
of Ben More, the Casley falls into the Oikel, and augments its
size considerably.

In the locality we are now treating of, there is a group of lochs
amounting to upwards of two hundred, varying in extent from one
to fourteen miles each.   These are all comprehended within a
comparatively small distance, say, perhaps, of forty miles in circumference.   It is an exceedingly delightful ramble to worm one's
way throughout this mighty maze of still sheets of water, and to
dip a line in here and another there, in such secluded and
picturesque lakes.   This is a favourite trolling district for many
of the noted Scottish anglers; and very large sized trout are
captured, weighing sometimes fourteen or fifteen pounds.

The river *Carron*, which enters the Darnock Firth at Bonar
Bridge, is a good angling spot.   There are good fishing lochs in

the neighbourhood, and there is likewise a good and comfortable inn for lodging and refreshments—matters of some vital import. ance in this wild and rugged country.

The river *Shine*, which flows out of *Loch Shine*, and has only a run of about seven miles as a mere river, is a place very much frequented by angling tourists. It contains trout of a large size, salmon, the *salmo ferox*, and char. There are two falls in the river; and it is below these that the angling is the most fruitful of sport. The loch is twenty-four miles in extent, and is connected with a considerable number of other smaller sheets of water, all of which are worthy of the notice of the tourist. A boat is requisite to fish them properly.

The river *Helmsdale* is twenty miles in extent, and is connected with several sheets of still water. It is full of large trout and splendid pike. Some of these lochs have an abundance of fine char. This is an excellent spot for rod-fishing.

A few miles to the north we fall in with the higher rivulets of the *Halladale*, which empties its waters into the North Sea. It has a run of twenty miles. There are several fishing lochs in the vicinity. The river *Strathy* runs parallel with the Halladale for some distance. It is also a very prolific stream. It contains salmon grilse, and very large trout.

In keeping by the sea-coast, we meet with the *Naver*, which arises out of a loch of the same name of about seven miles in extent. Here are likewise salmon, grilse, and trout in abundance. This river has the *Mallart*, the *Skelvick Burn*, and the *Langdale Burn*, for its feeders.

There flows at no great distance the river *Borgie*, which springs out of *Loch Craigie* and *Loch Looghal*. The fishing is here first-rate for salmon, grilse, and fine yellow trout. The *Kinloch*, the *Hope*, and the *Strathmore* streams are all good fishable waters, both for salmon and trout; and on the western side of the country, along its entire range of coast, there is a continued chain of lakes in which all kinds of rich and valuable fish are to be found. To enumerate them would fill several pages. Fly-fishing and bottom-fishing can be had in all of them; and those who are fond of the minnow, will find this a splendid district for their peculiar branch of sport.

The county of Caithness is comparatively flat, and not so fruitful of the wild and the sublime as the regions we have just passed through. We have the rivers *Langwell* and *Berridale;* the first about eight, and the latter about fifteen miles in extent. The river *Wick* has a good repute among trout fishers. It flows through *Loch Scharmlet*, which contains both large trout and pike. But the chief stream in this neighbourhood is the *Thurso*, which falls into the ocean at the town of the same name. In its higher waters there is beautiful trout and salmon fishing with the rod. The *Forss* is also a good stream.

Turning our faces now towards the south, we shall meet with a number of first-rate streams in the several counties lying between this extreme point of the kingdom and the cities of Edinburgh and Glasgow. Should the angling traveller, when he comes to the vicinity of the Murray Firth, take the whole route of the Caledonian Canal as a fishing excursion, he will meet with many interesting waters, where fine trout and salmon fishing can be obtained. He will likewise have an opportunity of ascending some of the high mountains in this locality, such as Ben Nevis, and the mountain of Mealfourvonie. "The view from the summit of this last lofty hill," we are told, "is of vast extent, and highly impressive. We stand in the midst of an amphitheatre of mountains, old as the creation, and command a view of the Caledonian Valley, or Great Glen of Albin. The whole course of the canal, with its chain of lakes—Loch Ness, Loch Oich, and Loch Lochy, are all placed at our feet, extending in a direct and silvery line of sixty miles. Six lakes, and numerous tarns and pools, lie in front; and in the gorge, through which the river Foyer rushes, the top of the fall is visible like a white streamer."

The rivers and lochs of Cromarty, Elginshire, and Banffshire, are in considerable repute among south country anglers. The *Findhorn* has a range of sixty miles, and affords the rod-fisher an exquisite ramble. It passes Forres about two miles to the west. The water springs out of high and mountainous grounds in Inverness-shire. It is a wild and turbulently running stream. The yellow trout are here found in great abundance. It has many considerable feeders, which are themselves connected with lakes full of trout, pike, perch, and all kinds of bottom fish. Salmon fishing with the rod has, of late years, been prosecuted with great success on this splendid river. The stream called the *Nairn* is in the same locality, and has a range of very fair angling waters in its course. It falls, like the Findhorn, into the Moray Firth.

The *Spey* is one of the chief rivers of Scotland; it rises from *Loch Spey*, in Invernesshire. *Lochs Alvie, Morlich, Rothiemurchus, Pittenlish*, and *Garten*, all containing large trout and pike, are in the immediate vicinity of the higher streams of this noble river. Its banks are, in many localities, extremely grand and imposing. It has several feeders, as the *Dulnain*, the *Fiddich*, and the *Aven*. All these are fine trouting waters; and some fine salmon-fishing can be, at suitable seasons, plentifully enjoyed. There cannot be a more interesting ramble with a rod than along the entire banks and tributary waters of the Spey. There are various convenient spots for lodgings and refreshments; and the masters of these establishments are very ready to give the stranger any information he may require.

The *Lossie* is an agreeable river to throw a line on: it runs through *Loch Trevie*, and has a connection with several other sheets of water. The length of the river is about twenty-five miles.

In entering Aberdeenshire, we have a ready access to a batch of splendid streams. From the town of Aberdeen, celebrated for its ancient and learned university, we have two considerable rivers, the *Dee* and the *Don*. The first has a range of one hundred miles, and flows through tracts of wild and beautiful mountain scenery, calculated to rivet its remembrance on the memory for a lifetime. Before the river arrives at Balliter, it receives the waters of the *Clunie, Gairn, Muick,* and *Geldie,* all abounding with swarms of smallish trout; and on some of whose banks we have rural scenes of surpassing beauty. The Dee fishing, on the whole, is excellent; and Castleton, Balliter, Aboyne, and Kirkardine O'Neil, are convenient stations for reaching its best angling localities.

The Don enters the German Ocean at the town of Old Aberdeen. It has a higher reputation among fly-fishers than even the Dee. It is sixty miles in length, and it has several tributaries of note, among which are the *Bucket* and *Esset.* The *Urr* joins the main river also at the neat village of Inverury. Trout are frequently taken here, of five and six pounds weight. Trolling is very successfully practised in the Urr. The *Kellack, Calpie, Shevock,* and *Gady,* are small streams, which are sometimes visited by travelling anglers. The trout in them are dwarfish. It has been surmised, by anglers who have frequented the Don and its waters for some years, that it has recently fallen off a good deal from its former prolific supply of salmon and trout. We think there is no good ground for this opinion. The best stations on the river are Alford, Inverury, and Kintore.

Pressing southward into the counties of Kincardine, Forfar, and Perthshire, we meet with many noble fishing waters.

One of the most enticing fishing localities in this direction is the river *Tay,* and its dependent waters. These embrace an extensive range of angling streams, both for the salmon and trout. To visit all these places would take a considerable time; but those who can afford that time need be under no apprehension of lacking any reasonable amount of sport. This river rises out of the high grounds of Larne. Soon after it leaves its parent springs, it receives the waters of many small burns and rivulets, and then enters into *Loch Dochart.* It falls into another sheet of water, called *Loch Tay;* and issuing from it at Kenmore, the Tay is joined by another stream, called the *Lyon.* They jointly proceed to Athol, receiving other two feeders, the *Logierait* and the *Tummel.* The main river then flows on to Perth, and enters the German Ocean at Dundee. There is splendid salmon and trout fishing in all these waters.

The *Garry* springs from *Loch Garry,* and is about thirty miles in length. The *Erochkie,* the *Bruar,* and the *Tilt,* are its chief feeders. There is capital trouting in all these places.

Near Dunkeld, there are a number of lakes which abound with trout, pike, perch, &c. The principal of these are *Loch Ard, Loch Craiglush, Loch of the Lows, Butterstone Loch, Loch Rotnel, Loch Aishnie, Loch Cluny,* and *Loch Drumellie.*

The river *Isla* is a good stream: it falls into the Tay. It has the *Dean*, the *Eright*, and the *Susan* for tributaries. The *Earn* is a considerable fishing river, and in high repute by tourists from the south : it falls into the Tay a short distance below Perth. The *Teith* and the *Allan* are fair trouting waters. The first passes through several lakes, and flows by Callendar. The *Keltie* is a small stream, but is well stocked with fish. Besides these, there are the *Bracklin Burn, Stanack Burn, Loch Watston*, and *Loch Maghaig*, in all of which the angler will find sport. There is abundance of char in several of these waters.

The rivers of Fifeshire, readily approached by way of Edinburgh, are worthy of notice. The rivers here are the *Eden*, the *Leven*, and the *Orr;* but the angling is not of a first-rate character in this district, therefore we do not dwell upon it.

The *North* and *South Esk* are clear and sparkling waters, and contain a fair portion of trout, and a considerable sprinkling of salmon and salmon trout. There is some very interesting scenery on the higher streams of these two rivers. They have several feeders, which abound in small trout.

The waters of the Forth, in Stirlingshire, open out a rich field of sport for a limited piscatory tour. This is a very pleasant district to make a ramble in with the rod. It is easily approached from Glasgow.

CHAPTER III.

IRELAND.

> " Islets so freshly fair,
>   That never hath bird come nigh them,
> But from his course through air
>   Hath been won downward by them.
> Types, sweet maid, of thee,
>   Whose look, whose blush inviting,
> Never did Love yet see
>   From heaven without alighting.
>
> " Lakes, where the pearl lies hid,
>   And caves where the diamond's sleeping,
> Bright as the gems that lid
>   Of thine lets full in weeping.
> Caves where Ocean comes
>   To 'scape the wild wind's rancour;
> And harbours, worthier homes,
>   Where Freedom's sails could anchor."—MOORE.

WHEN the angler crosses the Irish Channel, and sets his foot on the Green Isle, he will soon perceive that its general aspect is entirely different from that of Scotland. Ireland is comparatively a level country; its chain of mountains being of no great length, and the elevation of them slight.

Numerous lakes, rivers, streams, bays, havens, harbours, and creeks, diversify the landscape, and produce a pleasing effect upon the mind of the traveller.

. Ireland stands next to Scotland in angling resources; but, in the estimation of many sportsmen, the Emerald Isle is equal to the latter. My own opinion is, that Ireland is greatly inferior to Scotland as an angling country, but that the Irish trout are vastly superior in quality to those of Scotland. There is a peculiar richness about all trout in Ireland; whereas in the north of Britain, the fish are, speaking with many exceptions, white and poor. And this difference is easily accounted for. The Scotch rivers have a great deal of the impetuous mountain torrent about them, flow over great tracts of country of an open and rocky character, and therefore the food for trout is but scantily provided. On the other hand, the rivers in Ireland are less rapid, and flow through a comparatively level country, which yields a more regular and certain supply of those things on which trout generally feed.

Like Scotland, the angler feels the same pleasure in traversing Ireland with his rod, from the absence of all kinds of restraint. The country as a whole is thrown open to every sportsman; and this makes all movements pleasant and agreeable.

Ireland is divided into four provinces, which are divided again into counties. In our description of the rivers, we shall take each province, and give a general outline of all the most approved fishing waters which it contains. These provinces are Ulster, Connaught, Leinster, and Munster.

PROVINCE OF ULSTER.

This province has some most excellent trout and salmon rivers and lakes. It is the northern province of the island. The best route for an angler to go to it is by way of Belfast, which lies on the coast, nearly in the centre of the province, when you are in the immediate neighbourhood of excellent fishing water. The eastern coast of the province is very scantily supplied with rivers; for there are none worthy of an angling tourist's attention, from Callingford Bay to the mouth of the river Bann; a distance of more than one hundred and fifty miles, and embracing all the range of sea known by the name of the North Channel. There are certainly little rivulets in the course, but no river bringing down the waters from the interior of the country. In most of these rivulets, trout will be found, and even a few salmon.

This district embraces the two counties of Down and Antrim. The rivers in the county of Down are the *Bann, Lagan,* and *Newry;* and those of Antrim are *Bann, Lagan,* and *Bush.* In the Lagan and Bush, good trout are taken, and salmon in spring and autumn; but not in such quantities as to induce an angler to go much out of his route to visit these streams. Trolling is often successfully employed in these Irish streams. With the exception of the Upper Bann, all the rivers of Down discharge their waters into the Irish Channel. The navigable river Lagan, which throughout near half its course, has a direction nearly parallel to the Bann, turns eastward at Magheralin; four miles north-east of which it becomes the county boundary, and passing by Lisborne, falls into the Bay of Belfast, after a course of about thirty miles. The Ballynahinch or Annacloy river brings down the waters of several small lakes south-east of Hillsborough, and widens into the Guvile river, which is navigable for vessels of 200 tons, a mile below Downpatrick, where it forms an extensive arm of Strangford Loch. The Guvile is covered with numerous islands, and its windings present much beautiful scenery. The Newry river rises near Kathfriland, and flowing westward by the northern declivities of the Mourne range, turns south a little above Newry, and after a short course falls into the head of Carlingford Loch. Numerous streams descend from the district of Mourne immediately to the sea, and there is no part of the county deficient in a good supply of running water.

The following rivers fall into *Lough Neagh*, in Antrim, the *Ravel*, the *Braid*, the *Crumbia*, the *Glenevy*, the *Carey*, and the *Glenshesh*, all of which are full of fine trout.

In the county of Armagh, the following are good angling streams, the *Callan*, the *Cambin*, the *Cushier*, the *Fleury*, the *Fano*, the *Newton Hamilton*, the *Talwater*, the *Tan*, and the *Tynan*.

Lough Neigh is not more than twenty miles from the town of Belfast; and here fine lake fishing may be enjoyed. There are trout and salmon in this lake; and very large pike, though by no means numerous. When the waters are in good order, and curl is favourable, the fly is very successfully enjoyed on Lough Neagh; but the largest trouts are commonly captured by trolling.

The Bann is a good trout and salmon river. It enters the sea at Coleraine. The higher the angler ascends the river the fly-fishing improves. It is no uncommon feat for an angler to take ten or twelve good sized salmon, and a creel full of fine trout in a day; nay, it sometimes happens in a few hours. Good large flies may be used in the lower parts of the Bann, but as the water diminishes, smaller must be adopted. Trolling in this river is often successful. Large trout are taken after a fresh in summer by this plan. The angler will find a good supply of flies of all kinds, at Coleraine, and in almost every village on the banks of this river.

The *Bollinderry*, which flows from the west, and fell into Lough Neagh, is a good angling river. Large trout are frequently caught in it; and they are of a very rich flavour. The best station on it, is about three miles below its source. It here becomes a beautifu. fly stream.

The river *Foyle*, which divides the counties of Londonderry and

Donegal, and forms Lough Foyle, before its entrance into the
ocean, is a good angling river in its higher departments. Some of
its feeders come out of the mountains and boggy districts of the
county of Monoghan, and are full of trout, but not of any great
size.

The districts of the Foyle best adapted for the fly, and for the
capture of large fish, are those which lie between Omagh, in the
county of Tyrone and Strabane, which is situated on the river
Mourne, before it enters the Foyle. In all this range of water the
river is beautifully adapted for angling; and when it is in fair
order, and the fish in the humour, a good sized creel is soon filled.
Good large flies may be employed with advantage in the latter end
of March until the middle of May. Larger trout are invariably
caught with these during this season, than with smaller ones.
The river Mourne is also worth throwing a line into.

The river *Finn*, which is the chief feeder of the Foyle on this
side, issues from a lake four hundred and thirty-six feet above the
level of the sea, situated in the centre of the mountain chain
extending south from Erigal, and after a course of about thirty
miles eastward, joins the Foyle at Lifford Bridge, eight miles
below Castlefinn, where it is navigable for boats of fourteen tons.
Other feeders of the Foyle, out of Donegal, are the *Derg*, which
comes from Loch Derg, in the south-east extremity of the county
of Donegal, and joins the main stream in Tyrone; the *Deele*,
which has a course nearly parallel to the Finn, and descends
upwards of 800 feet in its course from Loch Deele to the Foyle,
which it joins a mile below Lifford; and the *Swilly Burn*, or
Brook, which passes by Raphoe, and is navigable for a few miles
above its junction. *Loch Derg* is about two miles and a half
wide each way, and surrounded on all sides by steep and barren
mountains; it is four hundred and sixty-seven feet above the level
of the sea, and its greatest depth is seventy-five feet. This lake is
subject to violent gusts of wind. It abounds in excellent trout.
The *Swilly* river, although it has a course of little more than
fifteen miles, brings down a good quantity of water through Litter-
benny to Loch Swilly. The *Scannan* river, which likewise flows
into Loch Swilly by Rathmelton, is a considerable stream, as is
also the Lackagh, which discharges the waters of the lakes of
Gartan, Loch Veah, Loch Salt, and Glen Loch, and into Sheep
Haven. The waters of *Loch Salt*, which is, perhaps, the deepest
pool in Ireland, descends 731 feet in a course of little more than
three miles to Glen Loch.

There are a considerable number of small rivers and rivulets
which flow into the Atlantic on the western side of Donegal,
which abound plentifully with good salmon and trout. If the
angling tourist keep by the coast, he will meet with all these
waters in regular succession. In the *Guibera*, and the *Oenea*,
good sport is sure to be found in the months of April and May.

The river *Erne* is a splendid salmon and trout stream. It issues from a small lake on the north side of the county of Longford, runs through the county of Fermanagh, and falls into the ocean at Donegal Bay. Many British anglers have considered the Erne at Bally Shannon to be one of the very best salmon rivers in the kingdom. A distinguished Liverpool angler caught, in 1834, twenty large salmon in four hours and a half in this river. This was a surprising feat. The gentleman does not wish me, through delicacy, to make his name publicly known, but I have the means of substantiating the fact beyond all question. There is a great variety of flies used on the Erne, some large and gaudy, others small and dull. The fish here do not seem to be very particular. In the higher parts of the river, in the county of Cavan, the trout-fishing is almost equal to the Tweed—and this is saying a great deal. There is no district in Ireland where a sportsman can spend a week or two more pleasantly and successfully than on the streams of the Erne.

On the banks of this river, where there are some fine woods, the scenery is exceedingly rich and interesting. We find at every step a constant succession of small trees and shrubs which shelter themselves beneath the larger sons of the forest, whose majestic figures are beautifully and tastefully ornamented with climbers running from tree to tree, and linked together, we would fancy, by the hand of an amateur botanist. When the foliage is fully developed in the month of June, the scene brings to your imagination some of the fictions of the " Arabian Nights," or some land of fairy establishment. Nothing can surpass the luxuriance of the view. We feel as if we could linger amidst these delicious shades for months together, gazing on the interesting combinations of light and shade. When we think of this place, the lines of Milton's description of the Garden of Eden rush into our mind:—

"Over head up grew
Insuperable height of loftiest shade,
Cedar, and pine, and fir, and branching palm,
A silvan scene, and as the ranks ascend
Shade above shade, a woody theatre
Of stateliest view."

The rivers *Woodward* and *Crohan*, in the county of Cavan, are good trout streams, and will afford to the travelling tourist a few days' good sport. The palmer and hackle flies will be found in these streams, taking ones in the summer months of June and July. Both these waters yield a plentiful supply of fine trout after heavy rains in the height of the season.

THE PROVINCE OF CONNAUGHT

Contains the counties of Galway, Leitrim, Mayo, Roscommon,

and Sligo; and is a good angling district both for salmon and trout.

The *Shannon*, which is the largest river in Ireland, rises out of *Lough Allen*, in the county of Leitrim, and divides this province from that of Leinster. It is, in the opinion of many experienced anglers, one of the most prolific salmon and trout streams in the British dominions.

The best stations for both salmon and trout fly-fishing, lie in that section of the river which bounds the province of Connaught. Here many parts can only be fished with boats; but still there are extensive districts of the river where an angler can do very well without them. Surprising feats are sometimes accomplished in the killing of salmon with fly in the Shannon. A gentleman in Bath, in 1842, caught one fish weighing forty-five pounds and a half, with rather small trout tackle. He took nearly five hours to exhaust him, and then was captured with some difficulty. All kinds of flies are used in these waters; and it is wonderful to see some of the country people kill large fish with the most clumsy imitations of the natural fly, and, apparently, with the most inefficient tackle.

All the small streams and rivulets which run out of this province into the Shannon, are full of trout. In fact, many of these places are equal to the main river.

The river *Moy* rises in the hilly and swampy districts of the province of Connaught. It abounds with salmon and trout, and is much frequented by anglers. The best localities are those which approach nearest to its source. Here the trout are very abundant.

The *Sligo* is a good trout stream. Very fine sport is obtained here after a summer's fresh. Trolling is sometimes practised with great success on these occasions.

There are a great number of small rivers and streams in the western parts of this province which afford excellent angling. The coast here is so indented with bays and creeks, that every rivulet abounds with fish, which being often within salt-water mark, are particularly rich and delicate in flavour.

The *Owenmore*, and the *Errive*, are among the most prolific of these waters. The scenery is also, in many parts, exceedingly interesting, and cannot fail to call forth the unqualified praise of every tourist who has a keen relish for the beauties of nature.

THE PROVINCE OF LEINSTER

Is furnished with many rivers, containing good salmon and trout fishing. The best route for this province is to go direct to Dublin; this brings the angler nearly in the centre of the province.

The *Tiffy*, which flows into Dublin Bay, is a rapid running river, and in many of its localities abounds with fine trout. It

M

takes its rise in the mountainous parts of the county of Wicklow, flows into Kildare, and then passes through the county of Dublin into the Irish Sea. The best angling district for fly, is that section of the river which flows through Kildare. There are many admirable streams in the locality, and the fish are really of a superior richness and flavour.

The river *Boyne* rises in the north part of the county of Kildare, crosses Meath, and falls into the Irish Channel at the town of Drogheda. This is good water for both salmon and trout, and some of the latter have been taken of great weight, both with the fly and minnow. The more elevated parts of the stream are the best for the rod. The streams are limpid and sparkling, and are finely adapted for single handed fly-fishing. The *Blackwater* is a considerable tributary to the Boyne, and is also a good stream. It has a run of full forty miles from its source in Cavan. The Boyne has many other small feeders also, which abound in trout, and some of them with salmon.

The rivers *Louth* and *Dee*, which lie north of the Boyne, in the county of Louth, are both good fishing streams. Salmon may here be taken in spring and autumn, and in the higher parts of the streams, will be found many districts of fine limpid and rippling waters. After a summer fresh, the Louth and the Dee will yield good success, both for fly and minnow.

Most all the small rivers and lakes in the county of Wicklow, are well supplied with trout; and the fishing in them is generally very good. Many spots, situated on rivers in this part of Ireland, are exceedingly romantic; such as Glenaloch, the Devil's Glen, and the wild glen of Dargle.

The rivers *Slaney* and *Barrow* are both good fishing streams. Salmon and trout abound in these rivers; but the higher parts of the streams are the best fitted for the fly. In the more mountainous districts through which they run, are most delightful landscapes.

The Barrow is a tributary to the Slaney, which falls into the sea at Wexford Harbour.

The river *Nore* takes its rise from the elevated lands in Queen's County, and has a run of more than sixty miles, before it falls into the sea. Salmon and trout are to be found in it, at all seasons of the year, and in considerable abundance. I have known the minnow successful in killing large fish in the Nore after a good fresh in summer. The best fly-fishing stations are those above the town of Kilkenny. The scenery is on many parts of the river, romantic and beautiful. Some anglers employ very large flies on the Nore, particularly in the spring of the year. But middle sized ones are equally as good.

Many of the rivers and small streams which flow through the western parts of the province of Leinster, are tributaries to the Shannon, which we shall notice afterwards. All these dependent waters are full of trout and salmon. The angler can experience no disappointment in visiting these waters; for if the weather be even tolerably fine, success is almost certain. Many of the small rivulets yield trout of surprising richness of flavour. They cut as red as beef.

All flies with gray drake, starling or woodcock wings, are good for these waters; and the hackle and palmers are quite standards especially in summer.

THE PROVINCE OF MUNSTER.

This province stands pre-eminent for its angling resources. A considerable portion of the waters of the Shannon, flow through it to the ocean. These bear away the palm over all the other parts of the province, for the prodigious quantities of salmon found in them.

The best locality for angling for salmon, on the Shannon, is above the city of Limerick. But it is requisite to have a boat, to command the waters.

The Blackwater is a fine salmon stream. Lismore is a good angling station. Trout are also very abundant; but the further up the river the more numerous they become, and the better are the streams for the fly. Any sportsman who knows how to handle a rod, may kill his ten or twelve dozen of trout in a few hours in the Blackwater. This river falls into the sea at Youghal.

The river *Suir* contains many salmon and trout, and is much frequented by Irish and English anglers. It is said that this river contains some of the finest and richest salmon stations in Ireland. The river is not, however, very eligible for angling. The navigable traffic upon it, makes the fish difficult to hook. The trout are excellent as well as the salmon; and immediately after a summer flood, a good day's sport may be anticipated. The small stream called the Anna, which empties itself into the Suir, two miles below Clonmel, is a good angling locality. The trout are here smaller than in the Suir. The Anna has pike, for which its broad, deep, and sluggish waters are very favourable. Trout have been caught, it is said, of seven pounds weight; but such captures are rare.

In the higher departments of the Shannon, there are some most delightful scenes, which it is impossible without the aid of painting or poetry to bring before the mind's eye. Imagine yourself seated on the top of an elevated promontory, and see the mass of waters striking against the foot of an island which they encircle, and where fine trees and the greenest verdure deck their edges with the loveliest hues, in which all the magic play of light and shade are reflected on their brilliant surfaces. Here they rush down a rapid descent, and break against the scattered rocks which obstruct their passage, and dash and send up their spray, in a thousand forms. Now you see them fall into a transverse basin, something like the shape of a cradle, and are urged forward by the force of gravitation against the sides of a precipice, which seems to stop them a moment only to increase the rapidity of their current. The rocks against which the volumes of water strike, throw them back in white foam and glittering spray; and then you see them plunge into deep cavities, and rush forth again in tumultuous waves, breaking against masses of stone, and, perchance, forming a little island, in the midst of which a few dwarfish trees or shrubs spread out their shaded branches.

The little wooded islands in the waters of the Shannon, are disposed in beautiful order by the hand of nature, and give a perpetual variety to the prospects. When the river is smooth and calm, and reflecting the dazzling rays of a bright sun like glass, the scenes are often most delightful; when the smiling hills are taken into view, and contrasted with those fine green pastures so often studded with clusters of thick and massy trees. We meet with such picturesque views every few miles, in some localities of these fine waters; and the effect they have upon the mind, is cheering and interesting in the highest degree.

Should the angler visit the city of Cork, he must take a ramble on the banks of the *Lee*, which is an admirable trout and salmon stream. All its tributaries are also full of fish. On wandering on the sides of the Lee, we cannot help thinking of the lines of Spencer:—

> "Here also was the wide embayed Maire,
> The pleasant Bauder, crowned with many a wood;
> The spreading Lee, that, like an island fair,
> Encloseth Cork with his divided flood."

The Bandon rises in the hilly parts of the country, and falls into the ocean at Kinsale Harbour. There are many anglers who visit this river every year, and find abundant sport both in salmon and trout fishing.

The whole of the western division of Munster, from the Bay of Galway to Cape Clear, is intersected with numerous small rivers and lakes, which are plentifully stocked with salmon and trout. At every four or five miles the traveller finds himself on the banks of some fresh lake or river, where he has nothing else to do but to throw in his line and take his fish.

Then there are in this province the Lakes of Killarney, which have long been celebrated for their angling capabilities. These are commonly divided into three parts; the lower, the middle, and upper lake. The lower lake is six miles long, and three broad. On the side of one of the mountains is O'Sulliven's Cascade, which falls above seventy feet; and opposite to this the island of Innisfallen, which contains about eighteen Irish acres. On passing into the upper lake, the tourist will meet with the Eagle's Nest, a steep rock, which produces the most surprising echoes. The upper lake is about four miles long, and two broad. Here numerous beautiful cascades meet the eye, and present a great variety of the most picturesque views. The middle lake is the smallest, and is greatly indented with bogs and creeks, surrounded with dark groves of trees.

There is splendid trout-fishing in these waters. Salmon are not so very numerous. Trout have been caught here of great size; and the quality is very superior to fish caught in many other waters in Ireland.

The kind of flies requisite for these lakes, depends greatly on the state of the weather. If the day be dull and the wind high, large gaudy ones will often succeed best; whereas the very reverse must be the case when the day is clear and little wind. A skilful angler can seldom make any serious mistake in this matter.

The upper lake of Killarney is encircled with mountains of vast height, and ornamented with wood; and from the bright surface of the waters emerge huge rocks, crowned with the arbutus, whose dark leaves form a beautiful contrast to its scarlet fruit. The islands of the lake are of fantastic shapes, a circumstance which has induced the country people to fancy resemblances between them and certain objects, as a man-of-war, the church, &c. The craggy summits of these islands give an air of sublimity to the scene which it is impossible to describe. Shrubs and plants, in immense variety, line the bold and lofty shore, and suggest to the mind the beautiful lines of the poet of nature :—

"Here spring the living herbs profusely wild,
O'er all the deep-green earth, beyond the power
Of botanist to number up their tribes ;
Whether he steals along the lonely dale
In silent search, or climb the mountain rock,
Fired by the nodding verdure of the brow.
With such a liberal hand hath nature flung
Their seeds abroad, blown them about in winds
Innumerous, mixed them in the nursing mould."

In travelling in the neighbourhood of the Lakes of Killarney, the most sublime views open out to the angling tourist among the mountains. Every league changes the landscape, and new and interesting objects pass in constant succession before the enchanted eye. Now we are directed to sublime heights and craggy eminences, the haunts of the eagle and other birds of prey, and then again look down on the glossy and tremulous waves, which reflect the aspiring and umbrageous trees, which clothe the giddy summits. Sounds are here repeated and retained with surprising and bewitching effect. They float along the agitated air with angelic harmony, and issue from the deep grottos and recesses of mountains like so many celestial voices.

The island of Innisfallen is full of interest and beauty. The prospects from it are exceedingly grand. The opposite shores of Glenaa rise into magnificent mountains, and clothed mid-way with thick forests. To the west we recognize the lofty Tornish, and around the numerous islands, some crowned with arbutus, others resembling rocks, pillars, and arches. The sublime and picturesque effect of O'Sulliven's Cascade, amply verify the imagery of Thompson.

> "Smooth to the shelving brink the copious flood
> Runs fair and placid; where collected all,
> In one impetuous torrent, down the steep
> It thundering shoots, and shakes the country round.
> At first an azure sheet, it issues broad,
> Then whitening by degrees as prone it falls;
> And from the land-resounding rocks below
> Dashed in a cloud of foam, it sends aloft
> A hoary mist, and forms a ceaseless shower.
> Ne'er can the tortured wave here find repose;
> But raging still among the shaggy rocks,
> Now flashes o'er the scattered fragments, now
> Aslant the hollowed channel rapid darts;
> And falling fast from gradual slope to slope,
> With wild infracted course and lessened roar,
> It gains a safer bed."

"On the whole," says Mr. Young, "Killarney, among the lakes that I have seen, can scarcely be said to have a rival. The extent of water in Loch Erne is much greater, the islands are more numerous, and some scenes near Castle Caldwell of greater magnificence. The rocks of Keswick are more sublime, and other lakes may have circumstances in which they are superior; but when we consider the prodigious woods of Killarney, the immensity of the mountains, the uncommon beauty of the promontory of Mucrus and the isle of Innisfallen, the character of the islands in general, the single circumstance of the arbutus, which grows here with unequalled luxuriance, and the remarkable echoes, it will appear, on the whole, to be in reality superior to all comparison."

A little below the bridge of Ballyshannon, is a beautiful and picturesque cascade: it is over a mass of rocks, and is twelve feet high at low water. This is considered one of the chief salmon-leaps in Ireland. The effect is much heightened when the waters are flooded. The number of salmon taken at this fall is so great, that the fishery lets for above 1,000*l.* per annum; there is also an eel fishery at the same place, which is rented at 400*l.* a year.

Lough Erne is, in many respects, a very interesting lake, situated in the county of Fermanagh, through which it runs from one end to the other. The limits are considered to extend about forty English miles, from Beleck on the north-west to Betherbet on the south-east. It offers, far above any other lake in Ireland, inland navigation to a great extent, though occasionally obstructed by shallows.

There is an abundant supply of fish in this lake, such as salmon, trout, perch, pike, bream, eels, and a vast quantity of smaller fish. Along its shores are to be seen the ruins of several ancient castles; and there is a round tower, still in good preservation, on the island of Devenish. The country is very thinly populated, and there is not one village on the immediate shores of this beautiful lake.

Lough Erne is divided into two—the upper and lower lakes, and there is a distance of seven or eight miles between them, consisting of a very circumscribed channel, which many have considered might, with more propriety, be called part of the river Erne. The lower lake, which has a depth of 230 feet in many places, is both larger and deeper than the upper, and is interspersed with many beautiful islands. It is not more than four miles distant from the sea, yet it stands at an elevation of nearly 150 feet above the tideway. The first fall occurs at the village of Beleck, from which to Ballyshannon there are many falls of picturesque beauty. There is in this lake a sheet of water, about ten miles in length and five in breadth, which is tolerably clear of islands.

The upper lake, in its most open part, does not exceed a mile and a half in each direction; and its depth is seldom more than twenty feet. It is elevated about two feet ten inches above the lower lake.

The general aspect of the surrounding country is barren, with many isolated limestone hills, which seldom rise above 600 feet except towards the west, where the Poola Fooka range of land reaches 1,000 feet.

The small river Erne, which runs out into the sea at Ballyshannon, is said to be one of the most prolific streams in the country. It runs rapidly, and is only about five miles in length. It abounds with salmon and trout, and a variety of other inferior kinds of fish.

A friend of ours, a gentleman well acquainted with angling in Ireland, has given us the following miscellaneous remarks from his note-book on the subject. They are thrown together without much order, but will be interesting to the tourist, notwithstanding.

Should the Irish angler wish for a day's sport in pike or perch fishing, he will find Loch Deig, on the Shannon, will afford him amusement. Pike of twelve and fifteen pounds have often been taken out of this piece of water. There are good trout in it, but not many of them. A few specimens of the *gillaro* trout may here be met with occasionally. Fly-fishing is here unworthy of the angler's notice.

Should he step aside, about ten miles from the banks of the Shannon, from Killaloe to Broadwood, he may, perhaps, have a chance of hooking some of the large pike, said to be sometimes found in the Broadwood Lake. The country people tell us, that

some years ago, a pike was taken here weighing *ninety-two pounds*.
This may be a fable; but certain it is, that fish of *forty* pounds and
upwards have not unfrequently been taken out of the waters in
this locality.

Twelve miles from Limerick, near the village of Newmarket, are
the Lakes Rossroe and Fenloo. These abound with trout, full
ten pounds weight, and as rich as the finest salmon. They cannot
be taken with anything but by trolling with a small roach. A day
or two spent on these waters will afford the angler great pleasure.

The Lake Inchiquin, in Clare county, is a celebrated place for
trout: they are of great size, and particularly rich flavour. There
are two species of trout in this water—the *red* and the *white*. The
flies used here are commonly of the middle size, with red and brown
bodies, gold twist, and longish gray wings. The red palmer is
here a killing bait.

The fishing about Galway is of the first-rate kind. The river
Castello, near to Spiddell, issues out of a little lake about two or
three miles from the sea. Four or five dozen of trout may here
be taken in a very short time.

At Castlebar, in the county of Mayo, is Lough Con. The scenery
of this piece of Irish water is magnificent. Bold and rugged rocks
surround its edges, which are here and there ornamented with
wood. The mountain of Naphine appears in the distance, and adds
a powerful effect to the distant landscape. The loch is about ten
miles in length, but very narrow in many parts. Here there is
excellent fishing, and the *gillaroo* may be often met with. The
river Moy, which runs into this sheet of water, is a delightful
angling station. Its streams, in many localities, are exceedingly
prolific of fine trout, and their banks will afford the lover of fine
scenery much pleasure. This is one of the richest emporiums of
salmon in Ireland: *seventy thousand* have been caught in a single
season.

Lough Gilly, in Sligo, is about six miles long, and from three to
four broad. The south side is skirted with picturesque and beautiful mountains, ornamented with fine, majestic timber. There
are a number of little islands studded on its surface, which give
the scene an extremely lively appearance. Salmon and trout will
be found in considerable quantities here.

Ballyshannon leads to the river *Erne*, one of the finest stations
for the rod in Ireland : plenty of sport for salmon, and those commonly of a large size. At Churchhill, the angler will obtain a fine
view of Lough Erne, the entire expanse of the water, which is
about two miles in breadth. There are interesting spots upon it,
characterized by bold and majestic scenery. Many gentlemen's
castles, seats, with rural and scattered villages, ornament the
borders of the lake. Flies of deep orange, silk body, gold tinsel,
and rich mixed wings, are good for both the river and the lough.

Lake Dulach is a nice piece of water, with beautiful scenery
about its banks. Lord Sligo has a fishing-station, or lodge, near

it. There are plenty of salmon, and rich and splendid trout. Lough Kylemore is about three miles long, and lies at the foot of some precipitous and picturesque mountains. There are fine salmon and trout here.

All the sheets of water in the locality of Ballinahinch afford abundance of salmon and trout. The scenery is grand, and of the most magnificent description.

Lough Luggen is a most surprising place for the quantity of trout which are taken from it: they may be said to live in myriads of shoals. It is no uncommon thing to kill eight or ten dozen in a couple of hours; in fact, the angler gets quite fatigued with hauling them into his basket. The trout here are commonly large, too; and it is impossible for a pedestrian angler to carry any distance the fruits of a few hours' sport. Almost all kinds of flies will answer the purpose in this lough.

The west coast of Ireland is particularly prolific of salmon and trout. The great advantages which an angler in this district possesses for the successful prosecution of his craft is, that every two or three miles from the sea-coast he finds a series of fine loughs, or streams, which are swarming with fish. On the eastern coast of the island, these advantages do not present themselves to the same extent.

In the vicinity of Dingle and Bantry Bays, the trout-fishing is excellent. For twenty miles inland, the lakes abound with immense swarms of fish. The scenery is delightful, and chiefly of the bold and rugged kind.

Few anglers ever traverse Ireland, but hear very strange and unaccountable stories about fish and fishing from various classes of people with whom they come in contact. If it should so happen that an English travelling tourist should require the assistance of any of the professed angling helps in this singular land of wonders and miracles, he will be sure to hear some stories very like the following, which we take, for its real genuine fun, from one of our British periodicals:—

" ' Wouldn't it be right, Paddy' (for, as a fisherman, there are few more skilful on the lake), 'to have a blue hackle? I'd like to try one.'

" ' Nothing for the gap but brown. There's a fellow' (holding it between him and the light); 'and they'll rise to it as fast as you can throw out.'

" ' The blue hackle I had from you the other day killed me a noble salmon, very near thirty pounds; and, what is odd, he gave me no play whatever—after a tumble or two he was gaffed. But the strangest thing is, that Doherty, in helping to get him in with the landing-net, caught a fine trout.'

" It may be readily guessed that the last circumstance was invented, for anything like skill or luck on Doherty's part (he was a rival) displeased Paddy exceedingly; but he took no notice of it, and said, 'Oh! the large fish never give play: a lively *pail*,* now, is worth twenty of 'em for that, sir. But, talking of large fish,' continued he, looking at the fire and then turning to me, 'I was fishing over there at Benson's Point one day. The boat was almost wracked to pieces on that blackguard little quay that the Madam has below; two or three of her ribs war broken, and so I was obliged to fish from the land. Well, just as I was thinking where I'd put her when she was mended, I feels a mighty heavy pull at the line, that I knew must be from a great fellow. I tried him, but not a stir could I get out of him for any money. Says I, "This must be the making of me, when he won't rise his head at all out of the sand; 'tis the way with the great salmon that they won't give any play at all." Well, we tried him again, and again, and again; but 'twas no use. I thought that may-be 'twas a rock, or a stump of a tree, after all; so I goes about every way to get the hook free, but nothing would do. At last he vexed me all out —I didn't care a farthing what became of the rod or tackle; I gave a terrible whip, and tossed something over my head into the bushes behind. "Yourself, and all that came before you, to the divil!" says I, going to see what it was. And, sure, I found that it was an anvil, and that the hook had stuck in its eye. But that wasn't the best of it: there was a fine stag (nine years ould by the horns) sleeping in the bush, and when I thrun back the anvil, I struck him with it in the middle of the forehead, and killed him as dead as a gurnet.'

"'Who the d——l,' interrupted Moriarty, 'ever saw a rod or gut that would pitch an anvil out of the lake at Tornies? Weren't Mr. Lynch and I raising an anvil the other day, for a wages? There isn't a rod in the world, unless a rod of iron or steel, that would do it.'

"Paddy never vindicates a story. I was unable, from laughter, to utter a word; but Moll, as usual, swore 'it was thrue for the lad. Wasn't the anvil a block by the fire, until she gave it to her sister's son-in-law, when he set up the forge at Fahah Cross? And, for the stag, didn't an Iveraghan give a full-bound of butter for his skin?'

"I saw that Paddy was in great blood this day; and willing to see how far he would run if line enough were given him, I requested Moriarty's silence by a look, and showed Paddy a volume containing some excellent drawings of fishes.

"'That one is a shark: he grows to be sixteen or twenty feet long, and is exceedingly ferocious. A man in full armour was once found in the belly of one. Did you, Paddy, ever see anything like that?'

"'A man in armour?—That's a soger, I suppose? No, indeed, sir; I never saw anything quare in a fish. A man in a shuit (suit) of iron! The only thing I ever saw out of the way was one day I caught a brown trout, between twenty and thirty pounds, and we

* A spring salmon.

found a wran's (wren's) nest and seventeen eggs in his gills. That was all I ever saw *in* a fish. I remember, indeed, that I caught below there, opposite Fussa Quay, a big salmon with an officer's cocked hat on his head; and trouble enough he gave before he was in the boat.'

" 'Man alive!' said Moriarty, 'how could he see the fly with the cocked hat?'

" 'Sure, sir,' says Paddy, ' 'twasn't by the mouth at all I had him; if it was, we'd make aisy work of it: but he wanted to drown the fly with his tail when I hooked him, and that was the reason he gev all the play. It must be, sir, you often caught a trout that way, and you know how hard 'tis to land him.'

" 'But, Paddy, what was the greatest bounce you ever saw a salmon make?'

" 'Why, thin, indeed, sir, I never saw anything out of the way that way.'

" 'Well—I've seen the salmon-leap at Leixlip, which is at least twenty feet high, and the salmon spring higher still; so that they are sometimes shot *flying*.'

" '*Gondouth!* Sure, I'll tell you what happened myself, the day they gave the stag-hunt to the Lord Lieutenant—he that had the Black with him here.'

" 'Oh, the black servant!—Lord Talbot, I suppose.'

" 'The very same, sir. Well, that day—may-be you were out yourself, and know it as well as I do? But I believe you weren't in the country that year; anyhow, the whole world seen it. The hunt was in Turk Lake; and as soon as it was over, and the stag was in the boat, all the boats were going down Brickeen Bridge, to dine at Innisfallen. Oyeh! what a show there was of 'em; and what a power of ladies and gintleman there was on the bridge! There war boats, too, coming up from Glenna and Innisfallen. Well, sir, just as the Lord Lieutenant came to the bridge, Mr. Herbert desired him hear the echo first, and the shot for the stag. "Paddy," says he to me, "let's have a noble shot; I trust you with it before any man." So I got the pattherraro—you know the place, sir, of course, where the best echo on the lake is, from the rocks about twenty yards above the bridge?' (To this I could safely assent.) 'Well; I loads it well with powder, and a sod of turf; makes a good *divil;* and was just going to put the spunk to it, when I hears the cry, "The salmon! the salmon!" and, sure enough, there he was, a huge fellow leaping over the bridge. I suppose he was caught between the boats coming up and going down, and the wather being shallow, he was obliged to jump over the bridge.'

" 'And what did you do, Paddy?'

" 'I claps the pattherraro to my shouldher, and kills him as dead as a herring.'

" 'Oh, b—— and o——!' exclaimed my friend William, in the agony of his soul; but Paddy went on. 'They weighed him, and found he was just twenty-seven pounds and a quarter. But, what do ye think the Lord Lieutenant gev me? The *raggeen* put a hand in his pocket, and hands me a tinpenny bit!'

"''Tis thrue for him,' said the never-failing Moll; 'shure, I have it in the box there yet; only the child lost the key yesterday.'

"This was enough on one day even for me; so we started for the Gap, having paid Paddy somewhat more liberally than his lordship. As soon as we got out, 'Did you ever,' said William, 'hear such a liar? Shoot a salmon with a patterrara a foot long? Why, the priming would blind him. Besides, how would the horse do without his back-bone?'

"''True. Then you do think he told lies?'

"''It's my opinion,' said he, stopping and looking like a man that had made up his mind, 'that you ought not to believe half of what he said to-day.'''

CHAPTER IV.

CONTINENTAL STATES.

In reference to *where to go* in our foreign tours, much might be written. The words embrace a wide range; for where do not Englishmen go? and where is the spot they do not carry their amusements with them, and enjoy them, in spite of all difficulties? There are scarcely any great sections of the globe wherein they are to be found, in which angling is not followed. They have, within the last half century, carried rod-fishing to all the rivers of India; they have thrown the fly upon the numerous streams of South Africa, six hundred miles north of Cape Town; they have sauntered on the banks of the Nile, and other neighbouring waters; they have carrried their rods and fly books to all our Australian possessions, and to all the islands of the Pacific Ocean; they have dropped their lines in the high waters of the Amazon, the Plata, and the Oronoco; they have naturalized their sport over the entire North American Continent, from the southern point to the frozen banks of Labrador; they have ransacked every nook and corner of Europe; and they are now taking their rods and tackle into Asiatic Tartary, Circassia, Turkey, and the Holy Land. Such being the case, we confess ourselves somewhat puzzled how to set about our duty of telling anglers *where to go* not from any lack of matter, but from its great superabundance. We must, however, cut our labours down to something attainable by the great majority of travelling piscatorians, and dwell upon districts within a reasonable and approachable distance from their own homes.

Now, to commence near our own door, France is a country possessing great angling capabilities, and where there has been a considerable portion of British enterprise in this line for the last forty years. But it is an extensive country, and possesses great and numerous rivers which it would be impossible for us here to describe. All we can do is merely to point out certain districts of the kingdom where rod-fishing will readily be met with, and leave the tourist to his own resources.

The department of the *Pas de Calais,* which embraces, among others, the towns of Calais, Dunkerque, Boulogne, and St. Omer, is a great *rendezvous* for British anglers—not that they make the "gentle art" a primary object, but they carry it with them to eke out the paucity of enjoyments for their stirring and excitable temperaments. But this section of France is not anything like a first-rate fishing locality. There is bottom-fishing, but not good river fly-fishing. There is a want of the mountain streams for this purpose. The country all the way to Paris being comparatively flat, the rivers are thick, puddley, and sluggish. But the English, when they go to the Continent, practise bottom-fishing much more frequently, and with a keener relish, than they do in their own country. This may partly be accounted for on the principle of necessity, for our national partiality for all kinds of manly out-door sports makes us rush into everything productive of excitement, without scanning very fastidiously the exact bearings or nature of the thing itself.

There is good bottom-fishing in the vicinity of Calais. A few years since we counted, within eight miles of this town, on the banks of the canal to St. Omer, *twenty-three* English anglers in one day, zealously prosecuting their calling. All were fishing for pike, or perch. On New Year's Day, 1843, a friend of ours caught nine pike of eight pounds and upwards each. They have been taken out of this and the Dunkirk Canal eighteen and twenty pounds. There are large roach, dace, and bream, in all the waters of this department. The fly-fishing about Calais is confined to two small streams, the Laracoise, and one that flows by Marquise. They are scarcely worth visiting.

There are a few trout in the river *Lianne* at Boulogne; and the higher the angler advances up its waters, the more numerous they are. It is, however, but an insignificant stream.

There is trout-fishing in the *Aa,* which flows by St. Omer, and very large and rich trout too. The higher sections of the stream are the most fruitful of sport. These are situated about ten miles above the town of Fauquembergues, near to the famous battle field of Agincourt, where our countrymen so bravely displayed their valour four hundred years ago. But the best fly-fishing district in the whole Pas de Calais is Hesdin, on the river *Cauche* and its tributaries. It is excellent fishing in all these streams, and the success from trolling is often great. The trout are taken here of eight and ten pounds weight.

There are English flies and English fishing tackle to be had in most of the towns in this part of the Continent; not in great quantities, but sufficient for cases of emergency.

We should recommend the angling in *Picardie* to that of the department just named. In no part of the north of France will the angler find, upon the whole, better and more agreeable sport than in this section of the country lying between the Cauche and the mouth of the Seine. The whole of the rivers, with the exception of the *Somme*, though small, have a pretty good trout bottom—are clear and sparkling—run through a comparatively hilly country, and flow directly to the sea. Most of all these rivers have also a considerable fall, and on this account the streams are rippling and continuous. The great road from Montreuil cuts them all at right angles; and, therefore, every facility is afforded, at a low price, for travelling expeditiously from one water to another. Besides, in no part of France, from Havre to Belgium, are there more picturesque and beautiful views than in this ancient province of Picardie.

There are three rivers which pour their waters into the ocean at Dieppe, the *Arques*, the *Eaulne*, and the *Béthune*. They have each a run up the country of about twenty miles. The two last named streams are the best for trout. From this town to Havre, the tourist will fall in with the *Durdent*, at a place called Cany, and with the *Fecamp* at a town of the same name. There is good fishing in both waters.

The part of France which, to English tourists, goes under the name of Normandy and Brittany, has, since the termination of the war in 1816, been a favourite place for the British angler. The sport, however, of late years, has fallen off a good deal. This part of the country is easily approached from Havre, by steam-boat or otherwise. There is no part of this kingdom that can be wandered over, rod in hand, with greater pleasure than these ancient, and to Englishmen especially, highly interesting sections of the French territory. We shall make no apology for introducing here a few notes from the journal of a friend who has recently traversed this tract with rod in hand and fishing-basket on his back. Though well entitled to be made public, it has never yet been set in type.

"After having had a pleasant run among the rivers and streams of old Picardie, I took up my abode at Havre for a few days, being somewhat dodged with an inward controversy, whether I should take the great river Seine, and its numerous tributaries, right on to Paris, or slip over the water and have a ramble through the old and interesting departments, which formerly went under the name of Normandy and Brittany. I ruminated within myself on this question for some time; and at length I made up my account for the Norman waters, as I flattered myself I should here find some of my angling countrymen; and would, beside, if the accounts I had previously received were founded in truth, receive no little pleasure and amusement from the varied and rippling streams, and lively scenery, of this division of France.

"Having furnished myself with a small stock of necessaries, two dozen of good Limerick flies, and half a score of cast lines, I set off for *Honfleur*; purposing to pay a visit to a friend there for two or three days, and then proceed to *Pont Audemer*—an angling station on the north boundaries of the province, of some little notoriety and reputation. And I shall take the liberty of mentioning here, for the comfort and convenience of angling continental tourists, that I derived much benefit in my subsequent rambles from a *tin digester*, which I had got made at Havre, and which enabled me to cook either fish or flesh with scarcely any trouble whatever. This utensil was made of block tin; round like a dish, and about nine inches in diameter; had three small feet, and a little tin cup to hold about an ordinary wineglassful of any kind of spirit, by the ignition of which the cooking was effected. I carried the entire apparatus in my fishing-basket among other articles. It did not weigh more than ten ounces; and it often was the means by which I obtained a comfortable and palatable dinner, when I would otherwise, to all appearance, have had to go without.

"Having arrived at the fishing stream of Pont Audemer, I took the rod, and ascended the waters some little distance from the town. I found several French gentlemen had been trying their piscatory skill in this locality a week before my arrival, and, according to report, had been very successful. One of the party had caught a trout with minnow, near the mouth of the stream, which weighed *three pounds ten ounces;* a very fine, short, thick fish, which had been preserved, and was about being placed in a glass-case to ornament one of the sitting-rooms of the inn. I found in my rambles that the streams were very rippling and finely turned for a single-handed rod-fisher, and that red bodies and gray wings were my most successful colours. The first day's sport yielded me ten very fine trout, nearly all of a size, measuring about eleven inches, and weighing, on an average, about three quarters of a pound each. On the second day I laboured at the streams, and with great care too, for full four hours, and never got a single rise; when, all of a sudden, a general movement took place in every direction, both in streams and still water, and in another hour I obtained fifteen; more varied, however, in size than those of the day preceding, and amounting to nearly the same weight. The black palmer was the favourite to-day. From all I heard, I was led to conclude, that all the trout in this river are rather uncertain and capricious in their tastes and movements;— a fact, connected with their natural history generally, I have often had opportunities of verifying, in reference to the finny tribes of our own rivers in Great Britain.

"I was not successful in hooking one of the small species of salmon *(saumoneau)* which are to be found in the Rille, and which, writers on natural history say, are only to be found here and in the Rhine. I had the good fortune, however, to see one of these rare

fish in the basket of an English gentleman, who had caught it
near Montfort, a delightful locality of the Rille, on which the gray
walls of the castle of Hugh de Montfort still stands, which with-
stood a thirty days' attack from our Henry I., in the year 1122.

"The river *Rille*, at Pont Audemer, is divided into several
branches, when it arrives at the town, which contains about five
thousand inhabitants. But in all the divisions of the stream, and
even within the confines of manufacturing works, trout of good
size and fine flavour are to be had. I killed two very fine ones
close to a mill-race.

"I set off in a day or two after for *Pont l' Eveques*, on the river
Tongues, a very fine stream. Here I tried minnow, though not a
favourite bait with me, and caught some fine trout, during about
two hours I wandered by the sides of the river. I then put on fly,
but met with but indifferent success. The fish were rising here
and there at, apparently, a very small gnat fly; but with all the
care I could exercise, they obstinately refused to have anything to
say to my bait, though I presented them in succession with nearly
the whole range of my fly-book. The next day was highly favourable in point of weather, being rather dull, with a gentle breeze
playing on the still pools. Here I had better success. I took
eight trout, six of which I gave to one of the cottagers of a small
village by the river-side, and the other two I had cooked in my *tin
digester*; and a delicious meal they made. But the English must
remember that the women who cooked the viands, put nearly half
a pound of butter along with them. How fond the French are of
this article!

"I went to *Contances*, a fishing station of some little note in Normandy. There are two streams in this vicinity, both well stocked
with trout, but not of a large kind. The waters were rather thick
and puddly, from some recent showers of rain, accompanied with
very loud thunder; and this rather spoiled the attempts at fly. I
took out my artificial minnow, and got four with it in less than
half an hour; and for other three hours, I never saw a single fish.
There was a good deal of brushwood and jungle about some spots
in the streams; and this, among other things, put me somewhat
out of humour with the place. I determined, therefore, to set out
for the *Orne*, in its higher waters, and to go down till I came
to the city of Caen, where I knew I should meet with some
kindred spirits of the angle.

"After a pretty stiff journey, I reached the *Orne* about five miles
above *Argentan*. I stopped here two days, and had some fair sport;
but I obtained the largest of the trout by minnow and worm. I
was much puzzled here about flies. The fish rose greedily each
day I was out about three o'clock in the afternoon, for about half
an hour, at some little insect; but with all my efforts I could not
get to see what it really was. I tried with all the small flies I
could muster, but they never deigned to notice me. What I did
catch, I got with large winged bait; and at the tail of strong and
rapid running streams. I fished down the river till I arrived at

Turi. The scenery in the neighbourhood of the stream was often highly interesting. There was an admirable diversity of woods, meadows, orchards, and villages. In some places I passed, I stood for half an hour at a time, and gazed upon the landscapes with intense interest. When fixed in this manner one laments the poverty of language: even the pencil cannot represent that outward picture which fills the eye and imagination, nor express those confused, those delicious sounds of rural life, nor make us breathe that fine air, which renders the spirits so buoyant and lively. We feel the necessity of transporting the reader to the very spot itself, and give up all attempts to paint natural beauties which are inimitable.

"At *Turi* I met with two French anglers, officers of the army, who had been rambling on the river's banks for two or three days. They had each a very fine basket of trout, which they kept in a moist state, by occasionally dipping it in the water. They showed me the flies they were using; and what ugly and grotesque things they were! They were full as large as bumble-bees, and were very rudely tied on the gut. Cast lines they had none. They made a regular splash at every throw of the line. Their great object was to mark whenever a fish rose, and then to post off to the spot, throw a little above the spot; a mode of proceeding often attended with success. I displayed my stock of flies, at which they seemed quite astonished and delighted. Being fine, agreeable, and gentlemanly men, I begged they would accept half a dozen each of any colour and size they fancied; a proposition which was politely accepted, and which united us into the closest bonds of angling brotherhood.

"Passing down the river to *Vieux,* I had some good days' sport; sometimes using the fly, sometimes the minnow, and occasionally the worm, which, when the weather is hot, the river low, and there is a goodly portion of shady spots, near or over deep pools, is by far the most interesting and exciting mode of angling. It is often, likewise, the most successful mode. The flies I used on this section of the *Orne,* were of a miscellaneous cast; sometimes large, sometimes small, with sometimes light gray, and some dark brown wings. I happened to have a good breeze; and when this is the case, the labour of the sportsman is comparatively easy, and his success more certain. In the ground I travelled over, there were several very long reaches of still water, occasioned by corn and other mills on the river; and in these there seemed to be vast collections of trout. In some of the more shallow and stony parts of these reaches, where trout delight throughout the day to bask and gamble, I could often see scores of them darting in all directions for shelter, whenever my presence was detected. This was proof that they were pretty numerous in most sections of the river. There had been several fine trout taken out of the *Orne,* a little above the town, and all by minnow and worm—one about a week before I arrived, of nearly seven pounds and a half.

N

This is no mean sport. For myself, I must say that I was not successful in capturing any large trout; but during five or six days I was out with different small parties, I got several fish which weighed about a pound and a half. I never tried bait, but kept to the fly. I found the general opinion of the anglers at Caen very much divided as to the most killing flies for the river; some zealously claiming the superiority for this colour, and some for that. As far as my own experience went, I killed the greater portion of my fish with a middle-sized hook, red body, and drab coloured wings.

"I set out for Avranches, and after a tedious and rather laborious journey, I reached the bottom of the eminence on which the town stands. The place is exceedingly beautiful and picturesque. On casting an eye over the surrounding objects from the terrace on which the old cathedral stood, for it is now in ruins, a more engaging and lovely landscape cannot be seen in all France.

"After spending about ten days at Avranches, I left for the borders of Brittany. I bent my steps towards *Pontorson*—but I must stop here, and remind the wandering angler that on leaving Avranches he has five small rivers to cross; and if he is induced to keep, what the English call, *low down* in their course, he may find crossing their waters very troublesome. The sands sink prodigiously, and the tide rushes with amazing velocity, so that a traveller may be placed in great jeopardy without much previous intimation.

"On arriving at Pontorson, I struck up into the country. I soon got to the eminence of a long hill, from which there is a most enchanting prospect to the traveller's eye. The varied and undulating nature of the country, the yellow corn fields studded up and down, and the clusters of apple orchards, present to the mind a variety of objects of great beauty and interest.

"Travelling onwards, I came to the higher parts of the river *Couesnon*, which forms the boundary between Normandy and Brittany. Here I readily perceived that I was entering upon a part of France considerably different from that which I had just left. Brittany is the country where the real portion of the Celtic character is to be met with in all its purity. The inhabitants of Normandy have, generally, long oval features, and very expressive blue eyes, and fair complexions; whereas the Bretons are characterized by a brown swarthy skin, sharp peering black eyes, short round faces, and broad jaw-bones. They are likewise of a lower stature than the Normans. In the manners and customs of the two people there is also a wide and palpable distinction. In Normandy the men wear almost universally a *blouse* of blue cotton, while the Bretons have a sort of coat, sometimes made of calf-skin, and sometimes of sheep-skin, with the hair or wool outside. This coat reaches a little below their knees, and gives a very uncultivated and savage appearance to the person.

The Normans are active, industrious, and thrifty, while the natives of Brittany are idle, careless, and improvident. The former are likewise very superior to the latter in all their domestic arrangements and habits, and are, in fact, a couple of centuries before them in everything that appertains to social comfort, cleanliness, and civilized deportment.

"I was anxious to throw a line in the *Couesnon*, and I ascended it a short distance, put on two flies, and ventured on the surface of its streams. I only obtained three or four smallish fish; but the deep pools seemed to contain a fair proportion of trout for the capabilities of the water. It is very clear and sparkling, and requires fine tackle, and a light hand.

"The river Ronce is an interesting one; it takes its rise from among the high division of the *Méné* range of hills, near to the town of *Collinée*, from whence it flows in an eastward direction till it approaches *St. Jouan*, the boundary line between Normandy and Brittany. The stream then runs north, through a rich and beautiful valley, which at one place becomes very narrow, and terminates in a sort of rocky gorge, through which the waters rush towards Dinon. The river is thus hemmed in between precipitous and lofty hills, and presents a succession of varied and romantic scenery which a painter would revel in for days together.

"I only stopped to breakfast at the little town of Dol, being anxious to reach *Dinon*, distant about fifteen miles. This I accomplished towards evening. The town stands upon a rocky eminence, and the river *Rance* flows at the bottom of it, through a deep and rocky valley. A great number of English were residing here, many of whom were keen anglers. Having letters of introduction to two of them, I was soon in the midst of a whole host of the disciples of 'old Izaak.' I found angling in all its phases, aspects, and dodges, to be a standard dish of conversation; and the successes and disappointment, the attributes of the gentle art, seemed to afford never ceasing themes of eloquence and declamation. Still, there is invariably such a vital sympathy among all men who have what may be called *the root of the matter* in them, that we feel always at home with the true and enthusiastic angler, and are ever ready to pin our faith and honour on his sleeve, be he in what part of the world he may.

"The *Arquenon* abounds with fine trout, not large, but rich in flavour, and of the most bright and shining colours. We tried fly, and of a pretty good size, but found the trout shy and sulky. We then put on our artificial minnows, and we succeeded, in some of the strong and rapid streams, in hooking three or four fish, but part got off before we could land them on *terra firma*. Trying the fly again, about three o'clock in the afternoon, we found our finny friends in better humour; and after about two hours' work, my friend and I counted a couple of dozen of as fine trout as a man would wish to see. I got all mine with spider flies, while he was equally as successful with large winged ones. So much for favourite flies.

"In the parts of the river we had traversed, we found its course very winding and tortuous, and we were very much incommoded by the system of irrigation which is carried on by the sides of the stream. We had to go plunging through pasture-grounds, sometimes half-leg deep of mud and water.

"In the evening, we bent our steps towards the village of *Crehen*, with a view to remain the night, and try the river the next day. We got rather uncouth, but comfortable lodgings; and by six o'clock in the morning, after a good cup or two of *café au lait* and some fresh eggs, we were on the banks of the stream, rod in hand. On leaving the village the stream turns wider, and not so well adapted for fly-fishing. We had throughout the day but very poor success; not obtaining more, and with great labour and toil in a melting sun, than half the number of fish we had caught the day previous.

"My next angling tour of any extent took me to the higher parts of the Rance. I stopped a day at the village of *Guenroc*, where the river is considerably narrowed, and its banks are very picturesque and beautiful. I had but an indifferent day's sport; having only taken nine trout, averaging about six inches in length. I saw, however, some very large in a long piece of still water; and had I been able to obtain worm, I have no doubt but I should have captured some of them. The weather was bright and hot; and the only place where a fly had a chance of doing anything, was in gurgling streams.

"A few days after this I was with my rod at *La Chèze*, and spent two days in wandering on the banks of the *Lié*. I had now provided myself with some worms, and was fully bent on trying the shade-fishing where it was practicable. I suffered dreadfully, however, from the heat, in making my way through the thickets and brushwood, that skirt the river sides. I succeeded in taking two fine trout about a pound and a half each, and of the richest hues I had ever seen, when they first came out of the water. But in half an hour after they became nearly black.

"After rambling for nearly fourteen days, and throwing a line, in passing, into several small streams, I arrived at the town of *Guimgamp*, on the river *Trieux*, one of the best streams for trout in all Britanny. I remained at this place about a week, and had capital sport, all with the fly. I caught nearly four dozen fine trout in as many hours; and extremely rich fish they were. I dined daily off the fruits of my spoil; and gave the residue to my landlady, who received them with many expressions of thankfulness.

"I preferred the higher parts of the stream to those nearer or about the town. A few miles from it, the river divides into two branches, but they both lead to the Méne range of hills, as their sources. Below the town the bed of the stream gets too broad for angling purposes, although I one day stood upon some stone steps —which are placed above a mill-weir, close to the town, for the purpose of enabling people to pass over to the other side—and, being aided by a pretty good curl, I got four very fine fish, with the spider black fly. They were nearly half a pound each.

"Having spent the winter at *Morlaix*, I started in the following April on foot, to fish the river *Vilaine*, and as many of its tributaries as I could find convenient or pleasurable. I had a rough passage to its upper streams, and met with some unpalatable meals, and not very luxurious beds; but the zealous angler abroad must not be too tight-laced on these matters. When they once get over they afford topics of interest to the mind, and give it that gentle shaking which improves both its strength and elasticity. My notice of this tour must necessarily be very limited. I was full two months with rod in hand almost every day; and one day's sport and scenery is so like another, that to give an account of everything as it really occurred, would be both unprofitable and wearisome. I shall therefore just dot down a few things, without any appearance of plan or method.

"In the upper streams of the Vilaine, minnow fishing takes well. At least this is in accordance with my own experience. There are large deep holes, and the streams are of such a character as to be in favour of this mode of angling. I did fish with fly here; but from the nature of the water I do not conceive this to be the best bait in the early portion of the season.

"I went a few miles up the streams of one of the tributaries of the main river, called the *Seiche*. The scenery was wild and rather barren; but the fishing was tolerable. What I caught here were but small trout, such as we often obtain from some of the minor rivers in Scotland. I touched likewise at another of the feeders of the Vilaine, called the *Senone*, and here too I found the fish small, but numerous. The water was remarkably limpid, and it required the finest tackle, and smallest flies, to do any good in it.

"As we descend the parent stream, it becomes better adapted for fly, and the fish become larger, and even richer in flavour. I ran a short distance up the *Chere*, which falls into the Vilaine, but I was so much embarrassed with short brushwood, and other obstacles, that I soon made a retreat. The other feeders are the *Lie, Ars*, and the *Don*; in all of which plenty of sport may be obtained both with fly, and with bait. There are many beautiful sketches of water in all these rivers, which please the angler's eye, and give a sure presage of his obtaining some success."

Many British anglers make Paris their chief point of operations. In this they have a ready command of the *Seine* and *Marne*, and their various tributaries. These latter are much better fly-fishing streams than the main rivers. There are a few salmon taken every year in the Seine, but they are very seldom indeed taken by rod-fishing. The best mode of fishing the tributaries of the river, is to go from Havre as the crow flies, to the metropolis. The tourist will find the rivers that enter it, on which ever side he takes, to be very manageable with the rod, and tolerably fruitful of sport. The Marne enters the Seine about five miles from Paris, and in its higher waters, is a good river. All its feeders abound with trout. English fishing-tackle is to be had in many shops in the capital.

The British anglers have not generally frequented the fishing rivers in the south of France. There are, however, extensive ranges of these, where the sport can be obtained in abundance. The *Loire*, and its numerous tributaries, more especially in their higher localities, afford a pleasant range of amusements. So likewise do the Garonne, and its feeders.

The *Rhone* and the *Saone*, with all their dependent rivers, are very full of fish; and the fly-fishing on some of the smaller streams is very good.

The various rivers of the Pyrenees are first-rate spots for agreeable rod-fishing.

Italy and Spain afford good fishing to those who can penetrate up the higher branches of the rivers of these important countries. Rod-fishing has been practised there for ages. Most all the old paintings and engravings of Italian artists, depict angling with a rod, as a standard item in their landscapes; and in Spain, the gentle art is of great antiquity. As a proof of this, there is a very fine copper coin in the British Museum, of the age of Augustus, bearing the mark of *Carteia*, a town in Spain, on one side of which there is a well-defined representation of a man angling with a rod and line, and a fishing basket by his side.

There is good angling in the *Meuse*, the *Moselle*, and in the higher waters of the *Rhine*, and in all their numerous feeders. There are several fishing clubs established in these localities.

The salmon fishing in Norway and Sweden, has been zealously prosecuted of late years by British sportsmen. They have penetrated even into Russia, and the various tributaries of the Danube. They have met with sport of both a varied and exciting kind.

odel showing Salmon in different stages of progress to maturity, p. 183.

EXPLANATION.

A Water supply from cistern, constantly running.
B Plate-glass tank, containing artificially produced salmon fry.
C C Pipes conducting water out of tank to model below.
D D Troughs in which ova are being hatched, filled with clean gravel.
E E Gratings through which water passes to gravel.
G Model of river containing Salmon fry.
H Weir across river.
M Fish-pass over weir, to enable the fish to ascend to the upper waters without terfering with the water power above.
ı River below weir.

Note A, page 32.

As we have mentioned the subject of the artificial propagation of salmon, and as it is a topic interesting both to the rod-fisher and the public at large, we beg to observe that the enterprise or experiment has been successfully carried out in Ireland, in the waters of Lough Carrib, by the Messrs. Ashworth. It may not be uninteresting to inform the reader that the young salmon which were artificially produced at Outerard last year (1853), and exhibited all the summer months at the Dublin Great Industrial Exhibition, are now (May 1854) still alive, and progressing most rapidly, some of them having reached the length of *five inches*. They are kept in the Fishery-office Customhouse; where, under the directions and superintendence of the Commissioners of Fisheries, a series of experiments are being made, the results of which must be, if no other good or result follows, to afford an amount of information hitherto unknown in the natural history of the salmon. The Commissioners have also deposited about 15,000 salmon ova in boxes in their office; and they confidently look for a proportionate return. They have carefully watched the progress of the ova with the aid of a microscope, and have succeeded in obtaining an amount of valuable information, which, if published hereafter, must prove highly interesting and important to the great fishing commercial interests of not only this country, but England and Scotland. The vivarium in the office of the Commissioners is very well worthy of a visit; and, as it is their intention to keep it open all the next year, for the benefit and information of those interested in the salmon fisheries, it will amply repay the tourists, during the summer, the trouble to visit this place, and learn how to breed fish. The Commissioners are at all times most easy of access, and give every information in their power to the inquirer; indeed, they feel only a pleasure in seeing an interest created in an object that is of such vital importance to a country like Ireland, which has the most invaluable resources in its fisheries, both inland and sea.

In two of the models erected in the Fishery Office, may be seen salmon in all their stages of progress to maturity. The annexed figure will give the reader something like a correct idea of the process.

184   NOTE.

From the explanation attached to the engraving, the reader will
have a tolerable idea of the process employed, and of the several
stages of piscatory incubation; but as every question, it is said,
has two sides, and as our chief desire is to advocate free discussion
on the main question itself, we shall give a few observations from the
pen of Dr. Knox, who is at this moment writing on the matter,*
and who seems to have entered into the entire question with his
accustomed zeal, energy, and knowledge.   He says :—
   "It is rapacious, all-destroying man who interferes, disturbing,
often unnecessarily, her plans and views. He thinks he can improve on them! You may try, but I rather think you will fail.
Still, there cannot arise any harm from endeavouring to protect the
ova and the fry resulting from them in artificial ponds until they
shall have acquired size and strength sufficient to protect themselves when turned into the main stream of the river.   Once there,
they must be left to themselves to find their way to the ocean.
Let me examine, for a brief space, what this interval may be. I
mean the interval between the period when the fry have quitted
the gravel, until the time when, having acquired the robe or
external salmon covering, they are about to proceed in groups and
shoals to the ocean. Since the experiments of Mr. Young, of
Inverness-shire, this period is now supposed to be *in one year* after
they have left the gravelly bed.   Experiments made prior to those
by Mr. Young, on the young of the salmon reared artificially at
Drumlanrig, led the world to believe that the young salmon remained *two years* in the river before quitting it for the ocean. I
think it probable, by restraining the growth of the young salmon,
you may in time make it three years; for the secret simply is, the
restraint you put on a young fish which nature never intended
should be restrained. Leave the fry in the river, in the gravel of
which they were bred, and be assured they will be ready to descend
the river to 'the streams of ocean' in three or four weeks from the
day they rose through the gravel.
   "I know that it is so in certain streams in the East Riding of
Yorkshire, with a large kind of sea trout, which ascends these
small streams during the spawning season. I do not fear being
able to submit to you shortly proofs that the same law holds good
in the true salmon.
   "As I do not suppose that the promoters of the artificial method
of supplying the rivers of Britain with salmon, propose to abandon
the protection of the ova and fry, when deposited and grown in the
bed of the river, agreeably to Nature's laws, so it seems right that
further inquiry should be instituted into the natural history of the
fish. For the length of time during which the fry remain in the
river as fry, if determined, would determine the nature of the protection to be given to the fry. If but for a few weeks, the necessary protection might readily be afforded them; but should it be

* The Illustrated London Magazine, January, 1854.

proved that they continue to reside in the fresh waters for a year or more, then protection seems to me impossible.

" Whilst experimenting on the salmon from 1830 to 1833, and subsequently, I could not fail to observe that soon after (in from three weeks to a month) the escape of the young salmon from below the gravel, the streams everywhere abounded with silvery, shining, well-fed smolts, *which were not there before*. This generally happened from three weeks to a month after the fry had left their gravelly bed. On considering whence these smolts might come, I was in some measure forced against my own belief to come to the conclusion that they sprung from the ova of the salmon deposited *in the November of the preceding year*. This opinion (for it is merely one) was not based, it is true, on a *continued series of observation ;* this deficiency I felt, and was as much alive to as any man living; but the difficulty was not to be overcome but by creating another, namely, by *restraining the young* fish in *artificial waters*, and thus interfering with the growth of the smolt at a time when nature required it to be in full possession of its natural food and native streams.

" This, then, is the objection I make to the experiments made at Drumlanrig, on the Shin and elsewhere. By such experiments, the free action of the smolt is retained ; they retard the growth ; they interfere with its natural development. As if in proof of the correctness of my opinion on this point, the experiments made at Drumlanrig give *two years* for the residence of the young of the salmon in the rivers prior to its becoming a smolt properly so called ; those made on the Shin give only *one year ;* and I should not be surprised at some future experiments showing that three years was in reality the period. What conclusion can you draw from such experiments, saving this : that by interfering with the habitat and feeding of the young *salmon*, you only retard the development into the true smolt for a year or more ?

" Foreseeing the objections that would be made to my opinion, namely, the " absence of a continuity in the observation," I naturally bethought me of every mode of obviating it. This was long before the Drumlanrig or Shin experiments were made or even thought of. The more obvious way to remove the objection was, the simple one, namely—to grow live smolt from the eggs, and retain them in a pond under your own eyes until they became smolts. This profound and original thought, I am bound to say, occurred to me simultaneously with some herd boys who tended their flocks on the banks of the Whitadder. I am willing to yield the honour to them.

" It will naturally be asked what induced me to adopt, and to maintain, *until refuted* by qualified men, my first opinion ? I shall tell you. I was aware that before assuming the silvery smolt dress, or in plain terms, before undergoing his latest metamorphosis in the river, prior to proceeding to the ocean, the young salmon is with difficulty to be recognized from the young of others

of the Salmonidæ, and more especially from the mysterious fish
called the parr. Following the great law of Nature—the unity of
the organization—the young of all the Salmonidæ I have examined
resemble each other in many particulars. They have all red spots
and dark spots, and parr bars or markings, and their dentition is
nearly the same in all. But as each species progresses it lays
aside certain of these characters, retaining those which, by their
permanence, mark the species. The salmon loses the parr markings and red spots, and most of the dark ones, nearly all, in fact,
below the lateral line; the salmon trout loses its red spots and
parr markings, but retains numerous dark spots above and below
the lateral line; one kind of river trout retains the red spots only;
another the red spots and parr markings; the lake trout retains
only the darker spots. Lastly, the dentition changes; from being
alike in all, it becomes specifically distinct. The trout, with certain
exceptions, retains only the mesial vomerine teeth in a *double row*;
the sea trout loses most of these teeth, retaining, however, a single
row of mesial teeth and the transverse, or those on the chevron;
lastly, the true salmon loses all, or nearly all, the mesial vomerine
teeth, retaining only those of the chevron. It was known nearly a
hundred years ago, that if you scrape the scales from off the sides
of a smolt you will find the parr markings below; of course you
will: you will find the colouring of the fry, from which it has but
just changed. Does this partial persistence of the appearances,
dependent on the universal law of unity of the organization, prove
the smolt to be a parr? With men ignorant of the basis of all
zoology, anatomy, or physiology it does, but scientific men merely
laugh at this.

"Convinced that no true legislation can take place in respect of
the salmon until the parr question be decided, I have continued my
observations up to the moment I now write this. Parr and smolts
are now before me from the Annan and from the Shin. Anatomical
inquiries do not bear out the idea that they are identical. How
does their natural history agree? I have opened, in April and
May, hundreds and hundreds of smolts, and without an exception
found the milt and roe at their minimum, with every appearance of
their never having altered from their ascent through the gravel.
Now, if these smolts of April and May (say 1853), were merely the
winter parr of the year 1851 or of 1852, what has become of the
numerous male parr which during the autumn and winter have the
milt fully developed? How inexplicable must it ever remain according to the present views, that the male of the parr, a young, a
very young fish—a fish which, according to their views actually has
not yet acquired the specific forms and robe of the salmon, retaining still its embryonic colouring and forms and habits, should, *at all
seasons of the year, remark*, enter into a condition, as to the *milt*,
which the full-grown smolt never shares, and which is only found
in the male adult salmon late in autumn, and at a season which
never changes. I have found in the rivers abundance of male parr

with the milt fully developed from June to January : could these be salmon so young as not to have laid aside their embryonic characters, and yet have a milt as fully developed as a fully grown salmon ready to spawn ? And why the *male* only ? Why not also the *female ?* "

These are very important remarks and statements which the doctor has here laid before the public, and are entitled to candid consideration from all who are interested in this grand piscatory experiment. We find the following information upon this interesting subject in the *Glasgow Herald,* of April last :—

" Mr. John Shaw, of Drumlanrig, has deposited in the Fruin, which flows into Loch Lomond, a quantity of ova, calculated to amount to between 8,000 and 10,000 eggs, each containing the germ of a future salmon. The ova were carried from the Nith in perforated zinc boxes, with gravel in which they had been deposited, after being duly fecundated. On the 17th ult., the ova alluded to were deposited in three lots, in as many gravel beds in the Fruin, selected by Mr. Shaw as those most likely to afford shelter to the brood during the hatching process. Should they escape the incidents of furious floods or the ravages of ruthless denizens of the streams, these units of roe will in early summer assume the appearance of the perfect fish, although of the tiniest proportions imaginable, thence rise into the parr, and again into the salmon smoult ; when at the end of about two years from the period of their being hatched in fresh water, the instinctive desire to visit the ocean comes upon them. In the case of the salmon fry from the Fruin, this seaward trip will be rather a roundabout one ; for, in the first instance, they must traverse part of Loch Lomond, then descend the Leven to the Clyde, and thence reach the sea. It is presumed that, following the laws of instinct, they will return from their salt water sojourn to the parent loch and streamlet, sufficiently augmented in bulk to gladden the heart of the angler or professional fisherman."

The following paragraph we extract from the *Globe* of the 26th May, 1854 :—

" TAY SALMON BREEDING PONDS.—The Perth correspondent of the *Daily Mail* says—The young fry in these ponds have now got entirely rid of the umbilical bag, and are very active and lively. The greater part have left the breeding boxes and taken to the pond, and it is extremely difficult to retain them even there, as they seek out at the sluice, evidently bent on reaching the river, which we have no doubt is the best place for them, as they are now perfectly able to protect themselves under the stones in the bed of the river. As yet no food has been given to them. Up to this date the experiment has been eminently successful."

ANGLING REGISTER FORM.

Date.	No. of Fish.	Description of Fish.	Weight.	Where caught.	Fly, &c. &c.	Wind, and Colour of Water.	Observations.

CPSIA information can be obtained
at www.ICGtesting.com
Printed in the USA
BVHW071359061118
532312BV00014B/542/P

9 781527 761544